Innovation and Marketing in the Video Game Industry

Innovation and Marketing in the Video Game Industry

Avoiding the Performance Trap

DAVID WESLEY AND GLORIA BARCZAK
Northeastern University, Boston, USA

GOWER

Gower Applied Business Research
Our programme provides leaders, practitioners, scholars and researchers with thought provoking, cutting edge books that combine conceptual insights, interdisciplinary rigour and practical relevance in key areas of business and management.

Published by
Gower Publishing Limited
Wey Court East
Union Road
Farnham
Surrey, GU9 7PT
England

Ashgate Publishing Company
Suite 420
101 Cherry Street
Burlington,
VT 05401-4405
USA

www.gowerpublishing.com

British Library Cataloguing in Publication Data
Wesley, David.
  Innovation and marketing in the video game industry :
  avoiding the performance trap.
  1. Video games industry--Management. 2. Video games
  industry--Public relations. 3. Video games--Marketing.
  I. Title II. Barczak, Gloria.
  794.8'0688-dc22

  ISBN: 978-0-566-09167-4 (hbk)
  ISBN: 978-0-566-09168-1 (ebk)

Library of Congress Cataloging-in-Publication Data
Wesley, David T. A.
  Innovation and marketing in the video game industry : avoiding the performance trap / by David Wesley and Gloria Barczak.
    p. cm.
  Includes bibliographical references and index.
  ISBN 978-0-566-09167-4 (hbk) -- ISBN 978-0-566-09168-1
  (ebook) 1. Video games industry. 2. Video games--Marketing. I. Barczak, Gloria. II. Title.
  HD9993.E452W47 2010
  794.8068'8--dc22

                                                        2009052395

Mixed Sources
Product group from well-managed forests and other controlled sources
www.fsc.org Cert no. SA-COC-1565
© 1996 Forest Stewardship Council
FSC

Printed and bound in Great Britain by
MPG Books Group, UK

Contents

List of Figures   vii
List of Tables   ix
Preface   xi

Introduction   1

1   Shigeru Miyamoto and the Art of Donkey Kong   9

2   Nintendo's Dark Age   29

3   PlayStation Dreams   47

4   Xbox Empire   65

5   The Brain Age: Handheld Consoles and their Impact on Adult
     Gamers   79

6   Rings of Death   101

7   The PlayStation 3: Sony's "Supercomputer"   113

8   Blu-Rays and Netflix: Defining "the Ultimate High-Definition
     Experience"   131

9   The Wii Revolution   143

10   Game Development and the Rise of Casual Games   171

11   Guitar Hero Nation   195

Conclusion   211
Epilogue   219
Bibliography   229
Index   257

List of Figures

9.1   "Higher Definition: Play Beyond" PS3 Trailer   151
9.2   Nintendo "Wii for All" Trailer   152

List of Tables

4.1	Microsoft Acquisitions 1997–2000	71
6.1	Entertainment and Devices Division Financial Results	112
7.1	Sony PlayStation 3 Manufacturing Cost (60 GB Model)	117
7.2	Monthly U.S. Sales of Video Game Hardware	124
10.1	Video Game per Unit Cost: Next Generation Console Estimates	173

Preface

Shortly after the launch of the PlayStation 3, a journalist from *Electronic Gaming Monthly* approached Professor Gloria Barczak, head of the marketing department at Northeastern University's College of Business Administration, to get her opinion about Sony's poor market performance. That initial contact prompted us to take a deeper look into marketing issues facing Sony and other video game industry leaders.

Our first goal was to create a series of case studies and instructor manuals for executive training and development programs. Those cases have proved very popular with undergraduate, graduate, and executive students alike. After several cases in the series won awards or were selected for inclusion in best-selling textbooks, we realized that there was a need for more material on marketing and innovation in the video game industry. Although some segments from those cases have been included in the present work, most of the concepts discussed in the following pages have never before been published.

While teaching our cases to students in executive classes, many of whom work in Boston-area technology companies, we discovered that several were grappling with *exactly* the same issues as those faced by Sony, Nintendo, Microsoft, and others. We also found that nearly all of the problems currently experienced by console makers and software developers are not new, but have historical precedents both within the video game industry and in other unrelated industries.

In preparing the lecture notes for our classes, we were struck by a general deficiency in business and management literature focused on video games. Plenty of titles examine the music industry, the film industry, and other forms of entertainment. Yet video game innovations have had a greater impact on our society than almost any other leisure activity. Video games not only consume a large portion of our free time, they influence cultural trends, drive microprocessor development, and help train pilots and soldiers. Now, with the Nintendo Wii and DS, they are helping people stay fit, facilitating rehabilitation, and creating new learning opportunities.

Nevertheless, many parents, educators, and politicians only see a dark side to video games. Video games make kids lazy and encourage them to commit acts of violence, complain detractors. Advances in video game graphics in the 1990s have certainly led to more realistic storylines and images. Although the video game industry released a wide variety of content, some of the most popular titles were indeed ultra-violent first-person shooters. When the American Psychological Association linked on-screen violence to real-life aggression, many Americans urged the government to impose restrictions.

U.S. Senator Joseph Lieberman spearheaded a campaign to restrict access to violent video games:

> *Most parents have no clue what kind of bloody gore exists in the most offensive video games on the market today. Kids not only watch realistic characters spurting blood and pulling heads, spinal cords and beating hearts out of bodies, but they are creating the mayhem and are rewarded with extra points for doing so. The video-game manufacturers should recognize they've gone too far and agree to stop making games that portray extreme violence or sexual activity. That would be the best holiday present they could give to the children of America. ... At the very least, give us information we, as parents, need to avoid the offensive games you create. And if you don't, I believe Congress can and will require warning labels. (Lieberman 1993)*

In 1994, the video game industry responded by creating the Entertainment Software Ratings Board (ESRB), a semi-independent review board responsible for providing an age recommendation for video games as well as content warnings, such as language, sexual themes and violence. Lieberman felt the warnings were not sufficient and urged stricter government regulation of the video game industry. "Too many games now on the market this holiday season are more violent, more antisocial and generally more disgusting than ever," he told a congressional committee. "The gift these products give is to communicate the unadulterated message that killing is cool and viciousness is a virtue" (*Globe and Mail* 1996).

The debate reignited after a series of school shootings were linked to violent video games, culminating in the April 20, 1999 massacre of 13 people at Columbine High School in the state of Colorado by two video game enthusiasts. A few months later, then-president Bill Clinton announced a government investigation into the marketing of violent games to children. The public outcry reached a peak with the 2004 introduction of *Grand Theft Auto: San Andreas*, one of the PS2's best-selling and highest rated games. The game featured corrupt cops, racism, drive-by shootings, pipe beatings and explicit sex. An earlier version of the game awarded points to players who made drug deals, killed police officers, and solicited and murdered prostitutes. Rather than limiting sales, controversies often fueled demand for such games, as teens and older children flocked to stores to purchase mature-rated games.

However, research has shown that the link between video games and real world violence was not as clear as detractors suggested. An Australian study showed that "only children predisposed to aggression and more reactive to their environments changed their behavior after playing" violent games, whereas normal individuals were unaffected (*Sydney Morning Herald* 2007). Although some murderers played video games, many did not. A U.S. Secret Service study found that only 12 percent of school shooters showed an interest in violent games, compared to 24 percent who read violent books.

In his best-selling book, *Everything Bad Is Good for You*, science editor Steven Johnson (2006) explained how playing video games can actually have benefits. Besides the obvious content lessons within historical simulation games, such as *Age of Empires* and *Civilization*, children learned specific problem-solving skills, even from games with apparently trivial themes. In addition, puzzle games, such as *Brain Age* and *Brain Academy*, were believed by some to have a therapeutic affect on individuals suffering from certain neurological disorders, such as Alzheimer's disease.

A different problem was childhood obesity and diabetes, which according to the National Institutes of Health (NIH), had reached epidemic levels in the United States, partly owing to video games and computer use. In response, the Centers for Disease Control and Prevention (CDC) urged parents to "reduce their children's TV and computer time and encourage outdoor play" (Centers for Disease Control 1999).

Game developers addressed such health concerns by creating games with a strong physical component. *Dance Dance Revolution* required players to dance complex steps on an electronic floor mat to gain points and beat competitors. On the Nintendo Wii, a new motion-sensing controller had gamers swinging virtual tennis rackets, tossing virtual balls and wielding virtual swords, instead of sitting sedentary in front of the screen. As more companies designed accessories for the Wii, such as tennis rackets, golf clubs and baseball bats, the lines between gamers and athletes were expected to blur even further.

Our purpose is not to advocate for or against video games, as we feel there are plenty of other books that address the moral issues discussed above. Instead we will look at how innovation is being used to make gaming attractive to more users. Games like *Wii Fit, Guitar Hero*, and *Brain Age* are putting consoles in the hands of people who would not normally call themselves gamers, including some who previously opposed video games.

At the same time, many developers continue to focus on advances in traditional first person shooters, role playing games, and action games. They are spending vast amounts of money competing for a relatively small audience of dedicated gamers, only to be outsold by cheaply developed titles like *Brain Age* or *Guitar Hero*. Nintendo's winning strategy breaks free from the race for better performance to focus on innovations that appeal to a wider audience and directly address many of the criticisms aimed at the video game industry.

The topics presented in this book will appeal mainly to marketing professionals, business managers, product design engineers, and video game enthusiasts. At the same time, most of the material is written to be accessible to a wide audience, and therefore we believe that anyone who wants to gain a better understanding of the business of video games will benefit from the discussions presented in these pages.

The authors wish to acknowledge the support of the Institute for Global Innovation Management (IGIM) at Northeastern University for providing funding for the case studies that inspired this book and Ivey Publishing for agreeing to let us incorporate segments of those case studies in the current work. Special thanks go out to IGIM Director Professor Harry Lane for his support, advice, and encouragement. We also want to thank Francesca Warren of Redit Publishing Services for agreeing to act as our agent. Without her hard work, this book may never have been written. Finally, we want to thank Martin West, Commissioning Editor at Gower Applied Research for taking a chance on us. We hope that our manuscript lives up to your expectations.

Introduction

The public has no sense of how fast things are moving ... It's like going
from bows-and-arrows to the space age.

Ralph Baer, inventor of the first video game console

For most of the video game industry's short history, console makers and developers have been searching for a holy grail of high performance and realism. However, the recent surge in popularity of underpowered consoles and simple games over cutting edge technology and big budget titles suggests that a new paradigm may be at hand. Examples include the success of the Wii over the PlayStation 3 and Xbox 360, the DS over the PSP, casual PC games over first-person shooters, and music games over big budget action adventure titles.

Everywhere one looks, simplicity and ease-of-use are triumphing over depth and complexity. Netbooks, portable music players, and point-and-shoot digital cameras are a few of the product categories that have emerged to serve the needs of the mass market of consumers who require simple and easy-to-use products and services. In his best-selling book *Crossing the Chasm*, Geoffrey Moore (2002) argues that success in high-tech markets depends on "making the transition from an early market dominated by a few visionary customers to a mainstream market dominated by a large block of customers who are predominantly pragmatists in orientation." This transition is called the chasm and the key to crossing the chasm is to make the mainstream market materialize. However, achieving this leap requires a different strategy than what one might use to lure early adopters of technology. The reason is that the mainstream market has different values and requirements than the early market. Although all industries are affected by this reality, the case of the video game industry is particularly compelling.

The Social and Economic Impact of Games

This book is the first attempt to understand the business of video games from a marketing and innovation perspective. Why academia has not given more consideration to an industry that has a revenue-generating capacity that rivals film and music remains anyone's guess. We suspect it has something to do with a reluctance to investigate a medium that is often considered juvenile.

Yet video games should no longer be viewed as the exclusive domain of antisocial teenage boys, but rather as part of the commercial mainstream. Their impact on society is far reaching. For example, leading edge innovations in processor design, computer graphics, and artificial intelligence are all being driven by the video game industry. Game software is used to train soldiers for battle, to train pilots in flight controls and navigation, and to provide rehabilitation services to hospital patients.

Video games have demonstrated resilience amidst the economic crisis that began in 2008, when the world economy suffered its worst downturn since the Great Depression. Countless retailers closed shop for good, including electronics giant Circuit City, which declared bankruptcy in late 2008. Millions of American homeowners were forced into foreclosure and unemployment reached levels not seen in more than 30 years. Yet throughout the crisis, the video game industry remained resilient, continuing to grow year after year. In 2008, worldwide sales of video game hardware and software passed $50 billion, more than double the annual sales posted in 2004 and 2005, and $5 billion more than in 2007.

In less than a decade, more than one billion video game consoles have been sold worldwide. Video games are now one of the leading forms of media consumption, with sales rivaling the most successful Hollywood blockbusters. Marketing executives in a wide range of industries are turning to video games to promote their products through movie tie-ins and in-game advertisements.

So what makes video games so appealing? Why are people willing to spend hundreds of dollars on a video game console and hundreds more on software at a time when they are being forced out of their homes and are cutting back on purchases of clothing, fuel, and other necessities?

One theory holds that as the cost of outside entertainment rises, more people choose to stay home and participate in inexpensive forms of entertainment.

When gasoline prices hit record highs in the summer of 2008, the term "staycation" was invented to describe the families who "are trading in their travel plans for a stay-at-home vacation." Petroleum was not the only product reaching record highs. Between 1996 and 2004, concert ticket prices increased by an average of 82 percent, five times the rate of inflation. In 2008, the average concert ticket cost $66. Movie tickets also rose to an average of more than $7. For a family of five, a night at the movies could easily surpass $80, factoring in popcorn, drinks and other incidentals. No wonder more people were choosing to stay at home.

Yet the "staycation" phenomenon only tells part of the story. If it were the only factor determining game sales, one would expect to see revenues rise and fall along with gasoline prices and other commodities. Instead we see a constant rise in game sales year after year.

Innovation has played a major role in the long term success of the video game industry, as game publishers and hardware engineers design products that meet the needs of ever widening segments of the population. In the past three decades, video game companies expanded their reach by offering violent adult-oriented games for men, social and fitness games for women, educational games for young children and, most recently, mental acuity games for senior citizens. In 2006, Nintendo became the first video game company to have a booth at the American Association of Retired Persons (AARP) Annual Conference, where it promoted memory games that may delay the onset and progression of Alzheimer's disease.

The Performance Trap

One would think that the largest and most well-known companies in the industry would be the ones to benefit most from this expanding market. Yet industry leaders Sony, Microsoft, and Electronic Arts (EA) find themselves struggling as development costs skyrocket and design problems result in product delays and unprecedented warranty charges. The most successful companies were not those offering state-of-the-art consoles and software, but those that provided innovative products that reached new audiences while keeping development costs low.

Ever since it transformed itself from a toy company into one of the world's leading providers of electronic entertainment, Nintendo has been a leader in product innovation. Its latest sensation is the Wii, a game console that has maintained high levels of consumer demand for the past several years. Manufacturers typically drop prices within a year or two of a product's launch in order to attract late adopters. Not so for the Wii. Three years after it was introduced, retailers continued to have trouble obtaining sufficient stock to meet customer demand. During that time, Nintendo console sales have outpaced the competition by an order of magnitude, despite the fact that the Nintendo Wii is easily the least powerful and least versatile among current generation consoles. Even the PlayStation 2, which was first introduced in 2001, offers features that are not available on the Wii, such as DVD movie playback.

Nintendo was able to reach new audiences by implementing product features that appealed to non-traditional gamers. Examples include the Nintendo DS touch screen console that can be used for education, museum tours, and traditional games. The most revolutionary innovation is the Wii console's controller, known as the Wii Remote (or Wiimote for short). It challenges the stereotype of inactive gamers by turning the game console into a fitness device that is used for physical therapy in hospitals and senior homes.

Why is it that Sony and Microsoft, two of the largest and most successful companies in history, find themselves unable to compete against Nintendo and its underpowered console? The history of technology provides us with some clues. It is not unusual to find technically superior products that failed or sold poorly relative to technically inferior competing products. Some failed because they used closed standards that limited external innovation and, as counterintuitive as it may sound, some failed because product development managers failed to make technological compromises that help satisfy customer needs.

How can making sacrifices in features or performance help satisfy customer needs? Don't customers want the best products that money can buy? Not necessarily. The Sony Betamax is a classic example. Introduced in 1975, Betamax tapes were smaller and provided better definition than the competing VHS format introduced by JVC the following year. When RCA sought a video format for its new home-movie cameras, it initially approached Sony. However, Sony engineers were unwilling to extend the recording time of Betamax tapes because it would compromise video quality. RCA then turned to JVC, which owned the VHS format. RCA knew that VHS was inferior, but because JVC was willing to accommodate RCA's request for longer recording times, it won the contract. RCA realized that consumers valued the convenience of not having to carry around spare tapes more than higher picture quality. JVC then went on to license its technology to other third-party manufacturers who significantly undercut Sony's price. In 1988, Sony abandoned the format and began manufacturing VHS players.

Designers and engineers are often energized by breakthrough technologies that allow them to accomplish tasks they only dreamed were possible. In the process, they often lose sight of the real goal—fulfilling a customer need. They succumb to what we call "the performance trap." In Betamax's case, consumers valued longer playback times more than video performance.

Some managers in our executive and high-tech MBA courses have told us how excited they were about a new technology, only to see it fall short of market projections. When they were developing these wonder products, they didn't consider that customers might not care about spec sheets. Even if the product outperformed the competition, was the difference enough to warrant a higher price or the effort needed to migrate over to the new product?

It doesn't matter if you are designing a $5 remote control or a $5 million supercomputer, the lessons are the same. When a technologically superior product fails to live up to its market potential, it is usually because it offers features that are inconsistent with consumer needs.

Sometimes new products have indirect costs that are known to the customer, but are not readily apparent to product designers. Microsoft Windows is a perfect example. Despite years of complaints about poor performance and security flaws, the operating system continues to dominate the home PC market. Although Linux, UNIX, and Apple OSX offer clear advantages over Windows, users have little reason to switch. Most are willing to accept the inherent problems associated with Windows if it means they can avoid installing and learning a new operating system. Other features, such as the ability to run popular software programs and share files with other PC users, often outweigh security problems, which can remain unnoticed for years.

Although this lack of knowledge about customers is occasionally the fault of the product engineers, more often marketing managers are to blame. Marketing executives need to be vigilant throughout the development process to ensure that customer needs are understood and clearly articulated to other functional groups. The best way to do this is to use cross-functional teams of marketing, engineering and R&D personnel to develop new products and services. By so doing, individual members can more easily share important information that can impact the design and development of the new product. Marketing's role is not to dictate the design of the product or worry about technical specifications, but rather to ensure that customer requirements are being met by the underlying technologies and design architecture. As we will see later, the reliability of the Xbox 360 was partially compromised when marketing managers decided to redesign the external case to make the console appear more attractive.

Despite the Xbox 360's hardware failings that are the focus of the chapter titled *Rings of Death*, Microsoft did several things right. For example, it decided to deliver content differently by building the Xbox 360 around an immersive online experience known as Xbox Live. Although Xbox Live got off to a slow start, with only 20 percent of original Xbox users subscribing, the strategy eventually paid off. The company's foresight and unwavering determination in online gaming have allowed it to become the leader in an important and quickly growing niche.

Sony's problems began long before the PlayStation 3 was released. In pre-launch announcements, marketing literature, television advertising, and industry trade shows, Sony repeatedly declared that its console was powered by a "supercomputer on a chip," with performance and graphics beyond anything the world had ever seen. And Sony was right. The problem was that all of the impressive benchmarks and specifications did not translate into real world differences. Games developed for both the Xbox 360 and PlayStation 3 looked and felt nearly identical. Lately, Sony has taken steps to remedy the problem by helping developers learn how to take advantage of the PS3's unique hardware and by improving its online services.

Historical Precedents and Future Directions

The lessons we are going to examine are not new. Almost every success and failure in the video game industry has historical precedents in other industries. In fact, long before video games became part of the human experience, we find countless examples of technically superior products that either failed or sold poorly relative to technically inferior competing products. Although we may occasionally draw upon examples from other industries, the focus of our discussion will remain centered in the video game industry as we examine how really new and radical innovations can be used to open new markets and win market share from technically superior products that have become mired in performance traps.

Early chapters will consider the history of video game innovation, including events that led to the great video game crash of 1983 and the subsequent rise of Nintendo as the dominant console maker. We will examine how Shigeru Miyamoto, a Japanese graphic artist and musician, reinvented the industry and became the tour de force behind Nintendo's ascendency. Later, we will see how Sony finally broke Nintendo's monopoly, when other more experienced console makers failed and how the Sega Dreamcast provided the blueprint for the eventual success of the Xbox and Xbox Live.

The last half of the book focuses on recent innovations in video game hardware and why low-performance consoles are outselling their high performance counterparts. In particular, we will try to understand why the Nintendo DS and Nintendo Wii are outselling the Sony PSP, Sony PlayStation 3, and Microsoft Xbox 360. We will look at innovators in game software and find out why small independent studios are creating games that put big budget titles to shame. Some major studios like Take-Two Interactive and Square Enix have found ways to thrive by adapting to the changing business environment, while others like Electronic Arts have faltered by clinging to outdated strategies.

Lastly, we will look at trends that will influence the future direction of video gaming and electronic entertainment. They include mobile games for smartphones, cloud gaming, and Microsoft's Project Natal, a product that promises to eliminate the need for game controls by responding to gestures, voice commands, and even emotional states.

1

Shigeru Miyamoto and the Art of Donkey Kong

Much of Nintendo's success could be attributed to Shigeru Miyamoto (b. 1952). In the early 1980s, he created several highly popular games that helped vault Nintendo into first place in video game entertainment. His innovations also launched a race for performance that drove microprocessor development for the next two decades and led to some of the most important advancements in home video game consoles, high performance computers, and handheld devices.

When IGN Entertainment announced its list of the top 100 developers of all time, Shigeru Miyamoto topped the list. "It wasn't a difficult selection. Nobody in the video game arena has proven as innovative and irrefutably influential as Nintendo's legendary game designer," IGN announced.

> *His track record speaks for itself. From the mind of a single, unwaveringly happy man comes such timeless franchises as* Donkey Kong, Mario Bros., *and* The Legend of Zelda. *Through the years, Miyamoto has had his hand in just about every major Nintendo series, including* Wave Race, Mario Kart, F-Zero *and* Star Fox. *Yet he has never rested on his laurels, continuing to develop new ideas and fresh game concepts, including the 3D sensation that was* Super Mario 64, *the ultra-accessible* Pikmin *and the simply addictive* Nintendogs. *He brought the analog stick and the rumble pack to console gamers and he was integral in the advent of Nintendo's dual-screen handheld. Even now, almost 30 years after* Donkey Kong *arrived in arcades, Miyamoto's new software and hardware advancements continue to redefine the industry* (IGN 2009).

Although Miyamoto's early innovations saved the industry from mediocrity, they also spawned a performance race that drove up costs and made games accessible to fewer people. As more companies succumbed to the performance trap, it was Miyamoto who finally helped reign in the industry with products like the Nintendo DS, Wii, and Wii Fit.

Miyamoto the Artist

Shigeru Miyamoto grew up near Kyoto, Japan where he passed the time exploring caves and taking trips to the city to watch films. Although his family did not have a television, he was fascinated with comics and cartoons, particularly those coming from Disney. He even started a comics club in school where he and his fellow students could work together on drawings and animation.

He began his career with Nintendo in the late 1970s. At first, the struggling art school graduate did not impress company president Hiroshi Yamauchi. When Miyamoto arrived for a job interview with a bag full of toys he had designed, Yamauchi protested that Nintendo needed engineers, not artists. Yet because Miyamoto's father was a childhood friend of the Nintendo president, Yamauchi offered Miyamoto a position as the company's first staff artist.

Miyamoto spent the first years of his career at Nintendo designing artwork for arcade game cabinets. Then, in 1980, Yamauchi called Miyamoto into his office to get his opinion on a poorly selling arcade game called *Radar Scope*. Nintendo had produced 3,000 units of *Radar Scope* arcade machines, and most of them remained unsold. If something wasn't done, Nintendo stood to lose a considerable sum of money. Yamauchi also worried that Nintendo might lose its opportunity to break into the U.S. market, which at the time was dominated by Namco and Atari.

Based on his experience playing games at the local arcade, Miyamoto found that most titles suffered from overly simplistic gameplay and excessive violence. He told Yamauchi that games could be improved if only they would follow the examples of classical literature and offer interesting story lines and complex characters. *Radar Scope* was a perfect example. As a clone of *Space Invaders*, it offered nothing new to game players. Games needed to offer players something different, something that would draw them back to the game and make them want to continue playing it.

Miyamoto's ideas fascinated Yamauchi, who offered the young artist a chance to redesign the arcade game. There was just one problem. He had no idea how to create a computer program. Most people would have given up at that point, but not Miyamoto. He turned to the company's engineers for advice and assistance and quickly learned all he needed to know to produce the game that we know today as *Donkey Kong*. The new game featured a hero, known as Jumpman, who had to rescue a damsel in distress from the eponymous giant ape.

When Nintendo's U.S. sales force learned of *Donkey Kong*, they were dismayed. The game not only lacked proven features, such as bombs and missiles, it "had more in common with a Bugs Bunny cartoon than an apocalyptic science-fiction saga." Yamauchi ignored their complaints. "He believes marketing people will only look at what's popular right now, and if we make the game based on what's popular right now, the game will not be new and fresh," observed Nintendo managing director Hiroshi Imanishi. Yamauchi's instinct was right. Upon its release in 1981, *Donkey Kong* quickly became a best-seller, with first year sales of more than $100 million.

Donkey Kong was certainly not a masterpiece of storytelling, but it was surprisingly developed given the limited hardware Miyamoto had to work with. He had wanted to create a much more elaborate game, but many of his ideas were rejected by Nintendo's engineers because of the inability of the hardware to properly render the scene as Miyamoto envisioned it. However, the basic theme became a model for later titles that did conform to his vision, such as Zelda and Mario Brothers. "Gone was the open-ended 'highest score' criterion of previous titles and in its place was a more concrete goal: 'Complete' the game," observed Andrew Vestal in *The History of Zelda*. "Games had evolved from just-for-fun endurance tests to simple narratives with (in the best Socratic tradition) a beginning, middle, and end. Gamers had a reason to play beyond simple continued survival." *Donkey Kong* was also the first platform style game, the first game to use jump action, and the first game to use cut scenes to advance the plot and provide back-stories.

What was Miyamoto's key to success and why had it eluded so many skilled developers? When Miyamoto stepped in Yamauchi's office nearly 30 years ago, he certainly seemed an unlikely candidate for the title, "father of modern video games." He had no idea of the complexity of computer programming or the limitations imposed by the primitive hardware that was available at the time. Instead, he had a vision in his mind of what the ideal game would look like, a vision driven by his artistic and musical talent, his broad exposure to classical literature, and his childhood fantasies. Already with his first game, Miyamoto was thinking beyond the capabilities of current generation game consoles toward a future of high-definition video and sound. The idea was not to create more games, but interactive versions of the fantasy films and stories he enjoyed as a child, and as soon as Nintendo began taking steps toward achieving that vision, there was no going back. Experienced developers, on the other hand, only knew the craft as it already existed. They were mentally restricted by the processes and values of their respective studios as well as the industry.

This reluctance and inability to pursue disruptive innovations that create new markets is rooted in Clayton Christensen's perspective of firm capabilities. Christensen (1997) argues that capabilities initially reside in a firm's resources— people, equipment, technologies, money, etc. Over time, the firm's capabilities shift from resources to processes and values. As employees repeat tasks, processes are defined and embedded within the organization. As the business grows, strategies and priorities are established leading to the formation of values. When capabilities reside in processes and values, which are inflexible, sustaining innovations are possible and highly likely. However, this inflexibility makes disruptive innovation very difficult and often impossible to achieve. Thus, it appears that with many game developers, their capabilities supported the improved game graphics and performance that mainstream gamers valued. These same capabilities, though, prevented them from pursuing a disruptive approach to video games exemplified by the Nintendo Entertainment System and later by the Wii.

Robert Sutton (2002) of Stanford University believes that "another reason obsolete ways persist is that people become so skilled at doing things in old ways. Their deep competence at old ways and lack of skill at the new can mean that they perform worse when trying new (but ultimately superior) concepts, methods and technologies." When successful technologies, products, and strategies are reinforced, it is known as the "success trap." Companies that succumb to the "success trap" are often less equipped to deal with disruptive innovations that challenge the status quo.

One might be tempted to dismiss the success of *Donkey Kong* as a stroke of luck or genius, but what Nintendo did in the early 1980s has in fact been repeated many times throughout history. In numerous industries, profound leaps in product innovation often come from outsiders like Miyamoto. Patrick Regnér of the Stockholm School of Economics calls it "strategy making in the periphery." Regnér (1999) found that innovations often arrive from the periphery of organizations, from subsidiaries and satellite offices where employees had more contact with the outside world and therefore with ideas that were different from those of corporate headquarters or insular research laboratories. "New information needs to be assimilated from outside the organization and industry," notes Regnér.

Although Miyamoto worked at Nintendo headquarters, he was still an outsider in the sense that he was neither part of the senior level management team nor a member of the video game establishment. As an artist and musician with no formal training in computer programming or business management, Miyamoto was, in a very real sense, at the periphery of Nintendo's strategy making. In other words, he was just the kind of person to bring fresh ideas into the equation. "The benefit of opening up your problems to outsiders is that in fact you can get novel solutions—quicker solutions than what the firm or R&D lab might develop," explains Karim Lakhani of Harvard Business School. "It also opens up new domains for the pursuit of knowledge and activities" (Lagrace 2006).

Lakhani studied a number of companies in different industries and found that "innovations happen at the intersection of disciplines." He cites one example of a pharmaceutical company that uncovered an unusual toxicology problem. The best toxicologists in the company could not solve the problem, nor could the academic consultants the company turned to, who were also toxicologists. After posting the problem publicly, a crystallographer came to them with a simple off-the-shelf solution. "The pharmaceutical company had never viewed the problem as a crystallography problem," Lakhani noted. "What we don't know is whether some firms may be large enough by themselves to already have the requisite variety and heterogeneity inside the firm. Could they first start by broadcasting problems inside?"

This is, in fact, what Yamauchi did when he called Miyamoto into his office to solve a problem that normally would be considered the domain of programmers, engineers, or even marketing managers. More than anyone, he deserves credit for approaching the problem with an open mind and trusting the vision of a young artist over the protests of sales and marketing managers who saw Donkey Kong as childish.

Yamauchi was a visionary in other ways. When most console manufacturers were cutting back production and facing mounting losses, he moved aggressively to develop his own gaming console. Owing to the large fixed costs associated with semiconductor development and manufacturing, console makers needed to place large orders to keep unit costs low. At a time when incumbent Japanese console manufacturers were selling less than 30,000 units, Yamauchi's confidence in Miyamoto's ideas led him to place an order for 3 million microchips from Ricoh, despite the fact that Nintendo had never manufactured a console of its own. Although many people inside and outside Nintendo thought he was being irrational, to Yamauchi the opportunity was clear. "I guarantee that it will sell a lot because of the great games," he told a group of skeptical wholesalers. A few years later, Nintendo became Ricoh's largest semiconductor customer, accounting for between 60 and 70 percent of the supplier's production.

Mario to the Rescue

Nintendo licensed *Donkey Kong* to Coleco, an American toy manufacturer and one of the first companies to offer a home video game console. Coleco went on to sell more than 6 million units of the game. Nintendo then reinvested the earnings from its fledgling video game business into developing its own video gaming console. Meanwhile, Miyamoto was hard at work thinking up new adventures that eventually resulted in *Super Mario Bros.*, *The Legend of Zelda*, and numerous other games.

Mario Bros. was released as an arcade title in 1983 as a sequel to *Donkey Kong*. This time, the main character, known as Jumpman in *Donkey Kong*, was given a name (Mario) and a profession (plumber). He also gained a brother, known as Luigi, with whom he investigated strange happenings in the sewers of New York City. The game took place in expansive settings where pipes connected surface worlds with various underground locations. Previously, video games were set in confined areas that differed little from one level to the next. *Mario Bros.* rewarded players who explored new areas of the game. For example, a player could choose to travel over land, underground, or in the sky and arrive at the same destination. As such, a person could repeatedly play the same level and discover something unique each time.

The same year *Mario Bros.* was released, the North American home video game market experienced a precipitous decline as consumers grew tired of simplistic arcade games and diverted their attention to the newly emerging home computer market. Most console manufacturers exited the market either through bankruptcy or by refocusing on other product lines. One of the few survivors was Atari, which saved itself through drastic cost-cutting measures.

Between 1983 and 1984, it reduced its staff from 10,000 to only 200. Former Atari developer Chris Crawford (1992) reflected on the situation in 1984:

> *The video game industry died in 1983; home computer sales boomed in Christmas 1983. The damage was greatest in those areas of computer gaming that were closest to video gaming. Most of the smaller publishers, and all of those who had specialized in skill-and-action games, went out of business. Those that did survive did so by cutting costs and having something other than games, or at least something more serious, to keep them going.*

The reason behind the video game crash was not that kids had lost interest in games. Throughout the crash, video game arcades were busy as ever. The problem was that the video game industry was putting out too many mediocre games. Console games that were spin-offs of arcade games like *Pac-man* were poor copies of the originals, and original console games like *E.T.* were even worse.

Nolan Bushnell, the visionary behind Atari, sold his company to Warner Communications in 1976 and left the company two years later after Warner executives refused to heed his advice to lower the price of consoles and move aggressively into personal computers. "There was not a single innovation in the product line at Atari after the day I left," he said. "Everything they did was just a variation on the chip sets and the business I created." Unlike others who viewed home video games as a passing fad, Bushnell believed in the future of gaming. "Atari abandoned the game market to Nintendo, pure and simple ... Atari could have been Nintendo and Apple under one roof" (Sheff 1993).

Yamauchi wanted to repeat the success of the arcade versions of *Donkey Kong* and *Mario Bros.*, only this time in a home console. However, he did not want to repeat the mistakes of Atari, Coleco, and others. At a minimum, for a home game console to be successful, it had to offer players the same benefits and features as arcade machines.

Unlike previous home consoles, the NES would be no toy. In fact, Nintendo went to great lengths to build an advanced console with all the makings of a fully fledged computer, such as the ability to add a keyboard, modem, and other peripherals. With such capable hardware, software engineers had the flexibility they needed to develop stunning games, games like nobody had ever seen.

Among the NES launch titles was one title that would change the industry forever—*Super Mario Bros.* With its release, Nintendo had done the opposite of previous console makers. Instead of making a stripped down version of a popular arcade game as Atari had done with *Pac-man*, Nintendo made *Super Mario Bros.* better than the arcade game it was modeled after. In fact, it was better than any arcade game, period.

Super Mario Bros. excelled on many dimensions. Its improved graphics, intuitive controls, imaginative story, and multiple levels all helped to win over the hearts and minds of gamers. It at once reinvigorated a dying industry and established a new genre of "action" games. "There have been quite a lot of games in the action genre," noted Jun Takeuchi, a senior Capcom developer and creator of the *Resident Evil* franchise, "but I think the greatest achievement was *Super Mario Brothers.*"

> *This game really laid down the control fundamentals of action gaming. Mr. Miyamoto really understood the importance of the feeling of responsive controls when designing action games and put incredible effort into creating his control schemes. Pressing the jump button too soon or too late is no good. You have to be precise with Mario. This is something that has stayed with action games up to this point. (Stang 2007)*

The title went on to sell more than 40 million copies and was one of the main driving forces behind Nintendo's worldwide success. By 1990, Mario was more recognizable to American children than Mickey Mouse, and Nintendo was the most profitable public company in Japan.

People buy consoles to play interesting and popular games, just as they buy computers to run specific software programs. Hardware provides the raw power that allows games to perform their magic, but without the software, game consoles are nothing more than lifeless blocks of plastic, silicone, and copper. Proof can be found in a New Mexico landfill where Atari dumped 14 truckloads of unsold consoles and game cartridges in late 1983 because gamers lost interest in the arcade titles available at the time. The demand for consoles did not die in 1983, but gamers wanted something new and different. They wanted Mario. *Super Mario Bros.* helped Nintendo sell more than 60 million units of the NES, thus proving that content is indeed king.

The Legend of Zelda

With the success of *Super Mario Bros.*, Miyamoto was placed in charge of Nintendo's software division, overseeing development of several titles at once. Development budgets mushroomed to over $1 million per title, and each game had between six and twenty developers working on it at any given time. One of those titles was *The Legend of Zelda*.

As revolutionary as they were, *Donkey Kong* and *Mario Bros.* remained limited representations of Miyamoto's vision of games that told epic stories. "*The Legend of Zelda* was our first game that forced the players to think about what they should do next," Miyamoto explained. "We were afraid that gamers would become bored and stressed by the new concept. Luckily, their reaction was totally the opposite. It was these elements that made the game so popular." (*Superplay* 2003)

The Legend of Zelda is set in a mythical world known as Hyrule, which is populated with dungeons, fairies, goblins, and gnomes. It is here that a young hero known as Link sets out on a quest to rescue Princess Zelda from the evil lord Ganondorf. Meanwhile, Ganondorf is on his own quest to acquire the fragments of the Triforce, a sacred relic of great power that will allow him to completely rule over Hyrule. To stop him, Zelda and Link must acquire the fragments first.

Prior to *Zelda*, games were designed for amusement and entertainment. Miyamoto had a grander vision for *The Legend of Zelda*, one in which players established an emotional connection with in-game characters:

> Link is a regular boy when the game begins, but destiny makes him fight evil. I think many people dream about becoming heroes. For me, it has always been important that the gamers grow together with Link, that there is a strong relationship between the one who holds the controller and the person who is on the screen. I tried to create the feeling that you really are in Hyrule. (*Superplay* 2003)

Not even *Super Mario Bros.* came close to the level of detail in Miyamoto's fantasy world, which in many ways was similar to J. R. R. Tolkien's epic tale *The Lord of the Rings*. And like Tolkien, who began with a simple story (*The Hobbit*) and built a multitude of tales and back-stories of increasing complexity based on that original work, *The Legend of Zelda* spawned a series of sequels and prequels from which an entire universe was constructed. When Nintendo sold more than 2 million copies of *Zelda* in its first year on the North American market, it confirmed that gamers were hungry for something more involving and intelligent than simple arcade games.

Building brand loyalty was easier with games like *Zelda* that appealed to players on an emotional level. For the first time, gamers as individuals could develop strong and deep connections with the characters they saw on their TV screens. It also made the games harder to copy. Anyone can make an arcade game about a space ship that blasts its way through asteroids or aliens, but adventure games like *Zelda* were works of art, like great literature or music. When writers and composers imitate the style of other writers and composers, the results are often mixed. Even when an artist does achieve something great by emulating someone else's work, the end result will usually distinguish itself in other ways. The same was true for games.

Successful titles that were styled after *Zelda* had different stories and characters and each appealed to gamers in different ways. On the other hand, games that were styled after the arcade game *Asteroids* were essentially all the same. If a gamer owned one Asteroids-style game, there was no need to buy another one. That is why games like Zelda and *Mario Bros.* became such strong franchises and games like *Radar Scope* failed. Fantasy and role playing games were continuations of ongoing sagas that kept gamers coming back for more. Today, when gamers purchase "classic" versions of titles from the 1970s and early 1980s that have been ported to modern consoles, they are basically buying the same game that players saw when the titles were first launched. In contrast, when someone buys a Wii game like *Mario Kart*, *Super Mario Galaxy*, or *Zelda Twilight Princess*, the gaming experience is completely different from the original *Mario Bros.* and *Zelda*. Yet all the characters from the original titles are still there, taking gamers on new adventures to new and fantastic worlds.

In all probability, the lack of emotional appeal in earlier arcade games had as much to do with the video game crash of 1983 as any other factor. With so many similar games on the market, gamers had no reason to continue investing in new titles. It wasn't that the games were boring per se, but they lacked the depth and diversity that was needed to keep gamers interested. With *Donkey Kong*, Miyamoto planted the seeds of a revolution against arcade-style gaming, but it was *The Legend of Zelda* that brought that revolution to fruition.

The Rise of Adventure Fantasy Games

At the same time Miyamoto was working on Zelda, Tokyo-based Enix Corporation was preparing to deliver *Dragon Quest*, a role playing game (RPG) that would have a similarly profound impact on console game development. Andrew Vestal (2002) describes *Dragon Quest* as "a seminal and revolutionary title that establishes many conventions and standards."

> *Many of* Dragon Quest's *innovations can be found in RPGs today: upgradable weapons and armor, major quests interwoven with minor sub-quests, hit points and magic points, an incremental spell system, turn-based battles, royalty, chivalry, and really frightening dragons. Unfortunately, many of* Dragon Quest's *shortcomings have also stuck with us: the nameless hero, the stereotypical medieval story, the eminently rescuable princess, the bland and unmotivated characters, and the ridiculously frequent palette-swapped enemies.*

The premise behind *Dragon Quest* was similar to Zelda, but most of the action took place in the form of scrolling text. Although *Dragon Quest* became wildly popular in Japan, it failed to win a following in the United States, perhaps because American gamers saw its text-based game mechanics as a step backward. Nevertheless, *Dragon Quest* went on to influence American gamers in other ways.

One place where *Dragon Quest's* influence was felt was in games like *Final Fantasy* that included both turn-based and action adventure elements. *Final Fantasy* was the brainchild of Hironobu Sakaguchi, Director of Planning and Development for Square Company. Square's first games sold so poorly that by the time it released *Final Fantasy* in 1987, the company was on the verge of bankruptcy. Never in their wildest dreams did they imagine that it would become one of the best-selling game franchises of all time, or that it would transform Square Company into one of the largest game publishers in the world.

The Legend of Zelda, Dragon Quest, and *Final Fantasy* became models for countless fantasy, role playing, and action games. More than anything else, they freed developers to recreate their own fantasy worlds in digital form. With each successive title, they "improved" the games with more features, more levels, more realistic graphics, and more controls. The only limitation was the hardware.

The RPG titles that were being produced for the NES were far more difficult to learn than old style Atari titles. To help kids navigate the various mazes and bosses, Nintendo created a magazine with tips about how to play NES games and unlock various secrets. In its first year in circulation, *Nintendo Power* had 1.5 million subscribers, making it the most popular youth magazine in America. In addition to game guides, the magazine featured previews of upcoming titles, interviews with developers, and stories about top scoring gamers.

Nintendo Power gave subscribers an edge over non-subscribers and provided them with a strong foundation of inside knowledge that allowed them to graduate to even more complex games. It also marked the separation of gamers and non-gamers. Before long, specialized publishers entered the fray with magazines like *Electronic Gaming Monthly, Edge,* and *Game Informer* that catered mainly to older, more advanced players.

The increasing complexity of video games also created a market for specialized game guides. These "strategy guides" were complete books that were laid out like training manuals for pilots or auto mechanics. In 1990, *Nintendo Games Secrets* was one of the first game guides devoted to console gaming. The 358-page tome by Rusel DeMaria, founder of Prima Games, provided tips for all the popular titles then available on the NES. As the guides grew in size, publishers began to separate them into individual books, each dedicated to a single video game title. Some recent game guides, like the *Official Pokémon Guide: Pokémon Platinum,* have grown to more than 600 pages, and although the guides usually include color graphics, they are packed with small font text that describes the steps that players must take to master the game and defeat their opponents.

The growth of magazines and books dedicated to older gamers reflected the fact that kids continued to play games well into their teens. In the 1980s, Nintendo's target market was children between the ages of 6 and 14. By 1994, Nintendo decided that it needed to change its strategy to focus more on teenagers. "We got stuck with the reputation that we were the brand parents wanted their kids to have, which is the kiss of death," said George Harrison, Nintendo's marketing director at the time (Lefton 1994). The company modified its advertising campaigns to have greater appeal to a segment of the population that it referred to as the "MTV Generation" of 9 to 24 year olds. By 2000, the average age of video game consumers had again shifted to between 18 and 34 years old, where it remained for most of the next decade.

As more complex games became available, they were held to higher standards. In the Atari days, games often reached the marketplace with nary a review by actual gamers. Marketing teams had the first and final say over which titles would be promoted, and the results were disastrous. As Nintendo grew, it assigned full-time employees to do nothing but play games and provide feedback to developers. Mediocre games that might have been acceptable a few years earlier were vetted by Nintendo's quality control team. Some were killed outright, while others were sent back to developers for revisions. Phil Sandoff was one of the Nintendo reviewers. "First you think every game is the greatest," he said. "Then you get more critical" (Sheff 1993).

Nintendo could have followed the route of Atari and sold as many games as it could. The short-term profits would have been enormous. Greg Fischbach, founder of Acclaim Entertainment, was one of Nintendo of America's first licensees. He found that his company could sell out every game it produced. And he wasn't alone. "Every company sold out every game no matter how good it was, no matter how well the company was managed," he said. "Anyone with product was able to sell it."

Fischbach may not have realized it at the time, but Nintendo's quality program saved companies like Acclaim from the fate of an unforgiving market. After Sony and Microsoft broke Nintendo's monopoly, content restrictions were relaxed and companies like Acclaim were once again allowed to produce lower quality content. Under such conditions, it was the market that decided which games would succeed. Fischbach may have reveled in this new found freedom—for a time. However, after his company began to release dismal titles like *BMX XXX*, a racing game laced with pornographic content, it began to feel the full effect of free market forces. In the highly competitive video game market, Acclaim's losses quickly mounted and in 2004 it was finally forced into bankruptcy.

The Impact of Games on Console Development

Before long, game development began to push the limits of available technology. Eventually, Sony's frustration with the limitations of the Nintendo system prompted the company to develop its own, more advanced console, a decision that had a profound impact on the direction of console development. One of the more important game franchises on the Sony platform was *Final Fantasy*, a series that first appeared on the NES.

By the time *Final Fantasy VII* was released, 10 years after the *Final Fantasy* franchise made its debut, it boasted an expansive 3-D world and a digital soundtrack complete with vocals. It also won praise from all corners of the industry. "*Final Fantasy VII* is both the culmination of the series' aspirations to date and the start of something completely different and exciting," extolled Vestal (2009) in the *History of Final Fantasy*:

> *Freed from the size constraints of a cartridge and armed with a $30 million plus budget, Square's team of 120 artists created a game with a size, scope, and vision far surpassing any previous title. The cinematic aspects of the series are pushed to the forefront via the most amazing CG ever seen in a game.*

Shortly afterward, Nintendo released *The Legend of Zelda: Ocarina of Time* with similarly impressive features. Both titles are still considered to be among the top 10 games ever made. Most of the "improvements" that have been made to games since the late 1990s have been in improved graphics and sound. When Sony announced in early 2009 that it would make *Final Fantasy VII* available for the PlayStation 3, the crowd roared in approval, despite the fact that the audio and video of *Final Fantasy VII* was antiquated when compared to just about any current game on the market. Meanwhile costs continue to skyrocket. By today's standards, Square's budget of $30 million for *Final Fantasy VII* is considered mainstream, and some big budget titles can cost several times that.

As technology progressed and video game developers felt less constrained, they succumbed to a phenomenon commonly known as "feature creep." "Unlike tangible product offerings, software theoretically has an almost unlimited set of features and functions," note Wind and Mahajan (2001) of the University of Pennsylvania's SEI Center for Advanced Studies in Management. "Therefore, it is difficult to combat 'feature creep' that arises from the gradual addition of marginal features and functions." Video games are particularly vulnerable, explains Alan Gershenfeld (2003), former global leader of entertainment software for Activision. "It is a common mistake for games to become bloated as feature creep sets in," he writes:

> *In the quest to make the best game ever, there is a tendency to toss in more elements, making the game even cooler (no guarantee) and even bigger (guarantee). What is overlooked in expanding the project is that every additional element has a rippling effect on every other aspect of the project.*

As the complexity of the hardware increased to keep up with the demands of the industry, console makers found it harder to maintain promised launch dates. Nevertheless, some developers still felt constrained by the photorealistic 3-D graphics of modern consoles. "Personally, I can envision a move toward holographs," predicted *Final Fantasy* creator Hironobu Sakaguchi. "What I find most annoying about 3-D is the need to decide upon camera position. With holographic games, that decision would rest with users."

Always the visionary, Miyamoto was one of the first to recognize the problem facing the video game industry. "A few years ago, people were saying that Nintendo had slipped off top place," noted Miyamoto shortly before the launch of the Nintendo Wii. "But actually the game market itself had lost touch with the real world."

> *An increasing number of people don't want to play games because they're hard, and a lot of people think games are irrelevant to them. We've lost sight of essential enjoyment, which is the basis of gaming. In developing the Wii, we asked ourselves once more, "What kind of game console do people want in their homes?" We think that game designers, including us, have hit a dead end.*
>
> *It's assumed you will develop for a given environment, and developers don't know what they should make. To break out of this stagnation, we first have to radically change the paradigm. We have to try destroying the paradigm ourselves, and see what is born out of its destruction. If this cycle isn't repeated, nothing new will be created. We decided to base a product around this idea and offer it as a challenge to game designers of the world. So, although I don't reject today's games, if we don't do [something], no new forms of gameplay will appear. (Wyman 2006)*

Not only were games becoming unwieldy for developers, the games were becoming so complex that only those initiated at an early age into the rite of gameplay felt comfortable around a game console. Gamers had to invest a minimum of several hours learning the simple gameplay mechanics for each title. Habitual gamers soon learned that similarities existed between titles, making it easier for experienced players to learn new game functions. However, for the uninitiated, titles like *Final Fantasy XIII* or *Grand Theft Auto IV* seemed bewildering. Just looking at the controller with its array of buttons was enough to turn off most non-gamers.

Both the Wii and the Nintendo DS portable console were Miyamoto's answer to the unwieldy complexity that he helped create two decades earlier. This cycle of simple games to complex games to simple games again is indicative of the product life cycle. The life cycle concept, typically applied to product categories, maintains that products go through different stages characterized by the sales revenue generated by the product.

In the introduction stage, the product is new. As a result, a basic product is offered and few versions of the product exist due to limited competition. The objective in this stage is to create awareness and build primary demand for the product category. In the growth stage, as sales rise and the customer base expands, more competitors enter the market, thereby increasing the number of products available in the category. As well, new features are added to attract new buyers. Simultaneously, however, they increase the complexity of the product.

In the maturity stage, as sales grow at a slower pace, competition gets tougher, often leading to lower prices. Even more features are added in order to help differentiate products from competitors, but with the unintended consequence of making products needlessly complex. However, other innovative efforts can also be undertaken in this stage in order to prolong the life of the product category. Miyamoto's vision of simple, fun games that could be played in different ways (for example, with the Wii remote) is an example of the kind of innovation that can occur in the maturity stage of a product's life cycle. As we will see later in later chapters, such innovations often take the product category in new and interesting directions. In Nintendo's case, a return to basics was what pulled the company back from the precipice of oblivion.

The Evolution of Sound

Before he programmed his first line of code, Miyamoto was an accomplished musician who played banjo in a semi-professional bluegrass group. When he became a developer, he did not set aside his love of music, but rather incorporated it into his games.

Most games from the 1970s and early 1980s produced monotone beeps and other basic sounds that helped enhance gameplay, but they lacked the digital soundtracks that we are accustomed to today. Miyamoto wanted to change that. Rather than just incorporate basic sound effects, he decided to compose songs for *Donkey Kong* that reflected the mood of each scene.

After the success of *Donkey Kong*, Yamauchi decided to hire more artists to work on game development. One of them was Koji Kondo, a musician who joined Nintendo in 1983. "When I was a senior at university, Nintendo sent the university a kind of recruiting message, a recruiting opportunity for the university students," recalled Kondo. "That notice said that Nintendo, for the first time in its history, was hiring men who were dedicated to sound and sound composing."

One of Kondo's first projects was the new *Super Mario Bros.* that was being developed under Miyamoto's direction. Kondo's iconic music became an integral part of the gaming experience. "If you don't believe it," writes Bendik Stang (2007), founder of gameXplore, "play with the sound muted and see if you can figure out when Mario's immunity star wears off." Although Kondo went on to write music for more than two dozen Nintendo games, he remains best known for his work on *Super Mario Bros.*

Development studios that began to imitate Miyamoto's game design soon realized that they too needed musical compositions to provide the same level of gameplay that was coming out of Nintendo. Before long, other studios began to hire musicians to compose soundtracks for their games. Square Company was one of the first studios to advance Miyamoto's innovations with plot based games, cut scenes, and stylish soundtracks. In 1986, the company's art director asked Nobuo Uematsu, a self-taught musician who had been working at a music rental store, to create a soundtrack for a soon-to-be released PC game called *Blasty*. "At that time, Square wasn't a huge software company," recalled Uematsu. "It was pretty much a group of university students and graduates ... I wasn't even sure of the direction that the company was going to go in. But it was a way to make money, and I wanted to create music, so I said yes" (Mielke 2008).

Like many studios at the time, Square was struggling to lift itself out of the great video game crash. That didn't matter much to Uematsu, who saw the job as a temporary gig on his way to fulfilling his dream of writing scores for movies. Then, just as the company appeared to be heading into bankruptcy, it hired Uematsu full-time to write the score for *Final Fantasy*, a title that not only saved the company, but went on to become one of most enduring franchises of all time. Since then, Uematsu and Hironobu Sakaguchi have become two of the most revered figures in the industry.

The greatest limitation facing Miyamoto, Uematsu, Kondo, and other game composers at the time was the sound hardware used in game consoles. Although the 8-bit five channel NES sound system was considered advanced at the time, it could produce a limited range of sounds. "Music was composed in a manner so that a short segment of music was repeatedly used in the same gameplay," Kondo noted.

> I'm afraid that current gamers can more easily get tired of listening to
> the repetition of a short piece of music. Of course, back in those days
> that was all we could do within the limited capacity. We were doing our
> best. (McDonald 2005)

As soundtracks became more important, the need to upgrade the sound system became more obvious. Yet it was those same limitations that allowed unknown musicians like Miyamoto and Uematsu to compose scores for some of the most important games on the market.

For its next console, Nintendo turned to Sony for a sound system capable of producing higher fidelity audio. Sony responded with the SPC-700 processor, designed by Ken Kutaragi, who would later become one of the key figures in the success of the PlayStation brand. The new sound system featured a 16 bit digital signal processor capable of reproducing high sample rate audio for realistic effects like wind. Although the Super Nintendo Entertainment System (SNES) still had an electronic sound, it was a vast improvement over the original NES.

The early 1990s saw accelerated development as new entrants to the console market tried to upstage Nintendo in video and audio performance. Companies like NEC, Sega, and SNK pushed the limits in hardware development. By the time Sony entered the market with the PlayStation, consoles were capable of producing near CD quality sound. "Improvements in technology have played a major role in Uematsu's work," wrote *Time Magazine* music critic Christopher John Farley. "The release in the U.S. in 1995 of the PlayStation platform, with its increased storage capacity and CD sound quality, enabled game developers to employ more sophisticated music."

The release of *Final Fantasy VI* in 1997, with a score considered by many to be the pinnacle of Uematsu's life work, was a watershed moment for the video game industry. Music was no longer merely background sound, but a central part of the game that reflected the joy, tension, and tragedy of the characters. "Music plays a key role in [*Final Fantasy VI*], with each major character having his or her own theme song," observed Eri Izawa (2000), Lead Game Designer at L5 Games:

> In fact, in the game's plot, one of the game's characters must sing her theme song in an opera! Most of the tunes are melancholy, reflecting the tragic histories of their characters. In the barren, snowy wastelands, the music is mysterious and lonely; in a bustling town it becomes lively and simple; when the hero's airship flies through the skies after the final victory, the music is proud and triumphant, yet still a little sad.

Although sound improvements continue to be made, by the late 1990s console audio was sufficiently advanced for composers to create almost anything their minds could imagine.

More than ever, music continues to be an essential part of the gaming experience. Sound quality has improved to such an extent that the soundtracks are often sold as separate standalone products in the same way as movie soundtracks. Uematsu and other video game composers tour the world giving concerts with major orchestras from Montreal to Moscow.

Today's games feature tracks by the music industry's leading artists, including names like Kanye West and the Beatles, while high capacity hard drives and Blu-ray disks allow games to include more extensive and diverse content to suit the individual tastes of each player. *Burnout Paradise*, for example, includes 92 high fidelity music tracks ranging from Mozart and Brahms to Guns N' Roses and Alice in Chains.

Eliminating Barriers

When Miyamoto began recording tracks for *Donkey Kong*, he connected an inexpensive keyboard to a portable tape recorder. Today, musicians have tools available to them that are every bit as sophisticated as the development tools used by game designers. However, there remains one important difference. The technological advances in sound are typically invisible to the end user, whereas graphics performance can have a significant impact on the way gamers interact with the software. For example, sound is not manipulated in the same way as objects presented in 3-D space. Controllers became more complex to match the complexity of the game environment, to control more weapons in more ways, and to simulate the intricate movements of the human body.

This dichotomy in the way complexity is perceived by gamers will be a recurring theme throughout the book. For some, the answer may be to return to simpler days; hence we see renewed interest in "classic games." For others, it means embracing technological advances in ways that challenge existing paradigms about the way games should be played.

In the nearly three decades since Miyamoto envisioned the first modern video game, gamers have had to contend with steadily increasing levels of difficulty to the point where today's games require users to commit a significant amount of time and effort to learning each title's assorted rules and control schemes. Fortunately, a few visionaries have stood up to challenge the way we think about games. The question is how far their vision of inclusiveness and simplicity will take us.

Once again, Miyamoto is leading the way. With the Wii remote, he has broken down barriers by making the controller a more natural extension of the human body, by reducing the number of buttons on the controller, and by designing games that are intuitive, yet challenging. As with his early innovations in games like *Donkey Kong* and *Mario Bros.*, other developers are building upon Miyamoto's ideas and taking them even further. Both Sony and Microsoft are working on technologies that will one day allow users to interact with game consoles without any controller. Apple has built motion-sensing technologies into its iPhone, essentially turning a telephone into a capable gaming device. Instead of using technology to make games more complex, they are using it to make games more instinctive and natural. Just as great music has no bearing on the ability to play a game, new technologies are paving the way to simplicity and removing the constraints that have prevented many people from experiencing great games.

2

Nintendo's Dark Age

Within a few years of the North American launch of the Nintendo Entertainment System in 1985,[1] Nintendo had reached the height of its success. Investors loved the company, and magazines like *Fortune* heaped praise upon its managers. Kids loved Nintendo more than anyone for creating the most imaginative and entertaining pastime of their generation. On the other hand, the creator of Mario and Zelda was also making numerous enemies. Parents worried that Nintendo was brainwashing their children, retailers and developers complained about the company's power and influence over the direction of the industry, and legislators worried about its monopolistic practices and about public accusations that it had ties to organized crime and illegal gambling.

By the early 1990s, Nintendo was on the defensive. New competitors entered the market with better graphics, less expensive games, and standard hardware that could be used for more than gaming. Early attempts to challenge Nintendo had failed, and as a result, Nintendo grew complacent. However, before long companies like Sega, Sony and Microsoft were coming out with better consoles that offered more features for about the same cost. Nintendo seemed to have little chance against giants like Sony and Microsoft. Its GameCube console was a dismal failure compared with the PlayStation 2 and Xbox. When Nintendo's market share fell below 16 percent, the company's very survival seemed to be in question. Yet in some ways, it was Nintendo's new competitors that were becoming less relevant. Just as Nintendo seemed to be on its last throws of life, it surprised the world with the DS and Wii, two of the most popular gaming consoles in the world.

This chapter will examine the many reasons behind Nintendo's fall, from its monopolistic tendencies that alienated retailers and developers to its obstinate refusal to adopt industry standards. In later chapters we will see how Nintendo

---

1   The NES was released in Japan in 1983 under the name Famicom, a contraction of "Family Computer."

was able to use product innovation to recover from this seemingly hopeless situation and once again lead the industry.

Education vs. Gambling

In the 1980s, Nintendo was one of the first companies to envision "the establishment of a large-scale network" that connected gaming consoles to each other and to information stored on centrally located servers. "Our purpose is not only to develop new exciting entertainment software, but to provide information that can be efficiently used in each household," declared Nintendo President Hiroshi Yamauchi (Sheff 1993).

To access that information, console owners only had to install a modem into the console's expansion port. As long as a network was available for users to dial into, the process of accessing information was relatively simple. In today's world, such capabilities might seem trivial, but at the time, they were no less than revolutionary. Most people had never heard of the Internet, and the few who had were mainly employed in large government organizations and universities.

With NES consoles installed in nearly a third of all households in America and Japan, Nintendo was poised to lead the information age. In Japan, many households embraced online services. They used it to check news and weather, to conduct online banking, and to trade stocks. In contrast, less than 3 percent of Americans used online services, mainly through PCs hooked into a service call Prodigy. If Nintendo had its way, that was about to change. An NES with online capabilities could provide families with an inexpensive way to access information in ways that most people never dreamed possible.

Online services had the potential to revolutionize education by providing universal access to limitless amounts of information. *Encyclopedia Britannica*, which was known for its aggressive sales tactics, told parents that an encyclopedia set would help their children achieve better grades. However, few families could afford to buy the 32-volume set outright. The cheapest vinyl-bound set cost $1,499, while sets with padded covers were $1,799, and sets bound in genuine leader were $8,000. World Book Encyclopedia offered its 22-volume set for as little as $579, still a hefty sum by 1980s standards. To help make their books affordable, Britannica offered monthly payment plans, but such plans paled in comparison to what Nintendo could potentially provide, or to what Prodigy was already providing to the few families who could afford a PC. Online services were not only cheaper, they included more up-to-date information, allowed text searching and provided audio and video clips.[2]

In 1991, the year Nintendo planned to launch its North American online service, an article appeared on the front page of the *New York Times* exclaiming that the NES could become "the catalyst that will encourage more people to use computers and phone lines to tap into a growing pool of information and services" (Shapiro 1991). Others predicted that Nintendo would soon dominate computer networks worldwide. "Nintendo's plan for America is to launch a network that will dwarf Prodigy and its competitors," wrote David Sheff (1993), author of *Game Over*:

> *It is a reasonable ambition. Hooked to the promise of access to the game players across town and across oceans, kids would be the pioneers, bringing modems into households. They would probably educate parents about the potential of a network, but even if they didn't, the generation of kids who grew up with the Nintendo Network will one day be trading stocks and making airline reservations for themselves.*

One thing that Sheff understood that Nintendo did not was that—at least for the present—the primary consumers of Nintendo's Internet service would be children. Unfortunately, Nintendo of America President Minoru Arakawa saw things differently. To him, the primary audience was "a growing user base of adults in the United States who are at ease sitting on the floor in front of the TV screen." It was a fatal mistake.

To assess the system's online performance, Nintendo teamed up with the Minnesota state lottery to test the console as an online gambling platform. Parents who viewed the NES as a toy were abhorred by the idea that Nintendo planned to turn their children into gamblers. "Kids are gambling now; this will allow them to gamble more," complained Minnesota's former gaming commissioner (Shapiro 1991).

Nintendo was certainly within its right to view the NES as a computer platform, and a very capable one at that. But in marketing, perception is everything. Perception is shaped by experience, from what we see and hear,

---

2   Bandwidth limitations restricted the amount of audiovisual content available to online subscribers. Such limitations were later addressed with CD-ROM based media and broadband Internet.

from our interactions with friends and family, and from what we learn in school or see on TV. In this case, parents knew that the NES was primarily sold in toy stores for use by young children. That made it a toy, not a computer. Bob Heitman, general manager of the Sierra Network, one of the first online gaming companies, immediately knew that Nintendo had made a bad decision. "I have a bad feeling for lotteries," he said. "As a family game company, I would not do it or advocate that our company do it" (Shapiro 1991).

Nintendo offered assurances that children would not be involved in gambling, but by then it was too late. The public outcry was unstoppable. Soon media reports surfaced that Nintendo itself was involved in illegal gambling operations in the United States. Nintendo tried to assure the public that its online service would be much more than an outlet for gambling, but skeptical parents and politicians had heard too many empty promises to be convinced. Nolan Bushnell, the famous founder of Atari, once said that "a video game can teach geography and history as a player moves through the course. A game can teach complex decision-making and critical thinking." Instead, many parents complained that video games had few, if any, redeeming qualities. Years later, Bushnell himself conceded that "video games have not fulfilled the promise that I envisioned. The repetitive mindless violence that you see on video games right now is not anything I want to be associated with" (Sheff 1993).

Nintendo's expansion of its online service into the U.S. failed to take into account cultural, moral, and social differences of the American market. A new product launch can be challenging, but not nearly as challenging as when cultural and moral factors become part of the equation. Globalization has allowed people to be exposed to different languages, cultures, and products like never before. Yet cultural differences still exist and need to be taken into consideration when introducing new products. Sengun Yeniyurt and Janell D. Townsend of Michigan State University note that "cultural norms and beliefs are powerful forces shaping people's perceptions, dispositions and behaviors." In the case of product decisions and new product introductions, it is these cultural factors that need to be taken into consideration "including their impact on attitudes and persuasion" (Yeniyurt and Townsend 2003).

Managers need to have a strong grasp of local norms and beliefs that may impact an international product launch. In this case, Nintendo seemed oblivious to the fact that a storm had been brewing for some time over the expansion of gambling in the United States. In the 1980s and 1990s, casinos wanted to branch out beyond Nevada and Atlantic City to nearly every corner of the country, and cash-starved state governments wanted to use lotteries as a way to attract additional revenues.

Even before anyone had heard of Nintendo, parents, educators, and psychologists voiced concerns that the proliferation of legal gambling would have a corrupting effect on the nation's youth. By the time Nintendo entered the fray, the fury over gambling was reaching its peak. In *Futures at Stake*, Howard J. Shaffer, Director of the Division on Addictions at Harvard Medical School, observed that youth gambling had become an important moral issue in the U.S. in the late 1980s and early 1990s. Many parents were concerned that gambling organizations deliberately targeted children. For example, in one advertisement, the Massachusetts state lottery suggested that a young person had two alternatives in life, to earn a living the hard way, or to win the lottery. "While the advertisement was short lived, it did represent the way that gambling is often portrayed to young people" (Shaffer et al. 2003).

Senator David Durenberger of Minnesota, who in 1984 chaired a hearing on the legalization of state lotteries, questioned whether it was appropriate for the state to promote an activity that "for most of our history the states punished as a vice."

> For large segments of the American Public, gambling—whether promoted openly by the State or conducted outside the law—is, and always has been, a moral question. That's why it is against the law in most States—against the law unless some lawmaking body of the State finds itself pressed for funds. (Shaffer et al. 2003)

In Japan, where the prevalence of problem gamblers was lower than in the U.S., youth gambling has never been viewed as an important social concern. In fact, few western countries struggled with gambling's moral implications as much as America. Consequently, the controversy surrounding Nintendo's partnership with the Minnesota State Lottery must have come as a shock to the company's Japanese managers. But by the time they discovered their mistake, there was little they could do. Ultimately Nintendo decided that the potential risk to the company's brand reputation outweighed any potential gain. Dominating the global Internet, it seemed, was less important than Nintendo had led its investors and partners to believe.

The decision to exit the market for online services set the stage for future competitors to develop an online standard. When Sega tried its hand at online gaming a few years later, it too failed. Nevertheless, Microsoft, which had been working closely with Sega, planned to make online services the centerpiece of its own soon-to-be-launched console—the Xbox. Today, Microsoft's Xbox Live has become the de facto standard for online gaming and it is at Microsoft, not Nintendo, where the vision of the connected living room is coming to life. Meanwhile, Nintendo's online service has become its Achilles heel, as it struggles to keep up with the competition.

Retail Distribution and Licensing

Although Nintendo products made up as much as 20 percent of gross sales for toy stores in the late 1980s, the company's policies were unpopular. Retailers complained that Nintendo had too much power over them, and that it deliberately withheld inventory to create artificial demand. Retailers that normally purchased goods on credit were forced to pay cash up front in order to secure a small ration of game cartridges. One large retailer that was having financial troubles had to pay Nintendo one year in advance before it was permitted to place an order.

When Atari began creating unlicensed cartridges for the Nintendo system through a subsidiary known as Tengen, Nintendo went to retailers and threatened them with lawsuits and other remedies if they sold the cartridges. One remedy was to further limit supplies to noncompliant stores. Nintendo sent investigators to stores and when unlicensed merchandise was discovered, Nintendo followed up with threatening letters, phone calls, and meetings. Constrained as they were in the number of games they could sell, retailers could ill afford to have their meager allotment of games withheld.

Nintendo also forced retailers to sell games at a fixed price approved by the company. "One chain reportedly lowered the price of the NES [console] by a matter of cents and advertised it in Sunday newspapers. A competitor called Nintendo, which immediately froze shipments to the company offering the lowered prices" (Sheff 1993). A subsequent FTC investigation uncovered evidence of price fixing, and Nintendo was forced to abandon its policy of not shipping games to retailers who sold discounted merchandise. Nevertheless, Nintendo was able to maintain inflated prices for several more years. Retailers increasingly felt that Nintendo's monopoly had to be broken for them to reap the full benefits of the growing video game market. Only then would they be permitted to freely order as many games as they felt the marketplace could support and set prices as they saw fit.

In the early 1990s, Nintendo began to pursue any company that didn't follow its vision of how games should be consumed. When Blockbuster began to rent games, Nintendo tried to get the U.S. Congress to pass legislation that would ban game rentals. The effort failed. Then it tried to restrict rental stores from buying games from retailers by limiting the number of copies of one title that could be sold to a customer, and threatened to cut off any retailers that did not comply. That too failed. Nintendo then sued Blockbuster for copyright infringement because the rental stores sent out photocopies of game instructions rather than the originals. Blockbuster simply sidestepped the lawsuit by writing its own instructions.

Retailers were not the only ones to feel intimidated by Nintendo's growing power. Developers felt constrained by Nintendo's strict licensing terms which set out how many games a developer could produce in a year, how the games would be distributed, and whether or not they could be ported to competing consoles. One of the more outspoken critics of Nintendo was Masaya Nakamura, founder of Namco Ltd. Namco was one of the first Nintendo licensees to align itself with other console makers, first with Sega and later with Sony. Rarely did the heads of Japanese game companies publicly criticize each other, but Nakamura felt that Nintendo had gone too far. "Nintendo is monopolizing the market, which is not good for anyone," Nakamura told the Japan Economic Journal (Sheff 1993).

Independent developers were especially annoyed by Nintendo's insistence that they order at least 10,000 cartridges before their game could be considered for the NES. Developers also had to pay half the manufacturing costs in advance and pay additional royalties once the game sold. Most developers were forced to sign an exclusivity clause that prevented them from releasing the game for any other game system for a minimum of two years, and each studio could release no more than five games a year. For smaller studios the limit was a mere formality, but it restricted the ability of larger firms to produce the number of games needed to ensure profitability. At the same time, it encouraged developers to produce games for competing systems that did not impose such restrictions. The challenge was finding retailers willing to sell games without Nintendo's seal of approval.

Nintendo offered certain privileges to licensed developers that were meant to assuage their concerns and maintain their loyalty. They included access to Nintendo's marketing and customer services, a seal of quality stamped on the game package, product displays at Nintendo booths in trade shows, and the use of Nintendo's extensive retail distribution network. Nevertheless, some developers complained that Nintendo's own games seemed to get better coverage in promotional literature.

Nintendo Power was the most influential gaming magazine at the time. When favorable articles appeared in the magazine, game sales shot up. Although most games sold well regardless of coverage, third party developers often complained that they received less favorable coverage than Nintendo's studios. "Their games always get covers, always get page after page in the magazine, while we are made to feel privileged to be mentioned in passing," complained one developer (Sheff 1993).

When Colleagues become Competitors

The first real competitors to the NES were the Sega Genesis and NEC TurboGrafx-16 consoles, released simultaneously in August 1989. The TurboGrafx-16 was a joint venture between two Japanese companies, Hudson Soft and NEC. Hudson Soft was an early developer for the Nintendo Entertainment System with games like *Bomberman* and *Lode Runner*. In the mid 1980s, Hudson Soft worked on a technology known as the PC-engine, one of the first 16 bit gaming systems. At first, it tried to sell the concept to Nintendo for its next generation console, but Nintendo wasn't interested. "The problem for Nintendo, which was raking in a large part of its fortune from licensees, was that it had so much invested in the NES-Famicom technology," explained David Sheff. "If the company planned to release a new system, the game-designing companies would worry that the NES was obsolete, and the shift could precipitate an early crash of its bread-and-butter NES business" (Sheff 1993).

Nintendo's desire to hold onto its Famicom technology is a classic situation of a company ignoring emerging technologies because their product (based on an old technology) continues to generate significant revenue and profit. The problem with this strategy is that technologies mature before products. The time when a product is making large sums of money is exactly the time when the firm needs to be exploring new technologies. The theoretical foundation for this common problem was developed by Richard Foster (1986) who argued that technologies go through various stages. The idea is that as R&D spending increases, technology performance (in terms of features, speed, reliability, etc.) improves. However, at a certain point, performance hits a plateau and further improvement would be impossible or prohibitively expensive. It is at this point that the firm should switch to a new and different technology to achieve higher product performance. But, because new technologies can be slow at the beginning and have lower initial performance levels and because the existing product is generating significant cash for the firm, many firms continue to hold onto the existing technology rather than switch to the new technology.

Nintendo's concerns were not unwarranted. Transitioning from one generation console to the next involves an inevitable decline in sales as developers shift their efforts to next generation titles. The problem with that logic, however, is that if Nintendo didn't upgrade its console, other companies would eventually fill the void. Nintendo's 90 percent market share and its perceived power over retail distribution created a false sense of security. As with most monopolies, Nintendo believed that it didn't need to work as hard at being innovative; it could maintain the status quo and still remain the market leader. Although penetrating Nintendo's fortress would prove challenging to newcomers, it was not impossible.

If one were to use Michael Porter's Five Forces analysis to review the games market in 1989, Nintendo's position would have appeared unassailable. The only substitutes were personal computers and consoles that played none of the most popular games, like *Mario Bros.*, *The Legend of Zelda*, and *Final Fantasy*. Moreover, personal computers were far more expensive than game consoles. The most basic PC configuration with an Intel 286 processor and a monochrome monitor cost a minimum of $1,500. An NES console, by comparison, was only $199 and could be used with a color display. As we saw earlier, customers and distributors had little, if any bargaining power over Nintendo. Suppliers like Ricoh and Sony in hardware, and Hudson Soft and Tengen in software, relied too heavily on Nintendo for their revenue to pose a serious challenge. And when Atari tried to challenge Nintendo by making unlicensed cartridges, it was quickly defeated, setting a precedent that would cause other developers to think twice before crossing Nintendo.

For an electronics firm, Nintendo's position was enviable. Most technical products compete in commoditized markets where the only way to distinguish one product from another was through patent protection. Successful technology products usually have proven benefits that are clear to consumers, compete in a growing market, and have few competitors. Nintendo's fundamental flaw was that, outside the software innovations introduced by Miyamoto and his staff, the company was not a strong innovator. Nintendo, like Atari before it, was becoming complacent.

Blinded by its success, Nintendo failed to see that as games became more complex, gamers placed greater value on functional attributes such as color depth and image detail. When viable competitors first entered the gaming landscape in 1989, it was Nintendo's valuable software brands that kept gamers from defecting to other consoles. Gamers had too much invested in Nintendo franchises, both in terms of skill development and emotional connections to in-game characters. For competitors to successfully challenge Nintendo, they needed to find equally compelling content. Hardware performance and image quality alone were not going to topple the Mario franchise.

Indeed, it was the lack of compelling content, more than anything else, which sunk the NEC TurboGrafx-16. Gamers were impressed by its graphics and sound, as well as its ability to add an optional CD-player. The price, at $199, was also in line with Nintendo's less capable system. However, NEC only offered 94 games throughout the console's short life and none came close to challenging the best games for the NES.

The Sega Genesis, which was released at the same time as the Turbografx-16, offered many of the same technical advantages as the NEC console. Sega had long been a successful arcade game developer, but its early efforts to enter the home console market were less successful. The Sega Master System, which came out in 1986 to compete with the NES, never gained significant market share.

The Genesis system was different. This time, Sega borrowed advanced 16 bit technology from its successful arcade systems to create a more capable home console than either the NES or Turbografx-16. Unlike NEC, Sega already had a substantial software library to draw upon. In addition to popular arcade titles that Sega ported to the Genesis, gamers could play previous generation titles designed for the Master System. Although the system's backward compatibility would never be a main selling feature, it provided Genesis with a large library of launch-ready titles. Sega also found allies among third party developers who felt constrained by Nintendo's licensing terms and wanted the freedom to develop games the way they saw fit. Sega's more liberal licensing policies attracted some of the best known studios in the industry, including industry leaders like Electronic Arts and Tengen.

Sega was one of the first companies to use celebrity endorsements to sell games. For example, professional golfer Arnold Palmer lent his name to an eponymous golf game. One of the most recognizable celebrities to endorse the Genesis was Michael Jackson, who starred in a music video game titled *Moonwalker*. Endorsements, in and of themselves, were not enough to make Genesis successful, but they did help raise the visibility of the system. One of the challenges Sega faced was getting gamers to recognize the benefits Genesis offered over the aging NES. By keeping Genesis in the spotlight, Sega was able to demonstrate its capabilities to a wider audience.

Changing Demographics

Sega was one of the first video game companies to realize that gamers were getting older. Kids who had grown up on the NES were now in their teens and twenties. Sega went after these older gamers aggressively with titles like *Altered Beast* and *Golden Axe*. It also used more adult oriented advertising. Meanwhile, Nintendo of America imposed content restrictions that were far more conservative than those imposed on the Japanese market. If content might be viewed as offensive to American parents, it was removed. In Japan, games that included homosexuals or transvestites were changed to make them straight, blood was removed from battles, and cultural references were removed or replaced with American equivalents. Yet it was this kind of content that older gamers were clamoring for.

At the same time, Sega realized that the core market was still parents who purchased the consoles for their children. To broaden the Genesis' appeal, in 1991 the company changed its mascot from *Altered Beast* to *Sonic the Hedgehog*, a character in the self-titled game that would eventually become Sega's most successful franchise. Yet even with Sonic as its mascot, Sega imbued a more mature image than Nintendo, which continued to target young children between the ages of six and fourteen.

Instead of looking forward, Nintendo was looking backward. Marketing studies found that Mario was Nintendo's strongest asset, with 96 percent brand awareness. Therefore, Nintendo decided to continue emphasizing Mario with kids' games like *Mario Paint*. "We'll let the others fight it out," Arakawa said.

"We'll just continue to do what we do best" (Sheff 1993). The problem was that, even though people liked Mario, they were becoming bored with Mario games.

Companies often succumb to the trap of thinking that a successful product will remain successful indefinitely. They believe that all they have to do is tweak the product and customers will continue to buy it at the same level. They become victims of their own success when they fail to recognize that customers and their needs change. One of the more legendary examples of this trap involved a former Nintendo partner—Coleco. In the mid 1980s, Coleco introduced a toy known as the Cabbage Patch Doll. The doll became so popular that it generated more than $600 million in revenue for Coleco. Two years later, sales dropped as suddenly as they had risen. With so much invested in Cabbage Patch, Coleco was forced into bankruptcy. Other fads, such as the Rubik's Cubes, Hula Hoops, Pet Rocks, and so on, faced similar ends. Although such products don't always disappear from the market completely, sales declines are usually precipitous and severe. In the early 1990s, Nintendo was setting Mario up for a similar fall.

Instead of driving innovation with new unique games as it did in the 1980s, Nintendo followed the advice of marketing consultants who suggested that they exploit Mario for all he was worth. According to conventional wisdom, when a product reaches the maturity stage of its life cycle, variations and extensions of a strong brand should be developed to leverage the equity of the core product. However, those extensions should be introduced in moderation and be of the same quality as the original. Whereas in the 1980s Nintendo released an average of one or two new Mario titles a year, the 1990s saw a flood of ill-conceived Mario spin-offs, such as *Mario Teaches Typing*, *Mario's Game Gallery*, and *Mario's Time Machine*. Although some of the worst titles were produced under license by third party developers, such as Philips and Interplay, the onslaught of mediocre Mario games nearly destroyed Nintendo's most valuable franchise. If that wasn't enough, there was a 1993 Super Mario Bros. film, considered by many to be the worst movie ever made about a video game. The fact that Mario survived this avalanche of deplorable products stands as a testament to the quality and genius of Miyamoto's original games.

In the eyes of many gamers, Sonic was "cool" and Mario was "boring." Not even young children viewed Nintendo as favorably as they once had. "In America, younger children and even adults might imitate teens" in clothing, music, hairstyles, and other areas of popular culture, but teens are less likely to imitate children and adults (White 1994). In other words, by going after the teen market, Sega was doing a better job of convincing young kids that Genesis should be their console of choice.

Sonic the Hedgehog helped Sega to become the first company to realistically challenge Nintendo. In the 1991 holiday season, Genesis outsold Nintendo's systems by a factor of two to one. Nintendo responded with an upgraded system of its own, known as the Super Nintendo Entertainment System (SNES). Although the SNES lacked backwards compatibility, Nintendo released a number of compelling sequels to popular NES franchises, like *Final Fantasy III, Super Mario World,* and *Zelda III.* At the same time, Nintendo allowed retailers to discount poorly selling titles for the first time and it eased restrictions that it had placed on developers. Within a year, Nintendo was able to recapture the lead. However, its comeback proved short-lived.

The Demise of Cartridges

One of the main disadvantages of early Nintendo systems was their dependence on cartridges. By the early 1990s, console manufacturers were beginning to use CDs to distribute games. CDs offered more than 50 times the storage capacity of cartridges and could be manufactured for one tenth of the cost. Despite their many advantages, Nintendo resisted the move to CD-based media. The company had made a significant investment in developing anti-piracy measures, such as a special authentication chip. Although some companies found ways to disable Nintendo's security measures as a way to avoid licensing fees, doing so involved considerable effort. In contrast, anyone could copy a CD.

The biggest blow to Nintendo came not from NEC, Sega, or Atari, but from one of Nintendo's closest partners—Sony. Sony not only developed the sound system for the NES, it had been working with Nintendo since 1988 on a CD-ROM drive for the SNES. In 1991, Nintendo announced that it was canceling the project. Several Nintendo partners asked Yamauchi to reconsider his decision to stick with cartridges. They saw CD-ROMs as the next standard, a standard that Nintendo needed to support. "Nintendo believes in a standard, our standard," Yamauchi replied (Sheff 1993).

Rather than see years of hard work go to waste, Sony decided to enter the console market on its own. After all, it knew the hardware side of the business as well as anyone. The announcement was greeted with open arms by retailers and developers who were tired of Nintendo's strong-arm tactics. Sony not only had the electronics expertise needed to create a great product, it had relationships with enough retailers and wholesale distributors to potentially challenge Nintendo's grip on the market.

As early as 1993, critics had begun to complain that the NES was "dull." By this time, Sega Corporation of Japan and 3DO Company of the United States had each announced more advanced 64-bit CD-based consoles priced at $300 and $700, respectively. The new consoles would offer greater graphics capabilities and more adult-oriented games.

The first to market was the 3DO Player, launched in 1993 by the 3DO Company of California. The 3DO also played music, videos, and karaoke CDs, and could serve as a home computer with Internet capabilities. However, the $700 unit was deemed too expensive by consumers who saw its primary function as a video game machine.

Nintendo's greatest challenge came in 1995 when Sony introduced its PlayStation console. Although the $299 PlayStation was more than twice the price of the Nintendo console, it proved to be an instant hit.

Nintendo began to feel the heat in 1996, when Sony, Sega, and 3DO dropped the price of their consoles to $199. Nintendo responded by introducing an advanced system of its own, the Nintendo 64 (N64). Still, for most consumers, Nintendo's offering was too little, too late. When all its competitors had modern CD-based systems that could also play music, Nintendo chose to continue using bulky cartridges.

By 1998, the Sony PlayStation outsold the N64 by a ratio of 10 to 1. In addition, whereas Nintendo did much of its software development in-house, Sony used its status within the electronics industry to establish strong relationships with independent developers. As a result, Sony was able to offer PlayStation customers a constant stream of new game titles. In 1998 alone, the PlayStation had 500 new software titles, compared to only 40 for the Nintendo 64.

The Decline of Nintendo

In 2000, Nintendo's situation deteriorated further. That year, Sony released its PlayStation 2 (PS2) console. The PS2 offered improved graphics, a built-in DVD player, and, most importantly, backwards compatibility. That meant that owners of the original PlayStation could continue playing their existing games, while gradually upgrading to newer titles. By the time Nintendo's next generation game console, called the Gamecube, was released one year later, the PS2 was already well entrenched, with more than 5 million units sold.

Initially priced at $199, the Gamecube was $100 cheaper than the PS2. However, it did not play DVDs or CDs, and it could not play N64 games. Instead, it used a new proprietary minidisk format that was incompatible with games designed for previous generation consoles. By this time, nearly every other company had transitioned to CDs. Nintendo alone continued to insist that gamers adopt its standard. "The reason why we choose the new media format 8cm optical disks is because of widespread piracy of ROM cartridges, and even CD-ROMs," explained Nintendo managing director Hiroshi Imanishi.

> Some companies have previously tried to offset these problems by charging premiums on hardware, or give the hardware away for a loss, in order to increase the number of users. Sony has done that with the PlayStation. In some countries though, pirate copies of software are being sold more than genuine ones now. That's not a good position for the future (Shimbun 2000).

In 2001, the average price for a single disk DVD player was between $150 and $200. The fact that Sony included DVD playback in its PS2 made it a better value than the GameCube in the eyes of most customers.

Nintendo also faced stiff competition from Microsoft, which released its Xbox console three days before the GameCube. Although Microsoft was new to video game consoles, it was the leader in computer games. The Xbox reflected Microsoft's PC heritage, with hardware and software that closely mirrored existing personal computers, and like the PS2, it came with a built-in DVD player.

Gamers who compared the GameCube to the PlayStation 2 and Xbox consoles saw it as an underpowered toy with too many games oriented to small children. They wanted realistic graphics, more violence and more action. Titles such as *Grand Theft Auto* for the Sony PlayStation 2 became all the rage. Miyamoto, however, was unapologetic. Nintendo was more about "making good games that sell well," than seeking a holy grail of realism and performance. "If you look back at what we've done in the past," he explained,

"Nintendo has a unique strength in that it is very good at making games that kids enjoy."

> But these are also games that everyone can enjoy, and I think that by focusing effort on our development you're going to see that there are going to be a lot of games that are going to appeal to people of all ages.
>
> Gradually over the years, very simple gameplay and very simple rules weren't enough to keep gamers satisfied, and so the games got more complicated. With the evolution in hardware and graphics the worlds got more complicated and the graphics got more incredible, and so in one sense the games got better, but at the same time they got less simplistic and so fewer people were really able to get in and play them.
>
> At Nintendo, what we want to do is show to other developers and our third-party partners that you don't have to just make games more complicated or more beautiful, you can actually have very simple gameplay that will be fun and very exciting for people. (Miyamoto 2003)

Satoru Iwata, president and CEO of Nintendo, believed that games needed to be innovative, intuitive, and inviting. "Photorealism is not the only means of improving the game experience," he asserted. "It's just one path" (Chaplin and Ruby 2005).

At the time, both Miyamoto and Iwata seemed to be in denial. Nintendo was sinking fast and yet they all but conceded that they had no plans to challenge Sony and Microsoft with better photorealistic games. In 2003, Nintendo was forced to cut production of the GameCube in order to clear out 5 million units of excess inventory, as its market share slipped to 16 percent. Meanwhile, Sony and Microsoft increased their market shares to 55 percent and 22 percent, respectively. Miyamoto confessed that he worried about the future of Nintendo. "Of course my biggest concern is always that people's impression of Nintendo is going to decline, or that people will stop thinking about us," he said (*Nintendo Power* 2007).

However, Nintendo had two secret weapons up its sleeve: a handheld console that used a stylus for input and a home console based around a motion sensing controller. They were bold moves that would almost certainly have doomed Nintendo had they failed. Even after they were announced, some people remained skeptical that these innovations were anything more than gimmicks. The *San Jose Mercury News*, a journal that focused heavily on technology, appeared especially skeptical when it printed this 2005 review of the Nintendo DS:

> *Although [the DS] will be able to connect wirelessly to the internet, the stylus pen used as a controller in some games is seen as a gimmick rather than an innovation. You can expect it to sell by the bucket load in Japan but in the West you cannot help thinking that Nintendo's days are numbered. Sales of the GameCube have been pathetic and some places either no longer sell the games or offer them at bargain prices.*
>
> *You have to wonder if Nintendo's marketing policy has helped the GameCube. The* Sunday Mercury, *for example, hasn't had a game to review for the Japanese giant for over a year. Even if they did have some good games out in 2004, we wouldn't have been able to tell you about them. Meanwhile, Microsoft's X-Box console—still the only one to be made in the West—goes from strength to strength. (Leek 2005)*

3

PlayStation Dreams

In 1993, author David Sheff made a bold prediction. Despite their best efforts to capture a significant share of the multimedia gaming market, video game companies like Sega were going to fail. Sega "seemed too narrow-minded and lacked the resources to promulgate a standard on its own. Instead, the competition would be among computer and consumer-electronics companies, or among newly formed joint ventures between them and entertainment companies." Although Sheff postulated that Nintendo would survive the shakeup, it would be joined by new entrants, "companies such as Apple, IBM, Sony … and Microsoft" that "were scheming how to get shares of [the video game] market." Together, these companies would bring about a new era of multimedia gaming in which "players would enter a fictional world and perceive it not as an outsider looking in, but from within the game itself."

At the time, Sheff's predictions might have seemed almost ridiculous. Nintendo and Sega dominated the gaming market, Sony had not yet launched the PlayStation, and Microsoft limited itself to operating systems and business software. IBM, which today develops the processors for all major gaming systems, was known for servers and PCs, not video games. Yet in some ways, the writing was on the wall. Video game consoles were becoming less like toys and more like high-performance computers. Therefore, it made sense that companies with the most expertise in engineering, consumer electronics, and software would one day dominate the industry.

This chapter will consider how video game consoles made the transition from simple toys to high-performance multimedia centers and the reasons behind Sony's domination of the industry during those years.

Partnership with Nintendo

More than a decade before it launched the first PlayStation, Sony entered the video game industry surreptitiously through the efforts of a mid level Sony engineer known as Ken Kutaragi. After Kutaragi bought one of the first NES systems on the market for his eight-year-old daughter, he was struck by how bad the sound system was. Kutaragi had been working on the company's first digital camera and he had several ideas on how to improve the NES.

Initially, Kutaragi wanted Sony to build its own console, but he found little support for the idea. "When Nintendo introduced its 8-bit console, nobody at Sony mentioned it," Kutaragi recalled. "They hated the product. It was kind of snobbery. For people within Sony, the Nintendo product would have been very embarrassing to make because it was only a toy" (Hamel 2000). Instead, Kutaragi hastily arranged a clandestine meeting with Nintendo executives to see if he could somehow help Nintendo improve its console. The only other person at Sony who knew of Kutaragi's plan was his supervisor. Both men knew that if word got out about the Nintendo meeting, the plan would be killed.

One improvement suggested by Kutaragi was the inclusion of a floppy drive he had developed for the Sony digital camera; another was to develop a better sound system. Although Nintendo rejected the floppy disk concept, the company was interested in a new sound system. They knew that as more music and effects were incorporated into games, sound would become an increasingly important part of the in-game experience.

Before Sony could enter into an agreement with Nintendo, Kutaragi would have to make his negotiations known to Sony's senior management team. They were furious at Kutaragi for going behind their backs, but Kutaragi used the meeting as a chance to explain the opportunity that video games offered. Amidst all the skepticism, Kutaragi was able to convince the person who mattered most, then President Norio Ogha. Nevertheless, many within Sony viewed the young engineer with suspicion. "No one accepted our project," he recalled. "This was a very difficult time for me."

The Advent of Disk-based Media

In 1988, Kutaragi negotiated an agreement with Nintendo to jointly develop a new console that would be called the "Play Station."[1] According to the original plan, Sony would build the SNES-compatible system with slots for both CD-ROM disks and cartridges. The idea was that the Sony console could be used to promote Sony's music products. However, the terms of the contract specified that Sony, rather than Nintendo, would retain all the rights to CD-based games. Nintendo, it seemed, had underestimated the impact CDs would have on gaming. "I heard they gave the store away," said investment analyst Robert Kleiber when the agreement was revealed in 1991 (Shapiro 1991).

Rather than return to Sony to discuss possible modifications to the contract, Nintendo secretly decided to kill the project and negotiated a separate CD-ROM development agreement with Philips. In the meantime, a PlayStation prototype was nearing completion. When Nintendo announced the new agreement with Philips in 1991, Kutaragi was shocked. He has spent the last two years working on the project and suddenly Nintendo was pulling the carpet out from under him.

The Sony executives who had questioned the company's involvement with Nintendo saw the event as a vindication of their skepticism. In their minds, it was time for Sony to abandon this foolishness and concentrate on its core business of consumer electronics. Instead, Kutaragi went to Ogha with a proposition to do what he felt Sony should have done years ago—develop its own console. The PlayStation was not merely a toy as some would have him believe, but an entertainment device that was fully in line with Sony's other businesses, such as Walkman CD-players and Trinitron televisions. The PlayStation represented the convergence of technologies and could become the centerpiece of Sony's global entertainment ambitions. Kutaragi even went so far as to suggest that Ogha create a new division titled Sony Computer Entertainment. In the end, Ogha left the meeting convinced of the PlayStation's merit, and Kutaragi was given a new lease to pursue his dream.

Knowing how shaky Kutaragi's support within Sony was, Nintendo must have been surprised by the announcement that Sony was not only going to go ahead with the PlayStation project, but that it would be the focus of a new division devoted to gaming and entertainment. Nintendo initially tried to stop Sony by claiming that it owned the PlayStation brand, but a U.S. judge ruled

---

1   The space between the two words was later dropped.

that PlayStation belonged to Sony and the name could be used for purposes other than a Nintendo partnership.

After Philips was unable to deliver a product that met Nintendo's standards, Nintendo returned to Sony with a new offer—Sony could bring the PlayStation to market provided that Nintendo retained any rights and royalties to CD-based games. However, by this time, the SNES was beginning to look dated. Sony wanted to build a more advanced console and bring it to market on its own terms rather than Nintendo's. Sony was finished playing Nintendo's game.

The early 1990s saw rapid change in the video game industry. New technologies allowed companies to transition from cartridges to CDs, from 8 bit processors to 32 bit and 64 bit processors, and from 2-D to 3-D video. In addition, the Internet was beginning to move beyond academic and military use. New dial-up Internet services began to appear, led by companies like AOL, Prodigy, and CompuServe.

Sony viewed these changes with caution. With it came new competitors with competing technologies and standards. Companies like NEC, SNK, Atari, and 3DO introduced new advanced systems that, performance-wise, far surpassed anything Nintendo was offering. In such an environment, one wrong step could doom a company's chances of becoming the provider of choice in next generation gaming and entertainment. Even though Sony was ready to announce the PlayStation in 1991, it would be another four years before it would bring its console to market. During that time, Sony began to build a network of supporters that it knew would be critical to the ultimate success of the PlayStation. They included third-party developers, retailers, and suppliers.

Aside from Genesis and the SNES, all the consoles introduced in the early 1990s failed. The most advanced consoles were the Atari Jaguar and 3DO Multiplayer. Both were launched in 1993 with advanced graphics and processing capabilities. They were also overpriced, needlessly complex, and offered benefits that few consumers understood how to take advantage of.

The 3DO Company was founded by William M. Hawkins, former head of Electronic Arts, whose aim was to create more than a video game console, but a complete home entertainment system. The 3DO "Multiplayer" was manufactured under license by Panasonic and a number of other electronics firms, including Sanyo, Samsung, and Goldstar. "Its powerful cel engine" and its ability to "display full motion video, fully texture mapped 3-D landscapes, and other amazing visuals, all in 24-bit color" made it the most advanced console of its time (Beuscher 2009). In addition, Hawkins promised that the Multiplayer would eventually function as an advanced cable TV controller that would one day support high definition video playback on HDTVs.

Many developers embraced 3DO's liberal licensing. Compared to Nintendo, 3DO was a breath of fresh air. In its first year on the market, hundreds of new games were produced for the Multiplayer. They included legendary classics like *Need for Speed* and *Super Street Fighter*. However, the lack of restrictions also brought a flood of low quality games that made it difficult for gamers to see the true value of the Multiplayer platform.

Nevertheless, gaming was never meant to be the 3DO's main selling feature. Analysts, pundits, and journalists praised the Multiplayer not as "a new stand-alone video game machine, but a new kind of multiple home entertainment device." When *Time* magazine named the 3DO Multiplayer the "Best Product of 1993," it lauded its contribution to the coming "data superhighway."

> *If you think you've seen graphics, wait till you check out the jaw-dropping visuals offered by this interactive system. With its CD-quality sound and 32-bit processor, the Multiplayer is the most powerful video-game system yet. Designed by Silicon Valley start-up 3DO and made by Panasonic, the $700 device is being backed by AT&T, Time Warner and MCA.*

Another product that made it on *Time*'s list that year would prove far more resilient. The IBM PowerPC processor was *Time*'s sixth "best product of 1993." In the coming years the PowerPC became the brain of the Apple Macintosh line of computers, the Nintendo GameCube and the Nintendo Wii. It also gave IBM the experience needed to design the Cell processor and PowerPC Xenon processor that are behind today's Sony PlayStation 3 and Microsoft's Xbox 360, respectively.

3DO was not as fortunate as IBM. In the end, consumers remained unconvinced that the Multiplayer's non-gaming features warranted such a high price. Other console makers manufactured their own consoles and earned royalties on game sales that could then be used to subsidize further hardware development. Unlike Nintendo and Sega, Panasonic did not have the ability to recoup hardware losses with software royalties because 3DO made the mistake of licensing the software separately. Without some pricing flexibility, Panasonic simply couldn't compete against other lower priced gaming consoles. Faced with mounting losses and the defection of key partners, in 1996 3DO ceased development and support for the Multiplayer after selling only 2 million systems worldwide.

More than a decade after the demise of the Multiplayer, another console would face similar challenges. Like the Multiplayer, the Sony PS3 was more advanced and offered more features than any other console on the market. However, Sony had advantages that 3DO did not, namely a committed community of developers and lucrative software royalties. In addition, video games were only one part of Sony's very successful electronics business, whereas 3DO's revenue came almost exclusively from the Multiplayer and related products.

If the 3DO Multiplayer was a failure, the Atari Jaguar was a disaster. Although the Jaguar offered advanced 64-bit hardware and was competitively priced at only $250, it relied on antiquated cartridges to keep costs low. By this time, CDs were becoming the industry standard and Atari's decision both limited the ability of developers to take full advantage of the hardware and made development more challenging. Among the few games released for the Jaguar, only a handful was of the caliber that gamers came to expect. Despite the console's advanced graphics system, many games looked inferior to titles on less capable consoles. The fact that Atari employed a 15 button controller that was confusing and difficult to use only made matters worse.

Atari mistakenly believed that its advanced processor and low price would turn the Jaguar into an instant success. Indeed, one could overlook the fact that it used cartridges and had a terrible controller, if only it had good games. Atari ignored the maxim that content is king when it failed to take the time to develop relationships with key third-party developers. Instead, Atari's strategy was built upon the hope that developers would follow of their own accord. In the end, despite the console's low price, Atari sold fewer than 250,000 units. It was the final nail in the coffin of a company that was once synonymous with video games. In 1998, Atari's remaining assets were acquired by Hasbro for $5 million.

The Rise of the PlayStation

One of the reasons Kutaragi delayed the launch of the PlayStation was to avoid the types of mistakes made by Atari. When the original Play Station was to be announced in 1991, it was essentially a Nintendo product. As such, it would have a large well-respected library of titles to draw upon. However, without Nintendo, Sony had to find titles elsewhere.

At the time of the PlayStation's U.S. launch in 1995, an industry shakeout was underway that would leave Nintendo and Sega as the only survivors. The PlayStation was one of the most advanced systems on the market with 32–bit processing, 3-D graphics capabilities and a highly capable CD-ROM drive. Sony offered developers a number of incentives, including higher margins and advanced development tools. At the time of PlayStation's launch, Sony had 27 complete game titles and development contracts with 164 Japanese software companies.

Sony's main competitor was the Sega Saturn, a console that compared favorably to the PlayStation. Like the PlayStation, the Saturn was a 32 bit CD-ROM based system that also played music and video CDs. Both were released in Japan in late 1994 for around $400 and both sold better than expected. Sony's initial projections showed the PlayStation reaching one million units in its first year on the market. Instead, it took only six months.

Both Sony and Sega planned to launch their respective consoles in the U.S. in September 2005. Then in May of that year, Sega stunned the world by announcing the immediate release of the Saturn, four months ahead of schedule, for a price of $399. The problem was that most third-party developers had been preparing their titles for a September release. That not only left the system with just four launch titles, it angered third-party developers who were placed at a disadvantage relative to Sega's own in-house development team. Most had also hoped to take advantage of the promotional frenzy that often accompanies highly anticipated product launches. By launching early, Sega deprived them of media coverage that normally results when gamers line up in front of stores.

Soon after Sega's announcement, Sony fired back by announcing that the PlayStation would cost only $299. The console wars had officially begun. It was a war characterized by rapid advances in technology, frequent price cuts, and a drive to secure exclusive software from third-party developers. Winning exclusivity for a popular game title was sometimes enough to tip the fortunes of a console. Although most third-party publishers produced games for more than one console, it was not uncommon for them to develop specific titles exclusively for one system. One such title was Tekken, a 3D fighting game developed by Namco. In 1995, Tekken became the first title to sell a million copies for the PlayStation and helped drive sales of the console in its critical first year on the market.

The next salvo came from Nintendo, which announced that it too would bring a new console to market. Slated to be released in early 1996, the Nintendo Ultra 64 (N64) would boast a 64 bit processor and a price of only $249. Yet Nintendo stubbornly resisted the move to CD-ROM technology, preferring instead to continue its support of cartridge-based media.

Advocates of cartridges pointed out that load times were significantly shorter than CDs. However, Nintendo's main concern was not performance, but protection from piracy. A subsequent flood of pirated PlayStation games seemed to vindicate Nintendo's concerns. Nevertheless, cartridges also had major disadvantages, not the least of which was a storage capacity that was one tenth the capacity of CDs. The lack of a CD-ROM drive also limited the N64's ability to perform non-gaming functions, such as music CD playback. Nintendo's ill-fated decision to stick with cartridges was influenced by the company's historical need to control development and distribution and by the "success trap" that saw its strengths become weaknesses. In the rapidly changing competitive landscape, Nintendo continued with strategies that had been successful in the past presumably believing that they just needed to do these same things better or work harder. Unfortunately, Nintendo failed to realize that "rowing harder does not help if the boat is headed in the wrong direction" (Leonard-Barton, 1998).

By sticking with cartridges, Nintendo went against what had become a dominant design in console manufacturing. Standards emerge when an industry decides to adhere to a set of specifications and features, whereas dominant designs result from consumer acceptance. Dominant designs have occurred in many product arenas including the Qwerty keyboard, IBM-compatible PC, and Intel x86 chips (Utterback 1994).

Sometimes dominant designs can take years to materialize as in the case of LCD televisions. Consumer availability of LCD technology has been around since the 1980s, but LCD TVs are only now becoming widely accepted. There were several reasons for this. First, early LCD televisions performed relatively poorly compared to plasma TVs. In addition, their high cost placed them beyond the reach of most consumers. Over time, as LCD technology improved and costs declined, more people realized the advantages LCDs offered over other available display technologies, such as lower power-consumption and greater reliability.

In the case of CD-ROMs, consumer acceptance happened much quicker, because CDs offered clear advantages over cartridges and tapes. They were also priced within reach of mainstream consumers.

Regardless of how long it takes for dominant designs to emerge, once they do, competitors and innovators must adhere to them if they hope to command a significant market share. Firms that fail to adopt a dominant design often do so because they have built internal and external infrastructures to support an established technology and it is difficult for them to shift to a new technology or design. Such firms usually end up either exiting the product category or becoming marginal players, as Nintendo did in the late 1990s and early 2000s.

Rampant piracy didn't stop Sony from outselling Nintendo in software. In 1998, ten of the fifteen best-selling games were for the PlayStation. If piracy had been as big a problem as Nintendo wanted people to believe, developers would not have created as many games as they did for the PlayStation. The cost in lost sales would have simply been too great. Yet in 1998 more than 500 games were released for the PlayStation compared to only 40 for the N64. Consider *Final Fantasy VII* for the PlayStation, a game that cost an unprecedented $30 million to make. When it was first released in Japan, more than two million copies were sold in three days.

Stuart Haber (2003) and his colleagues at HP Labs in Princeton found that copy protection schemes are not effective at combating piracy. "The key problem is that if even a small fraction of users are able to transform content from a protected to an unprotected form, then illegitimate distribution networks are likely to make that content available ubiquitously." The only way to ensure that software is not copied is to employ "draconian" measures, such as "devices that only process managed content," devices like Nintendo's cartridge system. However, "such systems face significant, if not insurmountable, obstacles to deployment." In Nintendo's case, those obstacles included higher costs, less flexibility, a more challenging development environment, less storage capacity, and so on. Haber concludes that "the real solution to the piracy problem is largely non-technical. The most effective way for interested parties to defeat piracy may be to compete with it."

By adhering to the dominant design of CD-ROM based games, Sony made the PlayStation a far more flexible and valuable device than the N64. As a newcomer to console gaming, Sony didn't have a vested interest in preserving an existing technology. Moreover, developers seemed less concerned about piracy than Nintendo wanted the general public to believe. Most found they could compete with pirated software by offering benefits, such as product support, attractive packaging, game manuals, better looking disks, and the developer's assurance of quality. Although such features did not "defeat piracy," they were sufficient to ensure that games remained profitable, and in many cases *highly* profitable.

Consumers had other reasons to choose licensed software over pirated copies. Some were influenced by moral and legal concerns, even though the risk of prosecution was small. Legal copies could also be resold or traded to other gamers, while pirated copies had little or no resale value. Finally, dedicated gamers often purchased software to show support for the development community. Regardless of the motivation, sales of disk-based games have remained strong over the past two decades. Even the recent rise of file sharing services like BitTorrent seemed to have little impact on game sales. For example, *Halo 3* for the Xbox 360 set new records when it was released in 2007, despite its wide availability on the Pirate Bay and other BitTorrent sites.

Sony, like Sega before it, understood that gamers were getting older. It launched a focused marketing effort aimed at 18- to 24-year-olds who had grown up on the NES and SNES systems and who were considered an ideal demographic for game consumption. Not only were they comfortable with video game technology, as newly independent adults, they could purchase the games they wanted without parental approval. Lastly, they had more disposable income to spend on games since most had yet to start families of their own.

This age group is often seen as one of the most important for building brand loyalty. Consumer behavior specialist Michael Solomon (2003) notes that teenagers represent one of the most attractive age groups for marketers, who view them as "consumers in training." "A teenager who is committed to a brand may continue to purchase it for years to come. Such loyalty creates a barrier-to-entry for brands that were not chosen during those pivotal years." By successfully building a brand relationship with this segment of consumers,

Sony could become the brand of choice for a wide variety of consumer goods ranging from music and movies to televisions and cameras. This loyalty may also partially explain the more recent resurgence of the Nintendo brand among older consumers who were raised on the NES in the 1980s.

To reach its target audience, Sony attempted to win the support of opinion leaders by handing out as many as 5,000 free consoles. According to Everett Rogers' theory of diffusion, not all customers in a market are created equal when it comes to adopting new products (Rogers 2003). Innovators are the first individuals to adopt an innovation and have particular characteristics that facilitate this behavior. They are willing to take risks and try new things, are very social, are very knowledgeable about the product category of interest to them, and are heavily influenced by mass media with regard to their product interest. Sony was going after early adopters, who comprise the second group (after innovators) to adopt new products. It is in this group where one finds the highest number of opinion leaders. They are open to change but do not take as many risks as innovators, they are more accepted in social systems than innovators who can be considered deviants, and they rely on mass media for information about new products of interest to them. Opinion leaders are critical to the diffusion of new products because they are the ones who spread (hopefully) good words about the product to other members of the market who rely significantly on friends and acquaintances to help them make adoption decisions. The support of opinion leaders is usually considered to be critical to the success of an innovation in the marketplace.

In addition, Sony copied a Smirnoff Vodka promotional ploy when it sent out music videos featuring the PlayStation console to night clubs frequented by its target audience. Both approaches were deemed effective, but ultimately the success of the PlayStation boiled down to one thing—Sony's ability to attract large numbers of third-party developers. Developers like Square and Namco created some of the best-rated titles ever seen, such as *Final Fantasy VII*, *Chrono Cross*, and *Metal Gear Solid*. All told, they created an unprecedented number of titles for the new system, more than 7,000 in total, and helped Sony achieve unit sales of more than 100 million over the PlayStation's 11-year lifespan. By the late 1990s, Sony Computer Entertainment had grown to the second largest division within the company and accounted for nearly half of the company's profits.

Meanwhile, Nintendo relied mainly on its own development studios to deliver compelling sequels to established franchises, like *The Legend of Zelda:*

Ocarina of Time and *Super Mario 64*. That was enough to convince some gamers, but overall, the system's 300 games paled compared to Sony's extensive library of highly rated titles. In the end, it was a lack of third-party support that doomed once mighty Nintendo to a distant second place in the console wars, with just over 30 million units sold worldwide. That was still well ahead of the Sega Saturn, which came in just under 10 million. In each case, content more than performance determined the ultimate outcome.

Sega's Shattered Dream

Despite having fallen behind in the console wars, Sega and Nintendo achieved sufficient momentum to carry them into the next generation. By this time, Atari, 3DO, and NEC were distant memories and all eyes were focused on Sony.

By the time Sega introduced its Dreamcast console in 1999, the company's market share had fallen to two percent. The 128-bit Dreamcast promised to turn around the ailing fortunes of Sega by offering features that were well ahead of their time at a price ($199) that placed it squarely in competition with less powerful consoles. The Dreamcast was the first console to offer a built-in modem that could be replaced with a broadband adapter.

Sega learned from its Saturn mistakes and offered a respectable line-up of launch titles. They included some of the top-rated games of its generation, such as *Soulcalibur* and *Sonic Adventure*. Even though one of Dreamcast's main selling features was its ability to play online games head-to-head between Dreamcast owners, none of the launch titles could use the service. However, Sega introduced more than 20 online titles over the next two years, including the first broadband capable games. Most games came with a web browser that allowed users to access the Internet directly through their consoles.

Few users could take advantage of Sega's online service. Most homes still used paid dial-up service, which meant that online play incurred usage fees and tied up telephone lines that were needed to place and receive voice calls. Ideally, gamers needed a broadband connection to take advantage of the service, but broadband penetration in most parts of the world remained low. As late as 2001, less than four percent of U.S. homes had broadband. The most connected country in the world was Korea with broadband in approximately 14 percent of households.

The Sega Saturn was criticized for its difficult to use programming tools. This time around, Sega chose to partner with Microsoft to develop an operating system for the Dreamcast in the hope that it would attract developers familiar with the Windows environment. How much this decision contributed to overall game development for the Dreamcast remains unclear, but it significantly shortened the time to market. Numerous third-party studios lauded the decision, including Craig Galley, VP of technology at Acclaim, who said that it allowed his company to "get title development under way within a month" (Microsoft Corp. 1999). As a result, the Dreamcast enjoyed a steady stream of high quality titles.

At first Sega appeared to have a winner on its hands. In Japan, Sega sold a respectable 1.5 million units of the console in its first year. However, that was nothing compared to the U.S., where Sega sold more than one million units in only two months. The Dreamcast continued to post strong sales until Sony and Nintendo dropped the price of their consoles to $150 and $100 respectively.

Sega's costs were too high to respond effectively to the price drop, and the console began to lose momentum. Sales through March 2000 were 44 percent below projections. Eventually, Sega decided to match Sony's price, but by then the Dreamcast's fate was sealed. The Saturn debacle had left the company in a precarious financial situation and it simply could not afford to lose money on the Dreamcast. In January 2001, Sega announced that it would discontinue the Dreamcast and focus strictly on software development.

The decision left many gamers scratching their heads. The Dreamcast had everything that devoted gamers wanted—great graphics, great games, and new features like online play. For many, the Dreamcast was "one of the best systems ever." Analysts suggested a number of reasons for the Dreamcast's demise, including poor marketing support, a lack of compelling game titles, and a higher price relative to established competitors. They didn't consider that under normal circumstances, the Dreamcast would have been considered a success. "We had a tremendous 18 months," recalled Peter Moore, President of Sega America:

> Dreamcast was on fire—we really thought that we could do it. But then we had a target from Japan that said we had to make N hundreds of millions of dollars by the holiday season and shift N millions of units of hardware, otherwise we just couldn't sustain the business.

According to Moore, another factor that contributed to the Dreamcast's demise was a "pre-emptive guerrilla PR" campaign by Sony "where they promised the consumer something they probably believed they were going to deliver, but they never did." What that did in consumers' minds was create "fear uncertainty and doubt" (FUD).

> It was a massive FUD campaign. The consumer thought twice when they started to read, "Can the Dreamcast make it?" It had a tough time in Europe; it had a really disastrous time in Japan. It was like, "well, what do you do?" You just do it yourself. You start talking, you don't wait for the Japanese to give you messaging — because PR is something they don't do very well — the only thing we could do was be passionate. But it was too little too late unfortunately. (Stuart 2008)

Moore cited an "infamous" March 2000 *Newsweek* cover story about the PlayStation 2 as an example of Sony's campaign to discredit the Dreamcast. In it, Sony promised the ability to play online games, the availability of inexpensive titles priced as low as $13, and graphics and performance that were far beyond anything currently on the market. *Newsweek* reported that developers saw the Dreamcast merely as a "transitional platform" until the arrival of "the increased realism offered by PlayStation 2," while *CNN* told its online readers that the PS2's "emotion engine" would enhance 3-D full-motion video and be several times more powerful than processors used in most personal computers.

Boxes, Cubes, and the PlayStation 2

When Sony launched the PlayStation 2 in 2000 with a price of $299, it had neither the online capabilities of the Dreamcast, nor inexpensive games. "They just never delivered," noted Moore, who admitted that he was angry with Sony for destroying his business with empty promises. In fact, Sony didn't become serious about online gaming until after Microsoft launched its Xbox Live service nearly two years later. Moreover, the console's graphics and performance were, at best, on par with the Dreamcast. Nevertheless, by this time Sega had already announced that it was exiting the hardware business, which temporarily left Sony as the sole producer of high end consoles.

Despite the PS2's shortcomings, in consumers' minds it offered other important benefits that were not available on the Dreamcast. One of them was games. By remaining backward compatible with the PlayStation, the PS2 had a launch ready library that numbered in the thousands. It meant that millions of PlayStation owners across the world could upgrade to the PS2 without having to invest considerable sums of money in new titles—at least not initially. Over time, Sony hoped that most gamers would retire their PlayStation games as they acquired new games designed for the PS2.

Not only could the PS2 play existing PlayStation games, newly developed games were able to take advantage of the console's advanced graphical and processing capabilities and deliver enhanced content through a built-in DVD drive. As games became more complex, they often had to be delivered on multiple CDs that users would have to swap out in the middle of a game. The DVD's higher storage capacity meant that more content could be delivered on a single disk. It also meant that consumers didn't need to invest in a separate DVD player to watch movies.

Sony would not have the high end market to itself for long. Within a year, Nintendo and Microsoft introduced consoles aimed squarely at the PS2.

When Nintendo launched its GameCube console in November 2001, it seemed to sum up all the mistakes made by console makers over the past decade. Nintendo finally moved to disk-based media, but rather than choose industry standard CDs or DVDs, it chose its own proprietary mini-disk format. That meant that the GameCube could not play CDs, DVDs, or anything else aside from the games approved by Nintendo. Although Nintendo reiterated its longstanding concern about piracy, even the most promiscuous pirates purchase legitimate games occasionally. All that Nintendo's copy protection schemes did was drive paying customers into the arms of the competition.

On launch day, the GameCube only had 12 titles (there were even fewer in Japan), including some that had already been released on competing systems. That was better than the Sega Saturn, but not by much. Also, Nintendo continued to focus on younger gamers, who by this time represented a much smaller segment of the gaming population.

Finally, the GameCube was not backward compatible. Before they could use the system, gamers would have to invest considerable sums of money in new games. Since N64 owners had no incentive to remain with Nintendo, they could just as easily upgrade to a PlayStation 2, Xbox, or Dreamcast as they could to a GameCube. Among them were children in their teens who wanted to upgrade to a more "mature" console. That left Nintendo with a market that consisted of its most dedicated fans and families with small children who were just beginning to experience video games. However, because young children were more involved in outside activities than teenagers, they were less likely to be consumers of large numbers of games. Perhaps that was why the GameCube had a lower attach rate (number of games sold per console) than other consoles.

Sony's most serious threat came from Microsoft, which introduced its Xbox console the same week that Nintendo launched the GameCube. Although Microsoft was new to console gaming, it benefited both from its experience in PC gaming and from its partnership with Sega.

In many ways, the Xbox was the true Dreamcast successor. It extended several Dreamcast advantages, such as online play and a Windows-based programming environment, while remedying some of its shortcomings, such as the lack of a DVD drive. After Sega announced that it was discontinuing Dreamcast, Microsoft was the first company to call Sega to ask it to develop games for Microsoft's soon-to-be-launched console. Microsoft even recruited Peter Moore away from Sega to lead the Xbox division. Moore knew that if Sega had had the financial resources of Microsoft, the Dreamcast might have been a success. Xbox gave him a second chance to beat his old rival.

Microsoft was also able to leverage its relationships with developers to ensure a steady stream of content for Xbox owners. Prior to the launch of the Xbox, Microsoft acquired Bungie Studios, developer of the popular *Halo* series. It also enlisted the support of Electronic Arts, which had been notably absent from the Dreamcast. Inside, the Xbox was essentially a modified PC, which made the transition easy for developers who were already creating PC games. It also ensured that the Xbox had a formidable line-up of launch titles.

In terms of performance, the Xbox was comparable to the PS2. One area where Microsoft excelled was in online gaming. Unfortunately for Microsoft, the lack of broadband penetration limited the benefits of Xbox Live. Nevertheless, the stage was set for an eventual surge in broadband usage that would give Microsoft a significant advantage over its rivals.

In the meantime, Sony continued to lead the industry with well-established gaming franchises and the largest library of titles. By 2003, it owned more than half of the video game market (55 percent), compared to 22 percent for Microsoft and only 16 percent for Nintendo. Finally, in 2007, the PS2 surpassed the original PlayStation as the best-selling console in history. The fact that it remains in production today, almost ten years after its introduction, is a testament to the PlayStation's enduring legacy.

4

Xbox Empire

For many years, Microsoft Windows was the most popular operating system for playing computer games. However, the rise of inexpensive gaming consoles in the 1990s caused Microsoft some concern, as entertainment software sales began to shift away from home computers. Microsoft saw gaming as a way to maintain its dominance in computer-based home entertainment.

In this chapter we will look at the motivation behind the creation of the Xbox brand, the rise of Microsoft as a powerful competitor in console gaming, and the role of Xbox Live in Microsoft's ambition to establish Xbox as a central hub for home entertainment.

PC Gaming

For most of the history of video games, computers, rather than consoles, were the platform of choice for the state-of-the-art, and for the past quarter-century, that platform has been dominated by Microsoft. However, this story goes back much further to a time when computers were limited to the military, large corporations, and academia.

Nineteen sixty-one was a seminal year in the history of computer games. Microsoft founder Bill Gates had just entered grade school near his home in Seattle, Washington, when researchers on the other side of the country were developing a game called *Spacewar*. This ancestor of modern video games was the brainchild of a group of researchers at MIT who felt that *Spacewar* could demonstrate the capabilities of the university's new Digital Equipment Corporation (DEC) minicomputer better than conventional applications. *Spacewar* had all the elements of video arcade games of the 1970s and early 1980s. They included "simulated spaceships, aerial torpedoes, maneuvers and tactics, a sun with a gravity field, all shown on a cathode ray tube and played with complex controls" (Goodavage 1972).

Another influential program was the 1976 adventure game *Colossal Cave Adventure*. Unlike *Spacewar*, it did not involve flying objects, simulated gravity, or complex controllers. Instead, *Adventure* was a text-based game that unfolded like a story, only with prompts that players had to respond to. The original intention was to create a computer version of the popular role playing game *Dungeons & Dragons*, which enjoyed a substantial following among readers of fantasy fiction novels such as *Lord of the Rings*.

Eventually computers found their way outside the confines of large institutions and into homes and small offices around the world. The capabilities of home computers went far beyond early game consoles. When the rate of computer adoption surged in the early 1980s, it helped contribute to the great video game crash of 1983. Consoles like the Atari 2600 simply couldn't compete with inexpensive PCs, such as the Commodore 64. The introduction of more powerful consoles, like the Nintendo Entertainment System, temporarily closed the gap between computers and game consoles.

By the early 1990s, the gap between PCs and game consoles had once again widened and Microsoft emerged as the leader in PC operating systems and business software. The shift from DOS to Windows helped to further popularize computer gaming. Microsoft included a number of casual games with Windows and offered an inexpensive and powerful *Flight Simulator*. Although Microsoft's *Flight Simulator* was sophisticated enough to be used as a flight training program, the settings could be adjusted so that anyone could fly an airplane after spending a few minutes learning the basic controls. The popularity of *Flight Simulator* helped spawn an entire genre of 3-D flying games that ranged from historic games like the *Red Barron* to futuristic titles like *Star Wars Rebel Assault*.

Henry Lowood (2006), Curator for the History of Science and Technology Collections of Stanford University, observes that "during the 1990s, personal computers, not proprietary game consoles, paced the progress of graphical game engines." It was this cutting edge technology that allowed the creation of games like the 1993 title *DOOM*. Credited as the original first person shooter, *DOOM* combined story-telling with graphical gameplay in an immersive 3-D environment. It was also one of the first games to use networks for online gameplay, although the relative scarcity of broadband Internet limited its usefulness.

Microsoft understood the importance of games to its core PC market. It was the leader in business software with products like Microsoft Office, but games set the Windows operating system apart from competitors. Microsoft's dominance in state-of-the-art gaming began to change in the mid 1990s as companies like Sega, 3DO, and Atari released consoles that challenged the best computers of the day. However, it was the launch of the PlayStation in 1995 that created the first real challenge to Microsoft's dominance. Games on the PlayStation offered many of the same qualities first seen in *DOOM*, such as powerful 3-D engine, detailed graphics, and expansive settings. The PlayStation's inability to perform business functions didn't matter to gamers who rarely used their PCs for non-gaming tasks. The primitive state of the Internet in the mid 1990s ensured that the PlayStation's lack of online networking capabilities would have little impact on console sales. Yet Microsoft understood that it would only be a matter of time before that too became an integral part of the gaming experience.

Sony's rise to prominence gave Microsoft pause for thought. To combat the impact of leading edge consoles on computer gaming, Microsoft decided to implement a defensive diversification strategy by expanding into its competitors' core business. For Microsoft, the expansion into game consoles seemed natural. After all, consoles were becoming less like toys and more like computers. The problem, as we will see later in the book, was that Microsoft's core business was *not* computers, but computer software. Its lack of competence in hardware design and engineering would eventually prove to be its Achilles heel.

Initially Microsoft took a more conservative approach that focused on its core competency in operating system software. In 1996 it entered into a partnership with Sega to supply the operating system and development tools for Sega's soon-to-be released Dreamcast console.

The Sega Dreamcast: An Xbox Prototype?

Any time a company enters a new area of business, even a related one, it must anticipate certain startup costs and delays. It must build new partnerships with customers, suppliers, and contractors, and it needs to hire new people with different skills. Building game consoles was poles apart from developing business software and operating systems. Even though Microsoft had experience in game development, particularly flight simulators and casual games, building game consoles was an entirely different enterprise. If Microsoft wanted to have a console capable of challenging Sony's next generation machine, it would either have to create one quickly or acquire an existing console maker.

Cisco, the world's leading networking company, turned acquisitions into an art form, and in the process expanded its business at a staggering pace. Between 1993 and 2006, Cisco acquired more than 110 companies, while retaining more than 90 percent of the workforce. In the process, it successfully entered new lines of business ranging from home networking to telephony. Yet few companies were as successful as Cisco. As many as 70 percent of acquisitions do not live up to expectations and nearly 50 percent fail outright. Those that succeed often require years of integration effort. Microsoft had had its share of failed acquisitions, like WebTV, an ill-fated attempt to enter the cable TV market.

More troubling was the limited number of acquisition targets. Atari and 3DO had already shut down their hardware business. Sega was the most promising acquisition target. In the mid 1990s, when the Japanese console maker nearly went bankrupt trying to compete against Sony and Nintendo, Microsoft was one of a handful of companies willing to partner with Sega, developing the operating system that would power its new Dreamcast console. Moreover, Sega shared Microsoft's vision of a networked world as confirmed by Charles Belfield, Sega's VP of Marketing. "Dreamcast will evolve much more into a network environment rather than a standalone system. It's not about you and the machine any more. It's about you competing against your friends, your enemies" (Kennedy 2005).

Although some speculated that Sega and Microsoft could jointly develop a Dreamcast compatible console, Microsoft quickly dispelled the rumors. It knew that negotiating any form of purchase or partnership with the Japanese company would be impossible within the timeframe it had set for itself. Developing the software for Dreamcast was a logical first step that benefited both companies. Microsoft used the opportunity to learn about the console business and to establish relationships with game developers.

In return, Sega received one of the easiest operating system platforms to develop games on—Windows CE. It meant that developers could create games using software readily available for any Windows-based PC. Sega President Shoichiro Irimajiri believed that the partnership with Microsoft would create "an unequalled environment for developers." Irimajiri had good reason for optimism. When the Dreamcast was finally launched in 1998 (Japan) and 1999 (Rest of the World), it had one of the best collections of launch titles ever seen on a video game console. As a result, it became one of the quickest selling consoles in history. Unfortunately, as we saw in the previous chapter, Sega did not have the financial resources to compete against cash-rich Sony. The next year, Sega announced its withdrawal from the console market.

Microsoft could have ensured the viability of Dreamcast through loans, profit sharing agreements, an equity stake in Sega, or a combination of these alternatives. Each would have benefited Microsoft in different ways. Sega had a high quality product, an established customer base, and a console that was quickly winning consumer acceptance. Sega's library of exclusive franchises only strengthened the company's position relative to competitors. The continuation of Dreamcast would have extended these strengths and provided a much stronger challenge to Sony and Nintendo than Microsoft was able to provide— at least initially. The Dreamcast partnership would have given Microsoft the opportunity to focus on its core competency in software development without the distractions of learning to design and build consoles. One can only speculate about how the video game industry might have evolved had Microsoft backed Dreamcast instead of Xbox.

Nevertheless, there were advantages to allowing the Dreamcast to fail. For one, Microsoft could incorporate many of the marketing and design ideas from the Dreamcast into the Xbox and Xbox 360. Microsoft also avoided certain risks often associated with acquisitions, such as overpaying for the acquired company's stock, losing key employees, and failing to realize product synergies. When Sega discontinued its console business, several key employees moved to Xbox, including Peter Moore, who went on to be Microsoft's Corporate Vice President responsible for Xbox. "Sega had the option of pouring in more money or going bankrupt and they decided they wanted to live to fight another day," Moore explained. "So we licked our wounds, ate some humble pie and went to Sony and Nintendo to ask for dev kits. Actually, the only company that ever called was Microsoft and that became my link with the company" (Stuart 2008).

Xbox Ambitions

Microsoft began planning its own console in 1999, while it was still a Sega partner. The Dreamcast partnership was one way Microsoft could build relationships with key software developers as it readied its own console. In effect, Microsoft hoped to someday control a diverse empire of home entertainment products, of which video games were just the beginning. Evidence of Microsoft's broad home entertainment ambitions could be seen in the list of companies acquired in the late 1990s that mainly specialized in products for cable TV, e-commerce, video games, digital music, and mobile phones. Out of 32 companies acquired between 1997 and 2000, only three specialized in business software as shown in Table 4.1.

According to Seamus Blackley, the Microsoft executive who co-wrote the Xbox business plan, "If the Xbox successfully landed Microsoft in the world's living rooms, it could count not only on the substantial profits from big-time game publishing, but also on one day controlling an empire of movies and TV-on-demand, Internet, and … as-yet-undreamed services" (Chaplin and Ruby 2005). In essence, Xbox was to be the centerpiece of the company's home entertainment ambitions.

When the Xbox was launched in 2001, it retailed for about $40 less than it cost the company to manufacture and distribute, leading to some speculation that Microsoft could lose as much as $3.3 billion over the life of the console. On the other hand, the software giant hoped that by getting its console in the hands of as many consumers as possible it could earn enough revenue through software sales and third-party licenses to offset those losses.

Even though Microsoft had little expertise in hardware development, it was able to leverage its strong ties to hardware companies such as Intel, NVidia and Seagate. Also, Microsoft was consistently ranked as one of the top employers in the country in terms of job satisfaction, turnover, and benefits. Therefore, it would have no problem recruiting exceptionally talented engineers to work on Xbox development. Once that talent was in place, it could draw on its many corporate partners to design and supply components, develop software, and assemble the final product.

The process was made simpler by Microsoft's decision to build the Xbox out of standard PC components. This also allowed games to be developed simultaneously for the Xbox and Windows PCs, thereby allowing it to attack

Table 4.1   **Microsoft Acquisitions 1997–2000**

Date of Acquisition	Company Name	Product Segment
December 21, 2000	Great Plains Software	Business Software
December 5, 2000	Digital Anvil	Video Games
October 26, 2000	WebAppoint	
September 18, 2000	Pacific Microsonics Inc.	Digital Music
September 13, 2000	MongoMusic	Digital Music
July 12, 2000	NetGames U.S.A.	Video Games
June 19, 2000	Bungie Software	Video Games
June 12, 2000	Driveoff.Com	E-commerce
February 29, 2000	Peach Networks	Cable TV
October 29, 1999	Entropic	Speech Recognition
September 17, 1999	Softway Systems	UNIX Software Tools
September 15, 1999	Visio	Business Software
July 7, 1999	STNC	Mobile Services
July 1, 1999	ZOOMIT	Business Software
July 1, 1999	Sendit	Mobile Services
June 14, 1999	OmniBrowse	Mobile Services
June 7, 1999	ShadowFactor	Video Games
April 26, 1999	Jump Networks	Business Software
April 19, 1999	Access Software	Video Games
March 4, 1999	CompareNet	E-commerce
November 5, 1998	LinkExchange	E-commerce
August 25, 1998	Valence Research	Networking
April 28, 1998	The MESA Group	Email
April 9, 1998	Firefly Network	E-commerce
February 23, 1998	Flash Communications	Instant Messaging
December 31, 1997	Hotmail	Email
August 5, 1997	VXtreme	Streaming Video
June 30, 1997	LinkAge Software	Email
June 13, 1997	Cooper & Peters	Internet Software
May 7, 1997	Dimension X	Internet Software
April 6, 1997	WebTV Networks	Cable TV
March 3, 1997	Intersé	E-Commerce

Source: Microsoft Corp.

the competition on two fronts. The Xbox would appeal to the mass market with its low cost, ease of use, and portability, while PC games would continue to attract committed gamers for whom only the most advanced graphics and gameplay mechanics would suffice.

The problem with outsourcing component development was cost. "Instead of developing core components in-house, Microsoft outsourced the expensive parts to Intel for the central processing chip and to NVidia for the graphics chip," explained David Shippy, chief architect for the Xbox 360 processor.

> They were painfully aware that custom hardware would have allowed them to better control costs and achieve the best price-performance ratio, but [Microsoft's] production timeline simply wouldn't allow it.

> Since Sony parts were custom-made, they were able to reduce the cost of their hardware by combining the central processing chip and the graphics chip into a single unit for the PlayStation 2. Consequently, the price of the PlayStation 2 dropped from $299 to $149. Sony even made a small profit on the game console. Microsoft, however, could not motivate Intel or NVidia to reduce the cost of the Xbox chips, nor did they have the opportunity to combine the chips into one, as Sony had done, because they were dealing with two different vendors (Shippy and Phipps 2009).

Another perceived drawback of relying on third-parties was the inability to control product development. Each company released its respective components after extensive beta-testing and quality-control. A setback in any one component caused the entire project to be delayed. In this case, delays in the production of graphics chips and problems with the power supply forced the Xbox to miss its original launch date. Some believed that the delay made it more difficult for Microsoft to take market share away from Sony.

When it came time to develop the Xbox's successor, Microsoft avoided third party hardware developers as much as possible. This allowed it to reduce costs and shorten the development time, but at the expense of testing and quality control. The result, as we will see in later chapters, was nothing short of disastrous.

The Xbox Live Experience

Microsoft's strategy had always been to dominate the sphere of online gaming through its Xbox Live online gaming service. Online gaming increased the challenge and playability by allowing gamers to face off against similarly skilled opponents or form teams with other online players. Xbox Live also gave users the opportunity to download add-on content, such as new levels, landscapes, or characters. Finally, developers could test new games online and marketers could use the data gathered through online services to better understand customers.

Sega had the same idea when it launched the Dreamcast, but at that time, few people had heard of broadband Internet and dialup Internet had limited use. Streaming high-definition video, music sharing, and social networking were all unproven concepts that were beyond the reach of the average person with a 56k dialup modem. Even as late as 2001, attempts to launch online video-on-demand services failed from a lack of broadband penetration. In short, Sega was ahead of its time.

When it was first launched, Xbox Live faced the same challenges that Sega faced. However, it would only be a matter of time before broadband achieved widespread adoption. Microsoft had the financial resources and patience to remain at the leading edge of a global connectivity transformation. Sega did not.

Even though Xbox Live would not make money for several years, it gave Microsoft unprecedented information about its customers—something that Sony lacked. "We've got this consumer demographic nailed," observed Moore (2006). "We know exactly who they are, what they're doing, what they're playing, what they like, what they don't like every second of every day" (Microsoft Corp. 2006).

The 2005 launch of the Xbox 360 coincided with rapid growth in broadband Internet subscriptions in the U.S.. More than 60 percent of Xbox 360 owners subscribed to Xbox Live at an annual cost of $50. In May 2009, the total number of subscribers jumped to more than 30 million, a 300 percent increase over 18 months. Even though Microsoft was the only console maker to charge a fee for its online service, it had a strong lead over Sony and Nintendo.

Sony and Microsoft targeted the same demographic of males between 18 and 35 years of age who preferred to play military-style games, sports games, science fiction/fantasy adventures and first-person shooters. Many of the more successful titles in these categories were moving online. Some examples of successful online franchises were *Final Fantasy*, *World of Warcraft* and *Guild Wars*. As long as Microsoft maintained its lead in online gaming, both through Xbox Live and Windows PCs, it would continue to win customers away from Sony.

The challenge was to maintain a sufficient gap between Xbox Live and other services to justify the additional cost. Sony sought to unseat Microsoft by enhancing its own online service, but Microsoft's lead created significant barriers to entry. "Is it possible that Sony could create a network the size and scale of Xbox Live in such a short time?" asked Christopher Grant (2006), managing editor of Joystick.com, when Sony announced its decision to challenge Microsoft. "It has cost Microsoft, the world's largest software company, billions and taken years just to lay the framework for the current Xbox Live service."

> It seems unlikely they could take the crown from Microsoft on their first try, but any attempt is a huge relief. It was beginning to look like Sony didn't think the Xbox Live service was a valuable addition to console gaming, or a serious competitor to their hegemony.

Clearly, Microsoft made a wise decision when it made Xbox Live its central focus. When online gaming became an important part of the core gaming experience, it allowed Microsoft to maintain strong console sales despite significant shortcomings in other areas. However, Microsoft's lead in online gaming will not last forever. As networking costs decline, so do barriers to entry.

For many gamers, Sony's PlayStation Network had already improved enough to meet their needs. Online play was nearly identical for non-exclusive games. The fact that Sony offered its service for free was enough to sway some gamers toward Sony. "I think what we're doing is pretty cool," offered Peter Dille, Senior Vice President for Marketing and PlayStation Network.

> I also think it comes back to great value. There's an awful lot of content you can get on the PlayStation Network. We're not charging consumers a subscription fee to get online and play games head to head (Totilo, 2008).

In *The Innovator's Dilemma: When New Technologies Cause Great Firms to Fail*, Clayton M. Christensen (1997) anticipates Microsoft's problem in his description of performance oversupply. This phenomenon occurs when the rate of technological improvement exceeds the rates of improvement demanded by customers. In the computer industry, the pace of development of hard drives greatly exceeded the needs of customers. "Performance oversupply triggered a change in the basis of competition. Once the demand for capacity was satiated, other attributes, whose performance attributes had not yet satisfied market demands, came to be more highly valued." Christensen's research focused on computer drives, a product in which miniaturization rather than capacity has driven the market. In recent years, inexpensive thumb drives based on *lower* capacity flash-memory have become more popular than larger high performance drives.

Online gaming is limited in the number of features and services it can provide. As bandwidth increases and online service costs decline, Microsoft's competitors will close the gap between their offerings and Xbox Live. Many gamers remain loyal to Microsoft for one reason, online play. If Microsoft loses its edge over the PlayStation Network, gamers could quickly abandon the console in favor of the PlayStation 3, which is generally perceived as more reliable.

Sony faced similar challenges to those described by Christensen, but in other areas, such as high-definition movies (discussed at length in Chapter 8: *Blu-rays and Netflix*). The important lesson for the video game industry is that key success factors have moved away from performance (i.e., graphics and speed) toward services such as social networking (i.e., online play) and interactivity (i.e., motion-sensing controllers). In other words, customer requirements have changed as the industry has evolved and matured. Following the natural evolution of product-markets, continued success of firms in the industry depends on understanding and anticipating such changes and creating products and services that respond to them.

The Decline of Computer Games

At the beginning of the chapter we discussed the importance of Microsoft Windows to gamers who need to be on the leading edge. For them, game consoles simply did not cut it. In addition, the ubiquity of Windows on home desktops meant that few landmark games were developed for competing operating systems, such as Apple's OSX and Linux.

PCs have continued to play an important role in the video game industry. In 2005, 39 percent of U.S. households used PCs for playing games, whereas consoles were present in 37 percent of homes. To satisfy the appetite of hard-core gamers for more powerful computers, specialty PC makers, such as Alienware and VoodooPC, continued to offer customized gaming machines that typically retailed for between $2,000 and $5,000.

However, as consoles became more powerful, fewer gamers felt the need to invest in expensive computers. Consequently, we have seen PC game sales decline every year for the past several years as more gamers turn to consoles for their gaming needs. Most gamers continued to use PCs, but mostly for non-gaming functions, such as social networking, email, and other basic tasks that can be performed well on almost any modern computer, irrespective of hard-drive size, processor speed, or operating-system software. Similar to what is happening in online gaming, a performance oversupply in processing power threatens Microsoft's continued dominance in the PC market. The surging popularity of netbooks is indicative of a trend that favors low cost and convenience over performance. Netbooks represent the lowest performance ratings among any class of computers, and are mainly purchased by consumers who realize that more expensive high-performance laptops far exceed their needs. More worryingly for Microsoft, netbooks are helping to popularize alternative operating systems, particularly Linux. Reacting to the rise in sales of computers preloaded with Linux, Microsoft dropped the OEM price of Windows XP from around $50 to $15.

Buyers who were wary of the security risks inherent in Windows XP or the learning curve of Linux turned to Apple. Although Apple offered computers that were typically less powerful than similarly priced PCs, they were able to win market share by emphasizing ease of use and better security.

Taken together, the aforementioned factors contributed to Microsoft's first ever revenue decline since the company went public in 1986. As Microsoft Windows declined in popularity, so too did the demand for traditional boxed PC games sold at retailers like Best Buy and GameStop. In 2008, sales of PC games fell by 14 percent in the United States.

Finally, Microsoft's dominance was threatened by a new trend known as cloud computing that pushed common computing tasks onto remote servers owned by Google, Yahoo, IBM, and others. Computer owners who used these services found that they had less need for powerful computers. As long as they could access the Internet, almost any computer would suffice, including old PCs, smartphones, and netbooks. In 2009, a service known as OnLive began to offer "cloud gaming." According to Chris Baker (2009), senior editor of *Wired* magazine, cloud gaming had the potential to drastically reshape the video game industry. "Imagine being able to fire up your vintage low-end Mac laptop and play *Crysis*, a gorgeously high-resolution PC game that's famous for overwhelming the GPUs of $4,000 Alienware rigs" (Baker 2009). Even if OnLive doesn't work, similar services will eventually negate the need for anything more powerful than a standard Internet terminal. In time, it might become possible to play games like *Crysis* directly on Internet-equipped television sets, such as Sony's Bravia line of HDTVs. Once that happens, gamers won't even need a console to play advanced games.

For now, Microsoft hoped to defend its leadership in PC gaming by expanding the services of Xbox Live to include PC games. "Games for Windows – Live" was announced on March 14, 2007 as a cross-platform service that enabled gamers "to communicate online and play supported games across both of Microsoft's gaming platforms, bringing more players and their friends together to connect in new and exciting ways" (Microsoft Corp. 2007). Michael Wolf, Senior Marketing Manager for Games for Windows – Live, believed that PC gaming would continue to play an important role in the industry and that the drop in retail sales simply represented a shift from traditional CD and DVD media to direct online purchases. "The PC gaming industry is not in decline; it's evolving and it's definitely evolving to a more online market. I believe the PC is the cradle of innovation; there's always new things happening on the PC" (Brightman 2009).

Microsoft quickly learned that the online PC market was far more competitive than console networking. Initially Games for Windows – Live had the same pricing structure as Xbox Live. However, when new competitors emerged to offer similar services for free, Microsoft decided to drop its membership fee requirements and offer Live for free. The question is whether Microsoft will be forced to do the same for console gaming.

If Sony continues to close the gap in online services, Microsoft may find that the billions of dollars it has invested in network services and infrastructure will be for naught. In the 1990s, Nintendo quickly lost its leadership position through complacency and a general lack of innovation. Microsoft knows that it cannot afford to do the same. Developments like Project Natal, an interface currently under development that will eliminate the need for game controllers, may help preserve Microsoft's industry leadership and bring it closer to the elusive goal of establishing an Xbox empire.

5

The Brain Age: Handheld Consoles and their Impact on Adult Gamers

In the 1960s, electronic games were played by hackers and scientists who had access to large institutional mainframe computers and minicomputers. When the first home consoles appeared in the 1970s, they opened up gaming to children and teenagers from middle-class and affluent homes. Then, in 1989, Nintendo launched the $89 Game Boy portable gaming console and forever changed the video game industry. From that point on, games became part of mainstream culture. Not only were they affordable, they could be played anywhere by anyone.

The Game Boy came bundled with the popular puzzle game *Tetris*, a landmark title that brought gaming to the masses. In the era of video arcades, games were seen as a juvenile pursuit. Portable gaming turned it into a pastime enjoyed by children, parents, and adults of all ages, classes, and educational levels. In recent years, portable gaming has migrated away from dedicated consoles to smartphones, portable computers, and mp3 players. Similarly, portable game consoles have expanded into movies, music, Internet services, and telephony.

In this chapter, we will examine innovations that have made some portable devices wildly popular, while others struggled. In particular, we will show how less capable devices like the Nintendo Game Boy and DS have triumphed over more advanced consoles and how new entrants like Apple promise to redefine the way portable games are played.

Early Handheld Devices

The earliest handheld consoles were single game devices that played sports games such as football or basketball. Despite their limited features, devices like Mattel Football were popular with children and achieved sales as high as 500,000 units per week. The Milton Bradley Company launched the world's first cartridge-based handheld console, known as the Microvision, in 1979. However, the Microvision suffered from a number of design flaws that led to its early demise.

It wasn't until Nintendo launched its Game Boy in 1989 that handheld consoles became a mainstream part of gaming culture. The original Game Boy had a black and white screen, stereo sound and a communications port for multiplayer games. It also suffered from a number of technical deficiencies, including its large size, difficult to read backlit screen, and mediocre processor. Journalist William Burrill (1993) of the *Toronto Star* referred to the Game Boy as a "video dinosaur" with its "teensy, eye-straining, matchbox-sized dot matrix black and white screen [and] smudgy graphics [that] look more like green and gray—if you can see them at all."

Simultaneous to the release of the Game Boy, Atari launched a far more capable handheld console known as Lynx, which sported a color screen, better graphics, and the ability to connect up to 8 players simultaneously. *Business Week* declared Lynx the "hottest" video game system of the year, one that "leapfrogs Nintendo Co.'s $89.95 Game Boy." The Lynx came bundled with *California Games*, a popular sports title that featured skateboarding, Frisbee, surfing and BMX biking. At $179, it was also twice the price of the Game Boy.

However, price and performance would have little impact on the final outcome of the handheld console race. Instead, the winner would be decided by one of the most unlikely sources of high tech innovation—The Soviet Union.

In 1984, Soviet computer scientist Alexey Pajitnov invented a puzzle game called *Tetris*. Initially, Pajitnov had no intention of making *Tetris* into a commercial product. His position changed, however, when the game quickly spread among computer enthusiasts in Eastern Bloc countries. Eventually, *Tetris* was discovered by former British Member of Parliament Robert Maxwell. Maxwell immediately realized the game's potential and set out to secure the rights from Pajitnov to distribute *Tetris* in the west. With an agreement in hand,

Maxwell went on to sublicense the game to several computer and video game companies, including Atari.

Nintendo believed that *Tetris* would be ideal for portable consoles, but the company was unsure if the rights Atari had obtained applied to handheld devices. To find out, Nintendo sent its own agent, game developer Henk Rogers, to see if he could negotiate a contract with the Soviets. Unbeknownst to Atari, Rogers learned that the original license Maxwell had obtained from Pajitnov was not legally binding, because Pajitnov had not obtained the proper authority to negotiate contracts on the government's behalf. And since all intellectual property developed in the Soviet Union belonged to the state, the contract was deemed invalid.

Rogers used the opportunity to negotiate a new license with the Soviet Ministry of Trade that would cover all video game consoles, not just handheld devices. It proved to be a game changer for both Nintendo and Atari. A few years after the fall of the Iron Curtain, the rights to *Tetris* reverted to Pajitnov. However, by then, Atari was history.

Tetris was a landmark for bringing adults into the gaming sphere. The game was elegant in its simplicity. Organizing blocks of different colors or textures was something almost anyone could do. The more block sequences a player completes, the faster the blocks arrive. Eventually, the blocks arrive at such dizzying speeds, not even the most practiced gamers can stop them. It was this "easy to use, difficult to master" formula that made *Tetris* so endearing to adults. There were no complex rules to learn, no unusual character and place names, and no time commitments. *Tetris* could be played for five minutes or five hours. Before long, Game Boys became "frequent attachments to traveling executives who spend hours in first-class compartments dropping Tetris blocks" (Levy 1993).

Nintendo had long planned to expand gaming to adult audiences. In Japan, the NES was known as the Famicom, short for Family Computer, a device that would offer something to every member of the family. Although the NES never appealed to adults in the way it did to children, Nintendo believed the Game Boy could finally change the way adults perceived video games.

Many adults were intimidated by game consoles, but that was nothing compared to the embarrassment they felt when children outplayed them on a TV screen in full view of friends and family. The Game Boy allowed adults to learn to play games in private without having their mistakes "magnified on a 26-inch television screen," explained Peter Main, Nintendo of America Senior Vice President of Marketing, shortly before the Game Boy's North American debut (McGill 1989).

The next step was to convince adults to pick up games for the first time. One Nintendo television commercial featured three middle-aged white collar professionals each playing *Tetris* in a college stairway, a company boardroom and an engineering design studio to the accompaniment of classical music. At the end of the 30-second spot was an announcement. "You don't stop playing because you get old, but you could get old if you stop playing." The positioning seemed to have its desired effect. By 1993, 40 percent of Game Boy players were adults over 18 and 50 percent were female.

Meanwhile, Atari mistakenly believed that the Game Boy's success was due to its relative low price. After the Game Boy outsold the Atari Lynx by 10 to 1 during the 1990 holiday season, Atari decided to drop the price of the Lynx to $99. That placed it in the same price range as Nintendo's technically inferior console. "We recognize that maybe we set the price too high—we didn't have the luxury of pricing research," said Atari marketing manager Peter Staddon (Toor 1991). With both handheld consoles priced under $100, Staddon predicted that the "Game Boy will struggle along on the back of the Nintendo name until Christmas and then disappear. Once kids have seen color they'll never go back to black and white."

Not once did Staddon consider that launch titles like the air-combat game *Blue Lightning* or the arcade style shooter *Gates of Zendocon* no longer appealed to the mass market. Atari seemed stuck in the 1970s, years after *Donkey Kong* and *Zelda* redefined gaming. In contrast, Nintendo had an impressive line-up of launch titles that not only included *Tetris*, but also a portable version of *Super Mario Bros.* called *Super Mario Land*.

Recent attempts to explain the demise of Lynx seem equally misguided. Strategic marketing consultant David M. Carter (2003) suggested that "to a new generation of kids the Atari brand meant little" and therefore "sales of the Lynx were minimal." Meanwhile, video game historian Leonard Herman (2008) claimed that the Lynx initially sold well, despite its high price. However, because Atari used custom microchips that were in short supply, it could not produce enough consoles to meet market demand. When Atari was finally able to increase production, it was too late. "By that time, Nintendo dominated the market."

Although branding and logistics may have contributed to the Lynx's demise, the real reason it failed was its lack of compelling content. If a console does not have games that people want to play, color screens, better graphics, faster processors, and networking will not be sufficient to influence consumer purchasing decisions. When the Game Boy was launched, Nintendo already had a significant following of *Mario* and *Zelda* players. The Game Boy not only gave children the opportunity to take their favorite games everywhere they went, it provided parents with a tool to occupy their children while shopping or taking long trips. Unsurprisingly, Atari's price drop did little to stimulate sales. In 1994, it discontinued Lynx after selling fewer than 500,000 units. Meanwhile, Nintendo went on to sell 118 million units of Game Boy and Game Boy Color.

In 1990, NEC launched the most advanced handheld console of the day, the TurboExpress, which retailed for $249. However, like the Atari Lynx, TurboExpress offered arcade-style games that were no longer fashionable among gamers and did little to attract non-gamers. It also had several technical shortcomings, including short battery life and a high failure rate. NEC sold just over a million units before retiring the console in 1994. Industry watchers blamed the failure of TurboExpress on its high price. However, as we have seen throughout the book, consumers will pay more for a product if it satisfies a valued need.

Like so many technology companies, NEC and Atari had fallen for the performance trap, believing that faster processors and color screens would help them win against Nintendo's basic black and white offering. Yet in an industry where content is king, Nintendo could have priced the Game Boy much higher and still outsold the Lynx and TurboExpress.

Atari and NEC were not the only companies troubled by Nintendo's success in the portable gaming market. When the Game Boy was first launched, a Sony manager berated his engineers for not coming up with a handheld console first. "This Game Boy should have been a Sony product," he told them (Sheff 1993). After all, Sony was the market leader in portable entertainment with its Walkman line of tape recorders and tape players. The comparison was particularly pertinent in light of the Game Boy's visual appearance, which was remarkably similar to a Walkman. According to one source, several Sony managers were transferred to other departments or were forced to resign out of shame.

A few years earlier, Sony would have been unfazed by the launch of a portable console. However, by 1989, Sony had come to view video games as an important new medium in its quest to dominate the entertainment industry. Sony had recently acquired CBS records and Columbia Pictures and entered into joint development agreements with Nintendo to produce home video game consoles, such as the PlayStation. Yet the company's inability to compete in handheld consoles proved to be a temporary setback in Sony's ambition to become a major force in video games.

Sega's Lost Opportunity

Another company with portable console ambitions was Sega. Compared with Nintendo and Atari, Sega was a relative newcomer to video games. Like Nintendo, Sega had been an important player in video arcades, but was several years behind Nintendo in entering the home market. Nevertheless, Sega had high ambitions. It hoped that by offering better hardware at a reasonable price, gamers would soon realize the value in Sega products. More importantly, unlike Atari, Sega had compelling content with which to compete against the Mario and Zelda franchises.

When Nintendo and Atari came out with their handheld consoles, Sega scrambled to create its own portable console. A year later, it unveiled the Sega Game Gear. The $149 console first became available in North America in 1991 with a line-up of eight launch titles. One of those titles was a *Tetris* clone called *Columns*. Then, a few months later, the company revealed *Sonic the Hedgehog*, Sega's answer to the *Mario Bros*.

Like Atari's Peter Staddon, Sega seemed to believe that "once kids have seen color they'll never go back" to the Game Boy. This was highlighted in Sega television commercials that featured side-by-side comparisons of the Game Boy and Game Gear. "If you were color blind and had an I.Q. of less than 12, then you wouldn't mind which portable you had," began one commercial. Game Boy players were portrayed as obese, uneducated, and unsophisticated compared to Game Gear players, who were invariable healthy and attractive.

Nintendo executives were livid. According to Nintendo, the attack ads ridiculed the mentally handicapped. It urged several national organizations for disabled persons to rally against Sega. Sega of America president Thomas J. Kalinske responded by saying that Nintendo "should spend more time improving their products and marketing rather than working on behind-the-scenes coercive activities" (Levine 1993). The behind-the-scenes drama made for great news headlines, but had little impact on console sales. In the end, Sega was more successful than Atari and NEC because it had better content.

Then Sega made one of the biggest mistakes in video game history. After selling a respectable 11 million consoles, Sega retired Game Gear to focus on a different portable console called Nomad. The key selling feature of the Nomad was its ability to play Sega Genesis titles right out of the box. That gave it the best selection of launch titles of any portable. However, by this time, Sega Genesis owners had migrated most of their game collections to CDs and Nomad could only play older cartridge titles. Moreover, the unit itself was bulky and suffered from an extremely short battery-life. Owners had the choice of constantly feeding the console fresh alkaline batteries or purchasing Sega's pricey and unreliable rechargeable battery pack. Either option made the Sega Nomad prohibitively expensive. As a result, sales never passed one million units.

Sega had a winning formula with Game Gear, a console that not only offered compelling content, but also technology that was years ahead of the Game Boy. To compete effectively in the portable console space, Sega should have improved Game Gear by giving it a brighter screen and making it smaller and more energy efficient. Eleven million Game Gear owners would have been encouraged to upgrade to a Game Gear II console, knowing that their existing games would look even better. Finally, an ever expanding library of titles would have attracted new buyers. Instead, by shifting focus to Nomad, Sega gave Nintendo the opportunity it needed to dominate the market with a console that already looked outdated when it was launched in 1989.

Game Boy Successors

Gamers tend to be influenced less by brand than consumers of other product categories. A perfect example was Nintendo's ill-fated attempt to offer a 3-D portable console known as the Virtual Boy. The Virtual Boy consisted of a head-mounted unit that displayed a monochrome stereoscopic image. At $180, the

Virtual Boy was reasonably priced for a first of its kind technology. However, the console relied too heavily on its 3-D technology and offered little in the way of interesting games.

The film industry faced the same problem when it first began offering 3-D movies in the 1950s. Early 3-D films were successful, but only because moviegoers were fascinated by the new technology. As the novelty wore off, consumers began to lose interest in the low quality productions. Before long, 3-D became synonymous with "B movie." Today's 3-D movies continue that tradition with films like *Journey to the Center of the Earth* and *Spy Kids 3-D*, both of which are considered to be among the worst films made in recent years.

The Virtual Boy could not play any of Nintendo's popular titles. Instead it had a dozen titles, such as tennis, golf, and bowling, which were good at demonstrating the console's 3-D features, but offered little else. With such a small library of titles, gamers could rent a Virtual Boy from stores like Blockbuster and, for a fraction of the cost of purchasing a unit, play every game the Virtual Boy had to offer. Although some gamers "loved the 3-D graphics," the general consensus was that the Virtual Boy was "boring," "stupid," and "hard to see." Not surprisingly, Nintendo sold fewer than a million units.

Nintendo did not produce a color handheld console until the release of the Game Boy Color in 1998, nearly 10 years after Atari and NEC pioneered the technology. The Game Boy Color was backward compatible with all existing Game Boy titles. Although original titles could not be displayed in color, the new screen provided improved visibility for all Game Boy games. Ultimately, the Game Boy Color was little more than an incremental improvement meant to satisfy the needs of gamers until Nintendo could release the Game Boy Advance (GBA) in 2001.

Aside from the Virtual Boy, the GBA represented the first significant portable console innovation to be released by Nintendo in more than 10 years. The technology behind the GBA was roughly equivalent to the popular Super Nintendo Entertainment System home console. That made it easy for developers to port existing titles to the new system.

Almost immediately, hundreds of new titles and ports of NES and SNES titles became available to prospective GBA customers. Classics like the *Legend of Zelda, Super Mario Bros.,* and *Final Fantasy* made the GBA an instant hit. In addition, the GBA was backward compatible with the Game Boy and Game

Boy Color, making it easy for existing customers to upgrade without investing heavily in new games. In 2003 alone, Nintendo sold nearly 15 million GBA consoles in Japan and North America.

Another advantage of the GBA was a built-in rechargeable battery that provided up to 15 hours of continuous use. This reduced the cost of ownership over the previous generation, which used disposable batteries or an optional battery pack that added to both the cost and size of the unit.

Attempts by various companies to challenge Nintendo's dominance of the handheld market invariably failed for the same reasons as earlier attempts by Atari and NEC. Notable among them was the Nokia N-Gage, the first serious effort to create a convergence device with cellular phone, music and gaming functions. The award winning device proved to be a capable telephone and mp3 player, but came up short in games. Not only did it lack sufficient content to challenge Nintendo, it suffered from numerous design issues, not the least of which was a battery that had to be removed to insert game cartridges.

One of the more interesting challengers was the Zodiac, the first portable console to use a touch screen. Zodiac was the brainchild of Tapwave, a Silicon Valley startup that was founded in 2001 to create a "mobile entertainment console." The idea was to combine the functions of several popular devices into one. As a result, the Zodiac played games, music, and movies, displayed e-books and photos, and managed personal data, such as addresses and appointments. Essentially, it was to be a Game Boy, Palm Computer, and iPod rolled into one.

At $299, Zodiac was priced competitively with high end PDAs, but was beyond the reach of those who wanted to use it primarily as a gaming console. More damaging was that fact that, like the Atari Lynx, the console relied on arcade-style games, including clones of *Pong* and *Pac-man*. In the end, Zodiac was one of the worst selling consoles of all time. In 2005, after selling fewer than 200,000 units, Tapwave declared bankruptcy.

Although N-Gage and Zodiac failed to gain market acceptance, they introduced technologies that would become commonplace in the next wave of handheld devices, such as the Nintendo DS, Apple iPhone, and Sony PlayStation Portable (PSP).

In 2004, shortly after Tapwave introduced the concept of touch screen gaming, Nintendo launched the first of its Dual Screen (DS) line of portable consoles, which provided touch screen input using a plastic stylus. The DS had built-in wireless connectivity, voice recognition, and backward compatibility with hundreds of Game Boy Advance titles.

When Nintendo announced the DS, the company was faced with an increasingly difficult business environment. In the home console market, Sega, Sony, and Microsoft had taken most of the share, leaving Nintendo as a marginal player. Nintendo Director of Development Shigeru Miyamoto blamed his competitors' willingness to suffer major financial losses in the pursuit of market share for Nintendo's dismal performance. Although gamers benefited when companies subsidized their console purchases, Miyamoto felt that such behavior was harmful to the industry:

> We've reached an era that's almost a dream come true for gamers, because they're able to buy these high powered games consoles at less than cost. It's obviously not good for the companies that are doing it, because they're bleeding money, and it's going to raise questions as to whether or not they can survive as a business. (Davies 2003)

Instead of continuing to battle Sony and Microsoft for an increasingly limited market of core gamers, Nintendo sought to expand its market with less complicated and more versatile gaming systems. For non-gamers, video game controls were a significant barrier. The DS stylus and voice recognition replaced standard controls on some games with more intuitive inputs. Everyone who could use a pen or pencil could interact with a well designed DS game. One such title was *Nintendogs*, a pet simulator in which players raised virtual puppies. Players used voice recognition to issue commands to their dogs and they used the stylus to pet, wash, and play with their puppies. By 2007, Nintendo had sold more than 13 million copies of *Nintendogs*.

Another popular title was *Brain Age*, a puzzle game that, if used daily, promised to stimulate brain activity and increase mental acuity. Nintendo marketed *Brain Age* to middle-aged and older players who enjoyed puzzle games and related activities. Players answered questions by issuing voice commands or by writing words and numbers on the screen. By the end of 2006, Nintendo had sold more than 8 million copies of *Brain Age* worldwide.

The first time Nintendo used advertisements to sell consoles to adult non-gamers was after the launch of the Game Boy. Yet most Game Boy advertising remained focused on children. Nintendo took a different approach with the DS, positioning it as a device primarily for adult non-gamers. "We have been very clear in our positioning," explained Reggie Fils-Aime, Executive Vice President of Sales and Marketing for Nintendo of America:

> As you look at all the demographic data, this industry can no longer rely simply on more and more young men coming of age to try gaming, call it ten to twenty year old demographic. The fact is that that demographic is shrinking and the next cohort, their younger brothers, is even smaller.
>
> So, for us, we view it as critical to find new ways to bring gaming to the masses. That means women, as we've successfully done with Nintendogs. That means older consumers, as Japan has successfully done with Brain Age and that product's sequel. That is exactly what we will be doing here in this marketplace, not only with DS, but with Revolution as well, bringing innovation to the marketplace that satisfies the hardest of the hard-core as well as brings new consumers into the marketplace. (Rojas 2006)

Nintendo hired 60-year-old actress Olivia Newton-John to be the DS "brand ambassador." In television commercials, Newton-John was shown playing *Brain Age* with a much younger secretary. By practicing every day, Newton-John achieved a "mental age" of only 29, allowing her to make calculations more quickly. In one spot, her secretary leans over and says "More brain training?" to which Newton-John replies "It keeps me even sharper."

Even commercials for games that might normally appeal to children often portrayed young adult actors. For example, pop singer Beyonce was featured in spots for the beat matching game *Rhythm Heaven*. In the UK, television commercials for games like *Zelda* and *Donkey Kong*, which traditionally appealed to core gamers, featured young women followed by the slogan, "Great games for girls from the makers of *Nintendogs*."

Traditionally, the United States adopted new video game technology before other regions of the world. Yet it was the last major video games market to embrace the DS. "Although we launched *Brain Training* software in Europe and in the Americas almost simultaneously, Europe was constantly selling significantly more DS hardware on a weekly basis," noted Nintendo president Satoru Iwata.

> It was taken for granted that American markets would easily sell twice the number as Europe, but Europe was first in blooming and the Americas are yet to show their real strength. Of course, we anticipate the expansion of DS there thanks to Pokémon and other titles. We will be glad as more Pokémon are sold, but it is not enough when we want to expand the gaming population.

> When I received a report from the U.S. that they sold 1 million Pokémon games already, I asked them, "Why did you sell only 10,000 Brain Age last week, when Europe sold 30,000?" This is a typical example of how I communicate with our people in the U.S. We need constantly to make an effort to appeal to the new audiences. (Nintendo of America 2007)

To appeal to new audiences, Nintendo focused its development efforts on discovering new uses for the DS. For example, Tokyo art museums began using the DS to provide interactive tours of exhibitions. One screen displayed compositions, while the other provided detailed explanations of the art. At the same time, users could access an audio tour using the console's headphone jack. In Kyoto, public high schools used the DS to teach English using special character recognition software. In one school, students achieved 80 percent English proficiency, compared to only 18 percent for students who did not use the DS.

Iwata also believed that gaming consoles could become productivity tools. "Modern human beings have less time and energy to spend on any activity," he observed.

> A great many things are changing with incredible speed. The energy one can spend on entertainment has never been very big in the first place. We have a very unusual software program for DS, which tells you how to prepare a meal. I love to use this cooking software to help me prepare meals at home on my days off. I think it important for us to create this type of software that will keep the owners' interests for a long time...

> As the number of consoles with a single architecture increase, there will be a variety of different possibilities for the machine to benefit society,

and they can be steps toward making the DS the machine that enriches the owners' daily lives. (Nintendo of America 2007)

In Japan, Nintendo sold between 600,000 and 700,000 DS consoles per month, with a production rate that continued to be insufficient to meet market demand. Although the console had been on the market for more than two years, retail outlets continued to sell out as soon as new stock arrived. During peak holiday periods, supply shortages in Japan were critical enough to prompt Nintendo to issue a public apology to its customers.

In 2007, Nintendo began to phase out its Game Boy consoles to focus strictly on the DS platform. Although the Game Boy had enjoyed a life span of more than 15 years in its various iterations, Iwata hoped for even better results with the DS. "If we can continue our efforts with DS, to the extent it can be used as a social infrastructure, it may be able to enjoy a far longer lifespan than any hardware in the past."

In 2008, Nintendo released an improved version of the DS known as the DSi. Nintendo replaced the GBA slot with a Secure Digital (SD) media slot. SD was supported by the largest computer and electronics firms in the U.S. and Japan and could be found in many digital cameras, music players, and PDAs. This gave the DSi additional functionality, such as the ability to play music and store photos. A built-in camera gave DSi owners the ability to take photos and edit them using the console's standard software.

By early 2009, Nintendo had sold more than 100 million DS consoles worldwide, making it the second best-selling portable console after the Game Boy.

The Sony PSP

In 2003, Sony responded to the growing adoption of handheld devices, such as cellular phones, mp3 players and PDAs, by introducing its own handheld "entertainment center," known as the PSP. Sony's new console offered the most advanced portable gaming features available, as well as playback of full-length movies and digital music. In addition to its bright widescreen display, the PSP offered wireless connectivity, flash memory and Universal Media Disk (UMD) storage, and a wide selection of downloadable media from the PlayStation

Store and TiVo. Sony hoped that the PSP's multitude of features would allow it to directly challenge Microsoft, Apple, Palm and others.

PSP advertising was clearly aimed at core gamers. Television advertisements almost exclusively featured young urban males. In the "Dude, Get Your Own" campaign, a geeky 20-something male gamer pesters young attractive PSP owners in public locations to allow him to play their PSP. He goes out of his way to appear stylish, but clearly lacks the authentic self-confidence of actual PSP owners. In some spots, PSP owners were portrayed as being more attractive to women. However, commercials featuring female gamers and other non-traditional players were scarce. The most frequently advertised PSP games were shooters, sports titles, and sci-fi fantasy.

As a gaming device, the PSP faced several challenges. Whereas DS users could immediately access a large library of GBA titles, the PSP had no predecessor. Instead, PSP owners had to invest in new games. To ensure that gamers would have a large library of titles to choose from, Sony used a MIPS architecture that was very similar to the PlayStation 2. This made it extremely easy for developers who were familiar with the PS2 to create new games for the PSP and to port existing PlayStation titles. As a result, the PSP had an impressive number of launch titles, including a *Tetris* clone called *Lumines*, first-person shooters, and several racing and sports games.

The PSP was the undisputed leader in portable console graphics. *Wipeout Pure*, a futuristic racing game that was one of the PSP's launch titles was a perfect example. Critics gave the game some of the highest ratings of any portable title on the market. A review on *Gaming Age* called *Wipeout Pure* a "thing of beauty" on "the large, crisp PSP screen." "When you play your very first game on the first course, and start out in the detailed grandstand area before plunging into a twisty undersea tunnel, it's hard to realize you are playing this on a portable game system" (Cordeira 2005).

However, much like the 3DO Multiplayer, most consumers did not value the console's non-gaming functions. Instead, they viewed the $250 device as a more expensive alternative to the DS. Those who did purchase a PSP for its multifaceted utility found it lacking in almost every area. As a music and movie player, it was bulkier than mp3 players like the iPod and Zune and had less storage capacity. The PSP's reliance on Sony's proprietary Memory Stick storage media made it less versatile than devices that used industry standard

SD storage. Also, SD was typically less expensive and came in a wider variety of sizes and speeds than Memory Stick.

Jack Tretton, president and CEO of Sony Computer Entertainment of America, felt that content providers were to blame for not providing what consumers wanted. He particularly berated movie studios for not releasing reasonably priced movies in the PSP's proprietary UMD disk format. "We made the mistake of assuming the movie studios understood our consumers and their tastes, and that they knew what they were doing," he asserted.

> *They flooded the market with movies. I don't know that it was necessarily movies that appealed to our consumers. I know it wasn't at prices that appealed to our consumers. As a consumer, if you're charging me $19.99 for a DVD, why are you charging me $29.99 for a UMD?[1] I'll pay $20 for it, but I'm not paying $29. And I'm not buying On Golden Pond. We're trying to educate the studios as to who our consumer is, and what their price tolerances are. We feel that UMD could be a viable format for movies on the PlayStation Portable if it's handled right. (Hsu 2007)*

The PSP fared just as poorly as a music player. Its built-in memory could not hold even one album in mp3 format, and purchasing additional flash memory could cost as much as purchasing a new Apple iPod with the same storage capacity. Finally, its large size made it less portable than the DS, iPod, and most other music players.

Even the PSP's core gaming capabilities did not always live up to expectations. For example, PlayStation and PS2 titles often did not translate well to the portable console because of the different button positions. The most successful titles were those specifically designed for the PSP. Yet even well-designed PSP games were less intuitive than their DS counterparts that utilized stylus input and voice commands.

Despite its shortcomings, the PSP sold relatively well, particularly among male professionals between the ages of 20 and 40 who used it during commutes and business trips. A 2007 price cut to $169 placed the PSP closer to the $129 Nintendo DS and helped attract younger and less affluent buyers.

---

1   The Universal Media Disc (UMD) was mini optical disc developed by Sony specifically for the PSP. It had a capacity of 1.8 gigabytes and could be used for storing games, movies, music and other content.

Over time, the average age of PSP users declined. In 2008, Sony saw its new demographic as teens. The company also wanted to expand the PSP's appeal to female gamers. "The teen demographic we've kind of nailed," noted PSP senior product manager John Koller.

> *It's a good demographic for us. I think looking at the younger set, to a degree, as well as female, both those areas I would agree would be good areas for us to look into in the next few years. I think what'll dictate that is the quality of the games and quality of other content, so things like Skype, GPS and Internet Radio. Those appeal to more of a gender split than maybe God of War will. We look at ways to increase those opportunities. Japan in particular is really pushing for that; they're making a big push for the female demographic, as well. You know, we made no secret it's a male-dominated device right now, and if we add the female demographic, I think we'll be in very, very good shape. It's a push for us. (Klepek 2008)*

By early 2009, total unit sales surpassed 50 million. Although that was less than half the number of DS units sold over the same period, it ensured the PSP's position as the best-selling non-Nintendo portable console.

Sony hoped to further broaden the PSP's appeal by addressing some of the console's shortcomings. A new model called the "PSP Go" was significantly smaller and lighter than previous versions, a feat that Sony accomplished by trading the UMD optical drive for 16GB of internal memory, enough to store numerous game, video, and music files. Sony also moved the control buttons from the sides of the PSP to a sliding apparatus that could be hidden when not in use.

Unfortunately, the PSP Go's design improvements may not be enough to mount a serious challenge to the DSi. In particular, Sony made two decisions that place the PSP Go at a distinct disadvantage. First, it increased the price back to $249. Large price increases are not uncommon for new generation console launches. Yet the PSP Go is not a new generation, but an improvement on an existing design.

Sony also kept the Memory Stick slot as part of its ongoing effort to promote its own proprietary format over SD cards. The company's persistent refusal to accept the SD media was the latest in a line of failed formats that Sony promoted long after other dominant designs and industry standards emerged. Betamax,

SACD, and ATRAC are several well documented examples. In each case, Sony allowed competitors with inferior technology to win market share because of its unwillingness to license its technology to other manufacturers and provide customers with preferred formats.

The role media formats will play in future portable console purchasing decisions remains unclear. In the past, consumers purchased consoles that were less expensive, adhered to industry standards, and offered quality content and ease-of-use. The PSP fell short of the DSi in every dimension except quality content. And while Sony offered a large number of compelling games, it had fewer titles that appealed to the nontraditional audiences the PSP Go was designed to reach.

The biggest threat to the PSP may not come from the DSi or any other dedicated gaming console, but from the iPhone and other smartphones. The iPhone has become increasingly popular among 20- to 40-year-old male professionals who traditionally purchased PSPs. More importantly, it is quickly turning into a highly capable mobile gaming device.

Apple's iPhone Gaming Strategy

Apple's first attempt to break into the video game market was in 1995 with the Apple Bandai Pippin. Apple designed the Pippin around a standard PowerMac computer with controllers that could display video on a computer screen or television. This was similar to Microsoft's approach with the original Xbox, which was essentially a repackaged Celeron PC. The Pippin played CD-based multimedia software and games and provided Internet for a price of $599. After designing the console, Apple gave responsibility for production and marketing to its partner, Japanese toymaker Bandai.

Although Pippin was reasonably priced as a full featured multimedia computer, it competed less favorably with inexpensive gaming consoles, such as the PlayStation and SNES. Pippin not only had one of the worst line-ups of gaming titles of any console, the few titles it did offer were mainly drawn from the Mac's educational library, such as *Dr. Seuss ABC*. In the end, history will remember the Pippin as one of the worst selling game consoles in history, with fewer than 50,000 units sold.

On January 9, 2007, after years of speculation, Apple CEO Steve Jobs announced the iPhone. The iPhone was Apple's ambitious foray into mobile communications, one that turned the popular iPod music player into a fully functional Internet tablet and smartphone. The iPhone came equipped with a 2 megapixel camera, between 4 and 8 gigabytes of flash memory, an accelerometer, Bluetooth, Wi-Fi, quad-band GSM radio, a mobile version of the OS X operating system, and up to five hours of battery life. A 3.5 inch touch screen display made listening to music, checking voicemail, and browsing the web as easy as swiping, pinching, and tapping the screen.

On launch day, Friday June 29, 2007, Apple fans waited in lines for hours and, in some cases, days for Apple stores to open. Others waited in front of their computers in an often futile attempt to purchase the iPhone from Apple's online store or from its mobile partner AT&T. The majority of these customers were innovators and early adopters for whom price was a secondary consideration. For everyone else, the iPhone's $599 price tag ($499 for the 4GB model) was simply out of reach.

Initially, the iPhone's software was closed, which meant that only a few applications developed by Apple were available for the launch. That didn't stop some hackers and independent developers from creating an underground development community known as the "iPhone Dev Team." The community's first objective was to create a Jailbreak application that would allow them to run unauthorized code on the iPhone. Afterwards, they created a custom user interface that allowed Jailbreak users to easily download applications from various Internet websites. Another group of hackers focused on unlocking the iPhone to allow it to work with mobile providers other than AT&T.

The use of a closed-software platform for the iPhone was consistent with Apple's policy of strictly managing its hardware and software. Many developers decried Apple's strategy because it prevented them from taking full advantage of the iPhone's advanced hardware. Among them was video game developer John Carmack, founder of id Software. He thought the iPhone would be an enjoyable platform to create games were it not for Apple's close door policy toward gaming. In particular, the iPhone's accelerometer (a component that detects movement) made the device ideal for certain gaming applications like steering cars.

To date, no mobile phone maker had been able to create a device that excelled at gaming. The Nokia N-Gage was perhaps the most ambitious effort, but as we saw earlier in the chapter, it proved to be a miserable failure as a gaming device. Carmack thought that most mobile games were "crap." Talented developers who wanted to create mobile games faced considerable obstacles such as slow download speeds, platform and hardware variability, and dealing with multiple mobile carriers. "It's an ugly market from a developer's standpoint" (Brightman 2007).

Unlike Pippin, Apple never positioned the iPhone as a gaming device. Instead, it was the iPhone Dev Team that first introduced mobile gaming to iPhone owners with emulators like *NES, Genesis4iphone, gpSPhone* and *psx4iphone* that played many of the most popular previous generation console games. Problems associated with failed hacking attempts became a costly burden for Apple's support line. Apple spokesperson Natalie Kerris told *The New York Times* that the "modifications not only violate the warranty, they also cause the iPhone to become unstable and not work reliably." Despite the difficulty and risks involved in installing the necessary files, iPhone hacks proved extremely popular. "Apple's iPhone support department has received literally millions of reported incidents of software that crashes on jailbroken iPhones," complained Apple in a legal filing against the iPhone Dev Team (Wortham 2009).

The popularity of jailbreak applications demonstrated that consumers were hungering for more than the limited selection of productivity applications offered by Apple. In addition, it proved that Apple's attempt to control development on the iPhone had been misguided. As we saw in early chapters, closed systems and copy protection schemes inevitably fail. Not even hardware locks, such as the one employed by Nintendo in the NES, could stop a dedicated hacker. Instead, closed systems end up costing companies more as consumers turn to alternative sources for games, movies, and software. A good example was a program called SecuRom used in PC games like *Spore* and *Mirror's Edge*. Gamers complained that the program prevented games from playing properly, limited their ability to play games on multiple computers, and caused their computers to become unstable. Therefore, instead of buying official software, they turned to illegal download sites to obtain "better" versions that had been stripped of the offensive software. On Amazon, thousands of gamers gave *Spore* one out of five stars because of SecuRom, making it one of the worst-rated games in history.

In October 2007, Apple finally realized that fighting the hacker community was not in the company's best interests. Instead, it announced plans to open the iPhone to third-party developers. Beginning in February 2008, anyone could create programs for the iPhone with Apple's free iPhone Software Development Kit. Developers could choose to give their applications away or sell them through a new online app store. Shortly after the announcement, Luke Plunkett (2007) of the popular video game news site Kotaku predicted that applications, and particularly games, would "start raining down like cats, dogs and men." Although most of the programs would be "rubbish," Plunkett welcomed Apple's new policy of freedom and openness.

By the time Apple launched its App Store in July 2008, downloads of the iPhone SDK had topped more than 250,000. Developers praised the SDK for its elegance and easy of use. In as little as two weeks, publishers such as EA and Sega were able to deliver ports of popular game titles. Apple not only made it easy for large developers to quickly create iPhone applications, its App Store proved ideal for small independent developers who sought to market their products without incurring significant marketing costs.

Apple made the iPhone even more attractive by adding GPS functions, improving download speeds, and lowering the price to $299 for a 16GB version and $199 for an 8GB version. With its built-in multi-touch screen, networking, microphone, and camera, the iPhone was ideal as a mobile gaming device. It was particularly suited to the types of touch-screen games that had made the Nintendo DS popular among casual gamers. "Calling the iPhone's App Store a success is an understatement," says GameSpot's Sarju Shah (2009):

> In just under nine months, Apple is close to announcing more than one billion downloads, with the total application count rising every day. According to the mobile analytics company Mobclix, there are almost 37,000 applications in total and more than 8,000 games currently available for the iPhone.

As we saw with the 3DO Multiplayer, open standards and inexpensive easy-to-use programming tools can have a downside if consoles become flooded with low quality games. In the 1990s, gamers had no way to evaluate the quality of new games outside magazine reviews. Today, sites like Google, YouTube, and Amazon make it easy to evaluate games prior to making a purchase. Apple instituted its own rating program for the App Store to help customers share their experiences and evaluate applications.

Still, critics assailed the iPhone for its general lack of compelling game content, lack of button controls and imprecise touch screen tracking. Not even best sellers could compare to games currently available on dedicated gaming consoles. Instead, gamers who wanted to take full advantage of the iPhone's gaming functions continued to use Jailbreak applications to run unauthorized versions of Game Boy and PlayStation titles. Either way, the iPhone was the first portable gaming device to mount a viable attack on the Sony-Nintendo duopoly, and the first truly successful convergence device since the term entered the gaming vocabulary in the 1990s.

Apple's success brought with it many imitators. HTC, Palm, Nokia, and Research in Motion introduced touch screen smartphones with similar features to the iPhone. The challenge will be to create the same momentum that is currently keeping the iPhone in first place. In evaluating alternatives, developers need to consider the size of the user base and outlets for distribution. In both these areas, competitors will find Apple hard to beat.

A report by Jupiter Research predicts that revenue from mobile games is expected to reach nearly $10 billion in 2009, the bulk of which will come from smartphones (Holden 2007). The importance of gaming to Apple can be seen in the company's recent decision to hire former Xbox senior director Richard Teversham and the launch of new game titles for core gamers like *Metal Gear Touch*.

Throughout this chapter we have seen that content and ease-of-use are stronger contributors to the success of portable game consoles than performance features such as faster processors, 3D and color screens. Quality content allowed the Game Boy to outsell far more capable competitors and it allowed the PSP to mount the first formidable challenge to Nintendo since the demise of Sega's Game Gear. Ease of use enabled adults, both male and female, to use handheld gaming devices. The wide availability of content has also contributed to the success of the iPhone despite Apple's misguided attempt to keep the system closed. We also saw that some product attributes are unique to the success of portable consoles, such as portability and battery life. Finally, intuitive touchscreen interfaces helped the iPhone and DS expand the video game market to new audiences. Success for these products did not mean having the best technological product, but rather providing customers with valued features and benefits. They provide us with more proof of why firms need to have a keen and deep understanding of their target segment of customers.

6

Rings of Death

Common wisdom in the video game industry was that, above all else, performance mattered. Sony and Microsoft shared a belief that superior technology would lead to a superior gaming experience and each invested heavily in research and development to make that experience possible. As recently as 2006, neither company viewed Nintendo as a serious threat. In unit sales, Nintendo placed a distant third. And in terms of performance neither Microsoft nor Sony had anything to fear from Nintendo. The unveiling of the Wii only reinforced a widely held opinion that Nintendo no longer mattered. "The underpowered Wii can't run with the competition," proclaimed one reviewer.

> Some say Nintendo's hypercute system won't be able to hold its own once Microsoft and Sony roar into the realm of high definition gaming. My fearless prediction: both Sony and Nintendo will be crushed underfoot. (Todd 2006)

Sony and Microsoft attempted to differentiate their consoles from each other by emphasizing the advanced features each offered. For instance, the PlayStation 3 was the only system with a built-in high-definition optical drive and the Xbox 360 offered a superior online experience. Yet despite these differences, the technologies they employed proved remarkably similar. Both were powered by processors created by a single IBM design team, both offered high-definition graphics, and both shared a large library of non-exclusive game titles.

In the next two chapters we will explore how Microsoft and Sony lost their way as they struggled to deliver features that, in the end, mattered only to a small cadre of dedicated gamers. In the process, both lost sight of the market's needs and allowed Nintendo, with its "hypercute system," to once again become master of the game.

The Launch of the Xbox 360

In 2003, Steve Ballmer, CEO of Microsoft, asked Peter Moore to head the Xbox division. Up until this time, Moore had been managing Sega's video game console business, a business decimated by Sony. Moore relished the chance to get even with his rival, "to put on my suit of armor, get on my horse and take on Sony again—but with a little bit more money this time" (Stuart 2008). A month later, Moore installed himself at Microsoft, ready to take up the fight.

Not long after his arrival, someone suggested that Microsoft acquire Nintendo. However, the idea was immediately shot down. Nintendo was becoming too marginalized to be an important player in the video games market, they thought. "We were just completely fixated on Sony," recalled Moore. "Nintendo didn't even come into the conversation." And so Microsoft's sights remained squarely on Sony, even as Nintendo was focused on perfecting innovations that would one day revolutionize the way people play games.

Moore's primary task would be to oversee the development and launch of Microsoft's next generation console, the Xbox 360. Sega had spent vast sums of money publicizing the launch of the Dreamcast, only to see it fail. This time, Moore wanted to do things differently. "I'm sick of consoles being launched with massively expensive ad campaigns," he told his colleagues at Microsoft. "I'm going to do this differently" (Stuart 2008).

The console itself was remarkably similar to the Dreamcast. Both employed technology far superior to their competitors, both focused heavily on online gaming, and both used an operating system derived from Microsoft Windows. The ways in which they were promoted, however, were vastly different. In 2005, Microsoft was poised to make full use of a networked world that didn't exist when Sega tried to showcase its technical marvel.

Viral Marketing on the Internet

In the months leading up to the unveiling of the Xbox 360, Microsoft created an online video game known as *OurColony*. Information about the game was sent to Xbox fans around the world with cryptic messages and instructions on how to participate. The final step in the game was revealed on May 12, 2005. Users who successfully completed all the steps were shown a video demonstration of the Xbox 360.

That day, a global MTV special presentation hosted by actor Elijah Wood, star of the *Lord of the Rings* trilogy, revealed the Xbox 360 for the first time. The show provided fans with a first look at the console's specifications, capabilities, and online gameplay through a new version of the Xbox Live service. After the show, viewers were invited to get more information about the console from MTV.com, including product details and previews of upcoming game titles.

"Tonight's unveiling is a signal to the world that the next generation of gaming is here," Microsoft announced in a news release,

> *Every Xbox 360 game is designed for high-definition, wide-screen televisions. Regardless of the television Xbox 360 connects to, gamers will experience smooth, cinematic experiences that far exceed anything they've seen or felt in games before. And these experiences are never more than a click away. The Xbox Guide Button is the launch pad that connects gamers to their games, friends and music from the wireless controller. (Microsoft Corp. 2005b)*

The benefits of the console went far beyond gaming. The Xbox 360 was designed to be a high-definition entertainment hub that included games, movies, and music.

> *As high-definition entertainment becomes more pervasive, Microsoft will offer more ways to experience HDTV and movies in any room in the house, any way people want it. Whether it's by the dropping of an optical disk in a drive, streaming to Xbox 360, or through broadband distribution, Xbox 360 will let players choose how to light up their high-definition content. (Microsoft Corp. 2005)*

Microsoft knew that it did not need "glitzy" mass market advertising to reach its core audience of dedicated gamers between the ages of 18 and 35. The *OurColony* viral campaign appealed directly to these users, and the infomercial on MTV provided an inexpensive venue for creating awareness. The strategy rested on Gladwell's maxim that "mavens have the knowledge and social skills to start word of mouth epidemics" (Gladwell 2002). As "information brokers," gaming mavens sought out any source that could shed light on their favorite pursuit.

Dedicated gamers not only knew of the Xbox 360's existence, they eagerly awaited its benefits. No other game console came close to the performance of

Microsoft's new high-definition powerhouse. In fact, its only real competition was high-end gaming computers that cost several thousand dollars. Once word got out, gamers gravitated to gaming websites, online forums, and even late night television infomercials. In such an environment, Microsoft did not need to sell the console; the console sold itself.

Four days after the MTV unveiling, Microsoft presented the Xbox 360 at the Electronics Entertainment Expo (E3), in Los Angeles, California. E3 was the gaming industry's most important trade event, providing a venue for new product announcements and demonstrations. Two models of the Xbox 360 were to be offered. The "Premium" package included a hard drive and headphones for $399. A stripped down "Core" version with no hard drive was priced at $299. High-definition movie playback would eventually be supported through the Xbox Live store for downloadable content and through an HD-DVD add-on drive capable of playing high-definition video disks. At launch, Microsoft stood to lose $126 on each Xbox 360 it sold. However, by the end of 2006, lower component costs and operational efficiencies would help bring the console's production cost down to $323 per unit.

Sony and Nintendo also used E3 to announce their next generation consoles, which would not become available to consumers until the following year. Both companies hoped that by announcing the inevitable availability of their consoles, potential Xbox 360 customers would wait to make their purchases until all three were available. At that point they could evaluate the consoles side by side and choose the one best suited to their needs.

Those lucky enough to get their hands on an Xbox 360 prior to its release gushed over its visuals. "The 360 is a gorgeous machine, a far cry from its clunky predecessor, the Xbox," proclaimed reporter Samantha Amjadali (2006) of the *Herald Sun*. "It's fast, powerful and capable of churning out impressive graphics and thumb-numbing game play." And she was right. The Xbox 360 was gorgeous, and that meant that dedicated gamers were not about to wait another year for Sony to get its act together. On launch day, they turned out in droves.

Video game enthusiasts who lined up on launch day fell into two categories: those eager to experience the benefits of leading edge technology themselves and those wanting to exploit an arbitrage opportunity. Over the next few weeks, as many as 40,000 consoles ended up on eBay, where they were resold for as much as $1,000. Given that nearly everyone who acquired an Xbox 360 by the end of 2005 had either endured the lengthy launch day line-ups or the inflated prices of the grey market, one could safely assume that early adopters were the most dedicated gamers.

Microsoft clearly understood the importance of being first to market, relying heavily on early adopters to "start word of mouth epidemics"—to be mavens to the uninitiated. Once the consoles became entrenched in households, Microsoft could depend on a steady stream of royalties and licensing fees from movies and games. Initial numbers seemed to support Microsoft's decision. By launching one year ahead of Sony and Nintendo, Xbox was able to establish a customer base of more than 5 million users before a single Wii or PlayStation 3 hit store shelves.

Even after Nintendo and Sony brought their products to market, Microsoft continued to post impressive numbers. In December 2006 alone, U.S. consumers purchased more than a million Xbox 360 consoles, exceeding the combined sales of Wii and PlayStation 3 consoles. Microsoft's continued success could partly be attributed to a library of games that had, by this time, numbered more than 160. To dedicated gamers, game titles mattered more than pixel counts or the number of transistors on the CPU.

The other reason had to do with networking effects. Gamers who wanted to play against their friends had no choice but to own the same console. Traditionally, this meant physically going to a friend's house and connecting a second game controller. With Xbox Live, multiplayer games could be conducted remotely through a broadband Internet connection. As more people gained access to high speed home networking, Xbox Live became one of Microsoft's chief competitive advantages.

Most industry observers applauded Microsoft's first-to-market strategy. Analysts at Piper Jaffrey, an investment bank, predicted that the Xbox 360 would lead the industry through 2011. By the end of 2008, Piper Jaffrey predicted sales of nearly 20 million Xbox 360s, compared to 15 million PlayStation 3s and only 5 million Nintendo Wiis. "In 2001, [the original] Xbox launched many months after Sony, and the all-conquering PS2 by then had cemented its position in the local games market," observed *Herald Sun* journalist Greg Thom (2006). "This time the boot is on the other foot." It was Microsoft's game to lose.

Product Defects Show up Early

What the journalists, bankers, and business analysts that lauded the Xbox 360 didn't know was that Microsoft had uncovered problems with some of its early production units. With only 69 days from the Xbox 360's initial production date until launch day, Microsoft was faced with a difficult choice. It could continue product testing and give up its first-to-market advantage, or release the console in its current state and accept a higher than average return rate.

IBM's David Shippy remembers when Microsoft came to his company in late 2002 to request a processor for the next generation Xbox. Given the fact that the Sony PlayStation 2 triumphed over the original Xbox by being first to market, Microsoft was under enormous pressure to beat Sony to market this time around. "It was a risky proposition," Shippy recalled. "Sony had a two and a half year head start, so Microsoft knew they were late to the game again." Nevertheless, Robbie Bach, President of Microsoft Entertainment and Devices, was emphatic that the Xbox 360 would be launched before the PS3. "He let us know in no uncertain terms that Microsoft would achieve a Christmas '05 product launch ... Bach and the entire Microsoft team were laser focused on [that] end result" (Shippy and Phipps 2009).

Rather than miss an important window of opportunity, senior engineers decided to ship the consoles anyway. If some units came back defective, they could be repaired under warranty. Nobody grasped the full extent of the problems until months later.

For a company like Microsoft, which focused mainly on software, the decision to ship flawed units made sense. Software companies were constantly under pressure to release new versions of software ahead of competitors, even if the program contained some bugs. Jim Balsillie, CEO of Research in Motion, maker of the popular Blackberry Smartphone, called it the "new reality." Research in Motion, like most companies, had a policy of addressing customer complaints by issuing software updates and patches. Usually such updates were inexpensive to distribute and effective at resolving common performance and reliability issues. Bach, who rose through the ranks of Microsoft as head of marketing for the company's popular "Office" software suite, was a part of that tradition.

Manufactured goods were different, however. Design flaws could rarely be addressed through software updates and patches. Instead, manufacturers were forced to issue recalls or pay to have the problems fixed under warranty. If problems surfaced soon after purchase, manufacturers potentially faced massive returns of defective merchandise. In some cases, product recalls were enough to bankrupt a company, although with nearly $30 billion in cash, that wasn't a problem Microsoft would likely face for some time.

Even before the Xbox 360 prototype was ready, Microsoft believed that any hardware problems or limitations could be solved by modifying the software. "The Microsoft team never wavered," recalled Shippy. "They continued to believe that their goals were achievable. Whatever we messed up in hardware, they reasoned, they could fix in software." After the processor design was complete, Microsoft went "against the advice of IBM" and began fabricating chips before they were "fully verified in the lab."

> Usually clients wait until the final spin of a chip has been rigorously proven in the hardware lab before proceeding with their manufacturing plan. But Microsoft lined up hundreds of thousands of silicon wafers in the fabrication facility so that they would have a shot at having volumes needed for a Christmas 2005 launch of the Xbox 360.

> With several million dollars at risk, Microsoft was living on the edge. It was just like the motto that drove their Windows software business: "Get it to market first at all cost, worry about the bugs later" ... I repeatedly advised them of the danger of encountering a major bug that simply couldn't be worked around with software, but they just smiled and waved it off ... It was an almost unheard of risk; one that neither IBM nor Sony would have taken. (Shippy and Phipps 2009)

That's not to say that Microsoft was not concerned. In fact, product failures were causing delays in production that jeopardized Microsoft's ability to meet its planned launch date. In August 2005, when Microsoft's contract manufacturers were supposed to be producing thousands of consoles, only a few hundred units were rolling off the assembly line. An internal memo dated August 31, 2008 explained that 68 percent of production units were failing because of an "overheating graphics chip, cracking heat sinks," and other problems.

Publicly, Moore tried to downplay the problems.

> Nothing's perfect. You've got a complex piece of hardware that's got 1,700 different parts in it every now and again the line will slow down

because something's happened and there'll be a component that didn't make it that morning…That's just the way of the beast, particularly when you are ramping up factories from ground zero all the way up to full capacity. (Sinclair 2006a)

For many software companies, shipping imperfect products may indeed have been "the way of the beast." Hardware, however, was a different beast altogether, one that was far less forgiving. Shipping consoles that did not meet quality-control standards was bad enough, but Microsoft made the problem worse by pulling its best engineers from the project at the most critical time. Dean Takahashi, author of *Xbox 360 Uncloaked*, revealed that "Microsoft's engineers started working on the Xbox 360 at least a year after Sony's engineers began work on the PlayStation 3."

Yet Microsoft wound up shipping a year ahead of Sony. Everything Microsoft did was under time pressure, [and] considering all of the work, Microsoft had too few hardware people. Some of the designers of the Xbox 360, including engineering chief Greg Gibson, were stretched thin. Gibson and J Allard, who led the console design effort, had begun work on Zune, Microsoft's portable media player. Top brass had approved the project to dethrone Apple's iPod, but Microsoft kept Zune secret from the outside world until much later. Some engineers were pulled off the Xbox 360 at a critical moment to join Allard's effort to create a music player. Those who were left to work on the test team worked around the clock, traveling to China to work in the factory. (Takahashi 2008a)

Once they got to China, Microsoft's hardware engineers were powerless to rectify the problems. Between the time pressures and staffing shortages, the Xbox 360 project was like a runaway freight train. A former Microsoft engineer who had worked on the Xbox 360 design recalled some of the decisions that were made after his arrival in China.

Whenever something failed and there was a question about whether the test result was false, they would remove that test, retest and ship, or see if the unit would boot a game and run briefly and then ship. The 360 is too complex of a machine to get away with that. I'm sure [the management team] thought that somehow they would figure it out and everything would end up ok. Plus, they tend to make big decisions like that in terms of dollars. They would rationalize that if the first few million boxes had a high failure rate, a few 10's of millions of dollars would cover it. And contrasting that cost with a big lead on Sony, they would pay it in a heartbeat. (Metcalf 2008)

A few months later, as customers queued up for one of the bright green boxes emblazoned with the Xbox 360 logo, it may have seemed as though Microsoft had dodged a bullet. Although the company hailed the launch of the Xbox 360 as a great success, some industry watchers were skeptical. The results were "not pretty," wrote one analyst.

From unconfirmed rumors of near-riots as employees apparently hoarded Xbox 360 systems in front of waiting customers, to numbers of pre-orders that went unfulfilled, some are saying Microsoft mishandled the launch. But those who actually got the systems in hand are breathing easy and living it up, right? Some of them are. But others are posting a plethora of problems with their brand-new 360s, from game crashes to hard drives that simply don't work.

... Just how widespread is the scope of 360 problems, though? It's a little too early to call whether these problems are systemic or isolated bugs. (Pinckard 2005)

Even so, early adopters were not about to give up on the system. Most realized that any new product as advanced as the Xbox 360 was bound to have some hiccups along the way. The fact that the Xbox 360 was the only high-definition console on the market meant they had no choice but to accept a certain degree of unreliability. Many believed that a company as big as Microsoft could resolve any early problems within the warranty period.

In reality, the technical problems reported on launch day mirrored those uncovered during the design and production phase, and the repairs would prove more costly than originally anticipated. Before long, the company's most loyal fans became its most outspoken critics.

One of them was Rob Cassingham. For years, Cassingham had been the ideal Xbox fan. On launch day, he and his spouse attended the launch event with large "XBOX" signs hanging from their necks. Cassingham loved games and he loved the Xbox. He even had a personalized license plate that read "Xbox 360." That was in 2005. In 2006, his first unit stopped working after displaying a red ring of light around the power button. In early 2007, after returning his seventh failed unit to Microsoft, Cassingham surrendered. "Xbox live is great," he noted, but the general hardware failures were too much.

> When [the repaired unit] comes, I'm going to sell it... That's a hard thing to give up. I gave up cigarette smoking so I've been through worse. I've had game systems since the Coleco machine. Intellivision. The first machine I had was the Magnavox Odyssey in 1972. I have never had to send any of them back. (Takahashi 2007a)

Cassingham's experience was far from unique. An online survey conducted by CAG, a popular gaming website, found that 59 percent of registered members (2,111 people) experienced at least one Xbox 360 failure. Survey administrator David Abrams (2008) acknowledged that the failure rate represented in the survey was almost certainly higher than normal. "It's probably safe to assume that members of an online video game community use their systems more than others. I'd imagine that increased use could lead to increased console failures," he wrote.

Surveys of retailers and repair centers showed average failure rates of between 16 and 33 percent. However, such reports did not include console owners who returned defective units directly to Microsoft. By comparison, the failure rates for the Nintendo Wii and the Sony PlayStation 3 were estimated to be 2.7 percent and 10 percent respectively, according to a study conducted by Square Trade, the largest independent warranty provider.

Once gamers discovered how widespread the system failures were, they expected Microsoft to resolve the problem quickly. Instead Microsoft issued an official statement denying that it had a problem.

> The return rate is significantly lower than the consumer electronics industry average of 3 to 5 percent. Customer satisfaction is our highest priority, and we do everything we can to take care of gamers who may be having problems with their consoles. (Boyes 2007b)

Such denials only served to infuriate those who had fallen victim to a "general hardware failure," a condition gamers would soon begin referring to as the "Red Ring of Death" or RRoD, for short. The problem was so prevalent that the term RRoD began to be used as a verb, such as "My console RRoDed last night."

In the UK, Micromart Ltd., which handled video game console repairs for major retailers, was inundated with systems displaying the red ring error message. Finally, it refused to accept Xbox 360 units. "The problem with three red lights was there fairly regularly, but over two or three months it became a real issue," explained a Micromart representative. "These days, it's harder to find someone with an original 360 than it is to find one who has had problems," observed one journalist.

> *Everyone online is complaining about overheating, red lights of death, and being on their third systems (if not more). I've had two die... Other game journalists and reviewers have complained about having to replace the office system often. (Kuchera 2007a)*

The Power of Online Social Networks

When Gladwell (2002) spoke about how mavens were set apart "not so much [by] what they know, but how they pass it along," he referred specifically to their influence within social networks to start new trends. However, social networks can also work against companies. In the past, customers often had no way of knowing whether or not other customers were having similar problems with a product. Widespread defects were only uncovered when company whistleblowers revealed them or when an investigative journalist uncovered documents about the defect.

In the modern world, however, news travels at the speed of light. It took less than a day after the Xbox 360's launch for news to reach potential customers about red rings, scratched disks, and drive failures. When problems reveal themselves, companies do themselves and their customers a disservice by not immediately recognizing the problem. Customers want to feel cared for, and denying the problem only alienates them further. One way or another, most companies will have to pay for their mistakes. The price they pay can be in returned merchandise, higher warranty costs, recalls, or lost customers.

In early 2007, the Xbox 360 experienced a precipitous decline in sales. By April, monthly sales were down by more than 100,000 units, or about 40 percent, from the previous year. Microsoft knew that drastic measures would need to be taken to reverse the decline. The first step was to admit that the console had serious design flaws, which Microsoft did on July 5, 2007, nearly two years after it had first learned about the problems in its Chinese contract factories. That day, Moore published an open letter on the company's website. "You've spoken, and we've heard you," he wrote. "Good service and a good customer experience are areas of the business that we care deeply about. And frankly, we've not been doing a good enough job" (Moore 2007).

Microsoft then took the unprecedented step of agreeing to take "responsibility to repair or replace any Xbox 360 console that experiences the 'three flashing red lights' error message within three years from time of purchase free of charge, including shipping costs." Microsoft estimated the cost of repairs to be between $1.05 billion and $1.15 billion, contributing to a nearly $2 billion loss for the 2007 fiscal year (Table 6.1).

Less than two weeks later, Moore resigned from Microsoft for "personal reasons."

Table 6.1   Entertainment and Devices Division Financial Results ($ millions)

	2002	2003	2004	2005	2006	2007
Revenues	2,453	2,748	2,876	3,242	4,256	6,080
Expenses	(3,588)	(3,939)	(4,213)	(3,727)	(5,518)	(7,970)
Operating Loss	(1,135)	(1,191)	(1,337)	(485)	(1,262)	(1,890)

7

The PlayStation 3: Sony's "Supercomputer"

> *The PlayStation 3 was the most successful launch in Sony's history.*
> Jack Tretton, president and CEO of Sony Computer
> Entertainment of America (Hsu and Bettenhausen 2007)

In the days leading up to the November 17, 2006 launch of the PlayStation 3 (PS3), enthusiasts lined city blocks for the privilege of spending $600 for the most powerful video game console ever created. Its predecessor, the acclaimed PlayStation 2 (PS2), had already become the world's best-selling video game console with more than 100 million units sold. The unprecedented display of enthusiasm for the PS3 suggested that Sony had another winner on its hands. The company projected sales of 6 million PS3 consoles worldwide by March 2007, a level that the PS2 took almost a year to reach.

At the core of the PS3 was an IBM "Cell" processor, touted by Sony as a "supercomputer on a chip." "The Cell outperforms many of the latest PC processors and delivers up to ten times the performance of a typical home computer," stated a company press release.

> *In terms of real-world application, it means incredibly detailed and interactive environments, more enemies, larger battles, and hyper-realistic game play. The increased processing power of the Cell also means developers for the first time can create games closer to actual intelligence instead of artificial intelligence, giving them the ability to closely mimic human reasoning and movement. (Sony 2006)*

At IBM, chip designers were confident that the Cell's performance would revolutionize the industry. One of them, David Shippy, writes:

> [We] were about to set out to design the Holy Grail of computing; the
> highest frequency, highest performing microprocessor in the industry—
> better than anything any PC had ever offered. We were going to make
> a supercomputer on a single chip. If we could pull it off, a whole
> generation of gamers worldwide would pay us tribute... (Shippy and
> Phipps 2009)

However, that initial euphoria was short-lived. By February 2007, more than
a third of PS3 consoles remained unsold, and some retailers reported a higher
number of returns than sales. Instead of paying tribute, consumers said they
felt let down by Sony. The PS3 looked no better than Microsoft's Xbox 360, they
complained, even though the Xbox 360 had already been on the market for
more than a year, and sold for $200 less than the PS3. Customers also lamented
the PS3's lack of interesting games, spotty support for PlayStation 2 games and
uninspired online capabilities.

As the two market leaders squared off against each other, Nintendo never
entered into the equation. To Sony and Microsoft, the Wii was an interesting
novelty, but it was essentially a GameCube console with a novel controller.
Given the GameCube's dismal performance, they could not understand how
the Wii could compete with consoles that were the result of billions of dollars
in R&D expenditures and technologies that were advanced beyond anything
the world had seen. Yet within a year, Nintendo would have a solid lead over
both companies.

Most people believed that the PS3's price tag was to blame for the console's
poor market performance. Yet during the 2007 and 2008 holiday seasons, Wii
consoles often sold for double their retail price on grey market websites such
as eBay and Craigslist. That meant that many Wii purchasers were willing to
spend $500 or more from a third party, often with no warranty, when they could
have walked into any electronics store and purchased a PlayStation 3 or Xbox
360 for about the same price.

Even when the entry level Xbox 360 dropped to $200 in 2008, higher priced
Wii consoles continued to lead the market in monthly sales. At best, each PS3
and Xbox 360 price drop resulted in a temporary surge in sales, as the Wii
continued to dominate the market well into 2009.

Despite the evidence to the contrary, many game developers believed that
Sony's flagging sales could be improved by a significant price cut. Among them

was Phil Harrison, a former Sony executive and current president of Atari, who felt that price was the "most notable" cause of the PS3's flagging sales.

Although a high price is one factor that contributed to the PlayStation 3's poor market performance, product feature decisions appear to be even more critical.

The Launch of the PlayStation 3

As early as 2005, Ken Kutaragi, chairman and CEO of Sony Computer Entertainment, pledged to deliver a machine with twice the processing power of the Xbox 360. Like the Xbox 360, the target market for the PlayStation 3 was 18- to 35-year-old male gamers with above-average education and a high degree of comfort with new technology.

Technical problems related to the console's built-in Blu-ray drive caused Sony to delay manufacturing and push back the initial launch from spring 2006 to fall 2006. Despite the delayed release, Sony was unable to manufacture the anticipated one million consoles needed to meet market demand. By the time the PS3 was launched in North America on November 17, 2006, retailers had fewer than 200,000 units to distribute. Kaz Hirai, president and group chief operating officer (COO) of Sony Computer Entertainment, recognized the problem, but tried to downplay its importance over the longer term:

> We are going to ramp up production and try to get as many units into the hands of consumers as possible for the launch. That is also why we strategically decided to delay the European launch [until Spring 2007], so that we could concentrate more on the Japanese and North American markets. But the most important thing for us is providing compelling software for the long term, so that six or seven years from now we can have a platform that consumers can embrace and enjoy. (Doree 2006)

Sony attempted to mitigate the shortage by air freighting consoles directly from Japan. "We will continue to utilize airfreight delivery for the PlayStation 3 to assure a steady stream of systems for North American consumers through the end of the year," Sony assured retailers in an official statement.

Pricing

The Sony PlayStation 3 was one of the most expensive consoles ever launched, with a price tag of $600, or $500 for a stripped-down version with a smaller hard drive and no wireless module. Table 7.1 shows that despite its high price tag, Sony lost between $240 and $306 on each console sold. The basic console cost Sony almost as much to make as the premium model. Sony saved only $11 by using a smaller hard drive and $15.50 by eliminating the wireless adaptor.

Jack Tretton defended the console's higher cost relative to competitors. "I would point out a couple of things," he said.

> Historically our platforms have staying power. Not three years, not five years, but 10 years. So are you making an investment for the next 45 days, the next year, the next five years, or 10 years? The PS3 has the best gaming experience of any platform that's ever shipped, with great gaming, free online play, Blu-ray movie playback, the ability to go online and surf the Internet, the ability to download your pictures and videos and the ability to rip your music. (Hsu and Bettenhausen 2007)

In Tretton's mind, these features made the PS3 one of the best values on the market.

> I think the consumers that get their hands on a PlayStation 3 clearly see the value and not only want to buy one for $599, in some instances they're willing to pay ridiculous prices to buy one on eBay. (Yam 2007)

During the first few days after the U.S. launch, some consoles sold for more than $2,000 on eBay, but then prices quickly plummeted to just over $1,000. By the time Tretton was interviewed in early 2007, auction prices for new PS3 consoles were near or below suggested retail. More troubling were reports of excess inventory building up in retail stores. "Customers are disappointed," one retailer complained:

> They are telling us that too many of the launch games are also available on the Xbox 360, and first-party titles aren't innovative enough for them. We have 24 PS3s in stock right now and we're getting more returns than we are selling systems. (Hsu and Bettenhausen 2007)

Table 7.1   **Sony PlayStation 3 Manufacturing Cost (60 GB Model)**

Miscellaneous Manufacturing Components	$148.00
Reality Synthesizer	129.00
Blu-ray Drive	125.00
Cell CPU	89.00
I/O Bridge Controller	59.00
SATA Hard Drive	54.00
XDR RAM	48.00
Power Supply	37.50
Case	33.00
Emotion Engine / Graphics Synthesizer	27.00
Motherboard and cooling	22.00
Wireless Module	15.50
Memory Board	5.00
Bluetooth	4.10
Other Miscellaneous Components	4.75
Manufacturing Expense	40.00
Total Cost	840.85

Source: Bangeman 2006.

With standalone Blu-ray players costing as much or more than the PS3, some felt that Blu-ray capability alone justified the extra cost. Others were not so sure. "The decision to make the PS3 a Trojan horse for Sony's high-def Blu-ray disk technology could be backfiring," one analyst suggested. "Unless you convince consumers that this extra feature is something they truly want, they'll only view it as an added expense (Hsu and Bettenhausen 2007).

Peter Dille, senior vice president of marketing at Sony Computer Entertainment America, seemed eager to accommodate calls from developers to lower the price, but was prevented by Sony headquarters. "At Sony Corp the message was 'Let's try to eke out a profit,' which took certain cards out of our deck," he explained. "We're not going to make a price move for PS3; we're not going to be packing five free games into a promotional strategy" (Nutt 2009).

Given the console's product features including the Blu-ray drive, cell CPU, and reality synthesizer, Sony was justified in its belief that the PS3 offered consumers an exceptional value for the money. Yet when Sony launched the

European PlayStation 3 in March 2007, it was plagued by a lack of demand. In the United Kingdom alone, retailers canceled more than $20 million worth of orders in the days leading up to the launch. In an attempt to generate positive publicity, on launch day, Sony gave a free high-definition television valued at more than $4,000 to the first 125 people to purchase a PS3. Clearly, between the U.S. and European launches, something happened to cause gamers to lose interest in what had been touted as the most advanced console on the market.

The price in Europe (€399) was not significantly higher than the U.S. and therefore could not account for the drop in interest, particularly when one factored in the excessive prices paid to secondary market sellers in the weeks following the U.S. launch. More evidence that price was less important than commonly believed came from the fact that Wii consoles sold for as much as $500 on eBay for two years in row. Faced with such evidence, Sony was right to maintain its price premium, despite calls from developers to the contrary. To appeal to price conscious consumers, Sony continued to sell its enduring PlayStation 2 console for around $100, which in 2009 made it the least expensive fully-featured home console in production.

Sixaxis: Penny Wise and Pound Foolish

Putting price aside, an issue that upset many users was Sony's decision to not include the video cables needed to take advantage of the console's graphics capabilities and, more importantly, the decision to eliminate vibration feedback, commonly known as rumble. According to Sony, the elimination of rumble was a "strategic decision" aimed at reducing costs. "The issue is trying to isolate the vibration feature from the motion sensors," Hirai claimed.

> It is a balancing act to be able to present the controller to the consumer at an affordable price. We have one controller in the box, but many consumers will want to go out and get an extra controller. If isolating the vibration from the sensing means that the controllers are going to be expensive, then we're doing the consumer a huge disservice. (Doree 2006)

Phil Harrison, who was Sony's president of worldwide studios at the time, claimed that rumble was a technology from the past.

I believe that the Sixaxis controller offers game designers and developers far more opportunity for future innovation than rumble ever did. Now, rumble I think was the last generation feature; it's not the next-generation feature. I think motion sensitivity is. (Klepek 2007)

Thus, aligning with its strategy of providing the best technology and highest performance (i.e., graphics and complex play), Sony executives believed that they needed to delete the "old" rumble technology and include the "new" motion sensitivity feature. To some, however, Sixaxis felt like a rushed attempt to counter the motion sensing ability of the Wii and to further differentiate the PS3 from the Xbox 360. Randy Pitchford, President of Gearbox Studios believed that Sixaxis was "more of a gimmick than a new revolutionary gaming input" (*PlayStation* 2009a).

Skeptics of Sony's motivation for replacing rumble with motion sensing cited a 2005 lawsuit in which Sony was found guilty of infringing on a rumble patent registered by Immersion Corporation and was ordered to pay $90.7 million in damages as evidence that Sony was not being upfront about its reasons for eliminating rumble. Immersion also challenged Sony's claim that it would be costly to isolate the vibration and motion sensors. "The two signals can be differentiated using filtering and other techniques," noted Erin Freeley, a public relations representative for Immersion. Lastly, the fact that Nintendo spent approximately $5 on each Wii controller, which included both rumble and motion-sensing features, seemed to contradict Sony's claim that rumble was too expensive.[1]

Rumble was a feature that most gamers had become accustomed to and therefore they expected it. Xbox had it. PlayStation 2 had it. Even the GameCube had it. Without rumble, the gaming experience felt dead. To most gamers it felt like a step backwards.

The outcry against the removal of rumble eventually forced Sony to rethink its decision. In April 2008, the Sixaxis controller was retired and replaced with Dual Shock 3 (DS3), a controller that offered both rumble and motion sensing. The DS3 significantly improved the user experience to the level experienced in previous generation consoles. Yet by this time, Sony had lost numerous customers to Microsoft, which offered rumble in its Xbox 360 controller. For

---

1   "The Motion Sensing Accelerometer and the Rumble Pack Cost Nintendo Approximately $2.50 Each (O'Brien 2007)

users devoted to non-exclusive games, like Burnout Paradise and Call of Duty, the Xbox 360 controller offered a more immersive experience.

In the final analysis, Sony's focus on motion sensing at the expense of rumble proved to be another significant performance trap that only detracted from the gaming experience. Nintendo, on the other hand, made motion control the centerpiece of a completely redesigned controller that could be manipulated in one hand.

Although it is not always necessary to include previous features in the next generation, the decision to exclude a feature depends on understanding customer needs and expected benefits. It appears that customers expected rumble to be included in all controllers implying that it had become a basic need and must be included in order for customers to even consider the brand. The Kano model developed by Noriaki Kano provides well established tools for measuring consumer needs (Berger et al. 1993). If Sony had used such tools, it would have realized that by eliminating this standard feature, the company was ignoring a basic customer requirement and decreasing the value of the PS3 in the eyes of the consumer.

"Content is King"

Every console manufacturer understood that one of the keys to success was having a library of quality game titles to offer consumers. Consider the Sega Dreamcast. When the console was launched in 1999, it was far ahead of its time. Hard-core gamers were so enthusiastic that for several months after its release, the Dreamcast was almost impossible to find on store shelves. Yet the Dreamcast proved a failure and eventually had to be withdrawn from the market. In their book *Smartbomb*, video games journalists Heather Chaplin and Aaron Ruby describe the Dreamcast as, "one of the best consoles ever built."

> There are a dozen stories about consoles that were ahead of their time. . . . . The Dreamcast was discontinued after only two years, because Sega simply couldn't get enough machines into people's homes and couldn't establish a library of games quickly enough. (Chaplin and Ruby 2005)

The lessons of the Dreamcast and other consoles were not lost on Hirai. "Compelling entertainment content" was the most important feature of any entertainment device, he explained a few weeks before the launch of the PS3:

We all know—it's a cliché but it's a truism—that content is king. The most important thing for us is being able to provide a platform for content creators to really get excited about, so that they can take full advantage of what we bring to them in terms of a technological palette. The PlayStation 3 really brings so much more in terms of the raw processing power and so much more in terms of storage capacity with the Blu-ray drive. (Doree 2006)

Nevertheless, the PlayStation 3 launched with only 15 titles, the majority of which were franchise games that had previously been available for the Xbox 360. Among the handful of exclusive titles, *Resistance: Fall of Man* quickly became the console's best-selling title. It was also its most violent, garnering a "mature" rating from the Entertainment Software Review Board (ESRB) for intense violence, blood and gore, and strong language.[2]

Sony praised *Resistance* as its highest ranking and best-selling title, but users were less enthusiastic. Professional reviewers called it "mostly unoriginal," a first-person shooting game that borrowed heavily from previously successful games for other platforms. In contrast, the Xbox 360 boasted 12 titles that were ranked higher than *Resistance*, including several similar style shooting games. Even the Nintendo Wii, a console which had been on the market for about as long as the PS3, had higher ranking titles. For its launch, the Wii boasted 27 titles, including high-rated exclusive games such as *The Legend of Zelda: Twilight Princess, Wii Sports*, and *Metroid Prime 3*. And while the PS3's exclusive titles were mostly for mature audiences, the majority of Wii titles were targeted to a wide range of ages.

Tretton defended Sony's line-up of launch titles. In his opinion, the company's track record for best-selling titles spoke for itself:

Take a look back at the debuts of all the past consoles to compare launch line-ups. We have published thousands of great games for all our PlayStation platforms over the years, selling billions of units. That won't suddenly change for the PS3. You can expect a steady flow of exceptional titles for the PS3 for years to come. (Hsu and Bettenhausen 2007)

Although Hirai recognized the challenges of having the same content released on multiple platforms, he felt the PS3 offered advantages over other consoles.

---

2   Mature-rated games were considered suitable for ages 17 and older.

When you compare the PlayStation 3 version of a game to any other version of the same game, it's a completely different entertainment experience. It is an exclusive entertainment experience for consumers enjoying a game on the PS3 as compared to any other console. (Doree 2006)

Sony was dismayed by the amount of negative press the PS3 had received. Some blamed Sony for delivering a console that did not live up to the pre-launch hype. Even the editors of the *Official PlayStation Magazine*, a periodical that normally advocated on Sony's behalf, said they felt let down by Sony's "promises for better looking games." In their view, the PS3 offered few advantages over the Xbox 360:

Blu-ray. The Cell Processor. The RSX graphics chip. The PS3 was supposed to be the most insanely advanced gaming machine ever created. It was supposed to be able to deliver visuals well beyond anything capable on console or PC. According to Sony, the next generation wasn't supposed to begin until PS3 arrived. So why is it, then, that all these PS3 games look just the same as they do on the Xbox 360?

Tretton believed that many journalists simply did not understand the needs of gamers. Instead, they targeted Sony because of its undisputed position as the market leader. "Because we're in that leadership position, there are a lot of expectations thrust upon us, and some of them are a little unrealistic," he asserted.

Given the complexity of the PlayStation 3, consumers and reviewers may have been unrealistic in their expectations, but Sony, more than anyone, deserved much of the blame for overpromising and under-delivering. Development studios needed more time to work through the various programming and production challenges posed by the new system. Whereas Microsoft used a more standard processor architecture that allowed developers to work on programs before the release of the Xbox 360, the PS3's cell processor was a fundamental departure from any known design. At IBM, David Shippy was helping Microsoft put together a developer's kit for the Xbox 360. "Sony had no possibilities for a similar early solution for their game developers because of the radical new Cell architecture in the PlayStation 3," he observed.

There was no such Synergistic core-based beast in existence. The PlayStation 3 early game code development would have to be accomplished on much slower emulators that could never provide insight into the real-time behavior of the code. So most of the game development would have to wait until we delivered the Cell chip prototypes. (Shippy and Phipps 2009)

By using recognized standards, Microsoft was able to release a development kit using off-the-shelf hardware one year before the release of the Xbox 360 prototype.[3]

Major studios naturally assigned their most talented programmers to work on Xbox 360 games. Getting them to later switch to PS3 programming when Sony's development kit became available was easier said than done. For some of them, porting existing Xbox 360 games to the PS3 was an easier solution. Developers could also ignore the unique advantages of Synergistic processing elements that set the Cell processor apart from traditional designs. Although such a solution made programming easier, it limited the ability of developers to create games that looked unique when compared to PC or Xbox 360 games. Unfortunately for Sony, both approaches also diminished the value proposition of the PS3. And while the ability to watch high definition Blu-ray movies was a nice add-on feature, it was not the console's main selling point.

Deirdre Ayre, head of Other Ocean Studios, complained that the PS3 architecture "wasn't the best approach."

The hardware should enable engineers to create great games quickly and efficiently. It took some time for that to happen on the PS3. (PlayStation 2009b)

By early 2007, the problems of a high price, lack of rumble, and too few unique game titles resulted in the PS3 dropping to fourth place in sales in the United States, as shown in Table 7.2. Worldwide, the Nintendo Wii outsold the PS3 by a ratio of two to one and total global PS3s sales through to March 2007 numbered 1.5 million units, compared to 5 million units of the Nintendo Wii and more than 10 million units of the Xbox 360.

---

3   The Microsoft development kit was built around PowerPC processors used in Apple computers and the ATI Radeon 9800 graphics processor commonly found in gaming PCs.

When comparing the game playing attributes of the PlayStation 3 to other consoles, the Xbox 360 compared favorably to the PS3 in key areas such as content, graphics, and online services. Although the Nintendo Wii compared poorly against its competitors in categories such as performance and online content, it was a leader in the most important category—content.

Table 7.2   Monthly U.S. Sales of Video Game Hardware

Company	Platform	Units Sold		
		November 2006	December 2006	January 2007
Nintendo	Wii	476,000	604,200	435,503
Sony	PlayStation 2	664,000	1,400,000	299,352
Microsoft	Xbox 360	511,000	1,100,000	294,000
Sony	PlayStation 3	197,000	490,700	243,554
Nintendo	DS	918,000	1,600,000	239,000
Sony	PSP	412,000	953,200	211,000
Nintendo	Game Boy Advance	641,000	850,000	179,000
Nintendo	Game Cube	70,000	64,000	24,000

Source: Thorsen 2007.

Backward Compatibility

One way to compensate for a limited selection of launch titles is to offer backward compatibility. The Wii, for example, could play any of the hundreds of GameCube titles, thereby leveraging iconic franchises like Mario Brothers, Zelda, and Donkey Kong. Nintendo also made some of the more popular titles from its other consoles available for download.

According to David Shippy, Ken Kutaragi, former CEO of Sony Computer Entertainment, insisted that the PlayStation 2 have complete backward compatibility with the original PlayStation. That "led to another phenomenal success in the marketplace."

> *Backward compatibility meant that...nothing became obsolete. This brilliant marketing strategy pushed Sony far into the lead in the game console market, as the library of PlayStation games was enormous. (Shippy and Phipps 2009)*

During the launch of the PlayStation 2, Alan Welsman, UK marketing director for Sony Computer Entertainment, told reporters that backwards compatibility "shouldn't even be a consideration" because it was considered a key selling point.

> You should be able to use your old software on your new machine. It's a great thing to show respect for the consumers who've ploughed money into the first one. We're very keen not to lose our core support, and we're very mindful that, as you and others have said, nobody's ever done it twice. The backwards compatibility shows how we're thinking about our core audience. The last thing we need is a multimedia machine that no one understands. (Guardian 2000)

Yet five years later, Welsman's company delivered just that.

Sony initially advertised the PS3's backward compatibility with PS2 games as a major selling point. However, only a few titles worked properly on the system. Subsequent software updates resolved compatibility issues for the most popular games, but not soon enough for many consumers who felt that the company had been dishonest in advertising backward compatibility. When Sony later removed the Emotion chip that natively runs PlayStation 2 games, it removed the last link between its current console and the previous generation. Without Emotion, the PS3 could no longer be viewed as an upgrade, and PlayStation 2 owners could as easily switch to an Xbox 360.

Even before the PS3's launch, Shippy recognized that the system would represent a complete break from the tradition of supporting previous generation titles. Yet he believed that gamers were more concerned about achieving the "Holy Grail" of performance that could only be achieved by a complete redesign. "Chip designers seldom get to start with a clean sheet of paper," he explained, "primarily because the PC and server market demand absolute backward compatibility with previous generation hardware and software" (Shippy and Phipps 2009).

Gamers, however, were every bit as demanding as PC owners. If backward compatibility was "a brilliant marketing strategy" for the PS2, then why not for the PS3? Hax and Wilde (2001) point out that "it is essential to maintain backward compatibility to preserve the legacy infrastructure that represents the core value of the standard itself." And the "core value" of the PlayStation "standard" is its content. By failing to deliver its promise of backward compatibility, Sony alienated many customers. It also likely contributed to the high return rate in the months following the console's initial launch. Although backward compatibility can be a double-edged sword by limiting the need for customers to purchase new titles, it makes it easier for gamers to upgrade because they can continue to play favorite titles. Several successful franchise games for the PS2, titles like *Grand Theft Auto* and *Final Fantasy*, were no longer exclusives, leaving PS2 owners with one less reason to upgrade to a PS3.

Customer Perceptions of the PS3

In its advertising, Sony rightly focused on the PS3's proven features, such as processor speed, graphics performance, and memory capacity. With so many functional benefits, one would think that the PS3 should be leading the market. Instead it is in last place. The problem is twofold. Customers are not aware of the unique features offered by the PS3 and the benefits are not readily apparent in the real world applications (i.e. games) that are most important to end users. If users cannot perceive meaningful differences between console brands, they will stick with their existing brand or go with a lower price brand, regardless of how well a console performs on critical industry benchmarks.

In a survey conducted by the NPD group, only 40 percent of PS3 owners knew that their console had a Blu-ray drive capable of playing high definition movies, despite the fact that Blu-ray was one of the key selling points in the company's marketing campaign. In fairness, the same survey found that only 30 percent of Xbox 360 owners were aware of that console's high definition capabilities. Clearly, the ability to play high-definition movies was not an important factor in the purchasing decision of most console owners.

In areas that were more important to end users, the PS3 often fell short. For example, the Nintendo Wii Remote was easier to use and more versatile than the Sony Sixaxis controller and Xbox Live offered a superior online experience. In terms of graphics performance, the PS3 was far superior to the Wii, but virtually identical to the Xbox 360. Both Nintendo and Microsoft visibly differentiated their offerings from previous generation consoles. Sony's only unique selling proposition was Blu-ray, a technology that was evidently not important to most gamers.

The Impact of Product Decisions

When Jack Tretton, President of Sony Computer Entertainment of America, declared that the "vast majority" of 150 million PlayStation 2 owners would eventually "migrate" to the PS3, he echoed a commonly held belief that the PlayStation brand would be enough to ensure the console's long term success. And who could argue with them? One had to look no further than video game discussion boards to find devout defenders of each console, known as "fanboys." In an article titled "Ten golden rules of video game fanboyism," journalist Jim Sterling asserts that among "those who prove themselves obsessively loyal to any product or corporation … nowhere do they flourish more freely than within gamer culture."

In reality, gamers were among the most fickle consumers, eager to switch brands when competitors introduced advanced features or offered eagerly awaited exclusive games. Witness Atari, Sega, Nintendo, and Sony, all industry leaders at one time or another. Yet their seemingly unassailable brands experienced precipitous declines at the hands of new competitors. When Sony challenged Nintendo's near monopolistic hold on the U.S. video game market in the mid 1990s, it relied on the willingness of gamers to switch brands.

Unlike some other product categories (e.g., coffee) gamers are influenced by what Allen (2004) calls cognitive drivers. "These are more rational and may involve the customer's critical assessment of his or her relationship with the supplier. These evaluations may involve attitudes toward the supplier's product quality, price, problem resolution, or distribution structure." In other words, console owners are influenced by functional, rather than emotional, attributes of the product.

As noted in this chapter, Sony focused heavily on unique functional features that would purportedly provide important benefits to customers. In fact, if you consider the entire package of attributes present in the PS3, it provides more features and benefits than its competitors. Why then is it not selling as well as the others? One reason is that its most critical differentiating feature is the Blu-ray drive which many customers aren't even aware of and don't care about. A second reason is that the decision to include Blu-ray led to Sony's late entry into the market which, in turn, diminished the value of other functional attributes that were also present in the Xbox 360. As a result, customers do not perceive that the features and benefits provided by the PS3 are worth the high price. For most gamers, it doesn't provide good value.

This series of decisions forced Sony to concentrate on late adopters as their target market. "As you get further into a cycle, you've got folks who are more characterized as the followers ... Those are people who are going to make a decision and buy one or the other, and so it becomes increasingly important that we convince them to buy ours," admitted Dille (Nutt 2009). Yet the PS3 lacked features that appeal to late adopters.

In his classic book on the diffusion of innovations, Everett Rogers (1983) argues that early adopters tend to be educated, have higher social status, and are wealthy. On the other end of the spectrum, late adopters tend to be less educated, have lower social status and have less income. Thus, socioeconomic status and willingness to adopt innovations are correlated.

The cost, sophistication, and advanced features of the PS3 make it difficult for Sony to reach late adopters, who "are less comfortable with technology and are quite sensitive to price" (Ryans 2000). Microsoft was able to reduce costs by eliminating the hard drive and Wi-Fi on its entry level console, features that, along with Blu-ray, were integral to the PS3 experience. For Sony, matching Microsoft's cost cutting was simply not an option.

Sony's best hope for reaching late adopters is through PlayStation 2, which at $100 is more within the financial means of people in the socioeconomic class described above. Late adopters can also take advantage of the PS2's standard features, which include DVD and CD playback, and a large library of low-priced new and used games. Yet despite its price advantage, the PS2 is not without competition. For one, as a previous generation console, it must compete against the large availability of used consoles, including the original Xbox, GameCube, Dreamcast, and used PlayStation 2s. As more owners of these consoles upgrade, the availability of low-priced consoles will only increase.

The PS2 must also compete against inexpensive current generation consoles. The Xbox 360 Arcade, which had a retail price of $199 and could be found in stores for as low as $150, was well within reach of consumers who might consider a PS2. Although the Arcade console lacked a hard drive, Wi-Fi, and other advanced features, it had one significant advantage over the PS2. It could be upgraded.

When Wii sales eventually decline, Nintendo is certain to drop the price of its console to encourage sales and attract late adopters. From day one, the Wii has been an inexpensive console for Nintendo to produce. Therefore, a lower priced Wii that competes with the PS2 will likely remain profitable. Given the choice, most people will choose a Wii over a PlayStation 2 for the reasons we outline in Chapter 9. Moreover, the Wii's ease of use makes it is particularly suited to late adopters who are less comfortable with technology. That will spell the end of the PS2 lifecycle. Nevertheless, Nintendo has a long way to go before it topples the PS2 as the most successful console in video game history.

8

Blu-Rays and Netflix: Defining "the Ultimate High-Definition Experience"

Blu-ray will revolutionize the media industry.
Ron Stuart, General Manager, Verbatim UK

The very concept of physical media is racing toward obsolescence.
Steven Levy, author of *The Perfect Thing: How the iPod Shuffles Commerce,*
Culture, and Coolness

In developing the PlayStation 3, Sony had two strategic objectives. One was to make the PS3 the most advanced game console on the market. The other was to dominate the market for high-definition movies. The unrivaled precision of the blue-violet laser utilized in Blu-ray optical drives permitted the production of disks capable of storing as much as 50GB of data, compared to only 8.5GB on a DVD. As a result, a Blu-ray movie could be presented at roughly six times the resolution of a standard DVD and still have room for a plethora of extra features, ranging from picture-in-picture commentary to games and multimedia.

Microsoft originally offered its own high-definition movie player add-on in a format known as HD-DVD. However, because Microsoft chose not to use HD-DVD for video games, it proved uncompetitive compared to Sony's Blu-ray technology. When HD-DVD was eventually discontinued, Microsoft used the opportunity to partner with Netflix. Netflix began as a mail-in service for movie rentals, but later expanded into online delivery. For a single monthly fee, PC and Xbox owners could download and view as many movies as they wanted. According to Microsoft, disk-based media of all kinds were a thing of the past.

In this chapter we will consider the role of various proprietary movie formats in the adoption of new technology, particularly how the battle between Sony's Blu-ray format and Toshiba's HD-DVD format impacted video game console adoption.

From Betamax to Blu-ray: Sony's Effort to Dominate Home Entertainment

Sony Corporation emerged from the ashes of World War II to become the first Japanese company to build a tape recorder based on military technology licensed by Bell Laboratories. By the late 1950s, Sony had become one of the world's leading producers of radios, which provided the company with the resources to later expand into televisions, stereos and other home entertainment products. In 2006, Sony had an annual net income of $1 billion on $64.5 billion in revenues.

Sony had a reputation for product innovation that had resulted in well-known brands, such as Betamax, Trinitron and Walkman. The company was also very protective of its intellectual property and was therefore reluctant to license its technologies to competitors. As a result, Sony products often lost market share to inferior technologies offered by competitors.

The Betamax videotape format was perhaps the best known example of a superior product that failed to win consumer acceptance. Introduced in 1975, Betamax tapes were smaller and provided better definition than the competing VHS format introduced by JVC the following year. However, Sony was unwilling to adapt the technology to accommodate longer play times because doing so would degrade the video quality. Consumers, however, preferred the convenience of longer recording times over higher definition images. Moreover, Sony Betamax players were significantly more expensive than the VHS players being produced by third-party manufacturers under license from JVC. In 1988, Sony abandoned the format and began manufacturing VHS players.

A more celebrated brand was the Walkman portable music player, which Sony introduced in 1979. The Walkman played standard audio cassettes and was capable of sound reproduction on par with much larger players. The brand dominated the portable music market in the 1980s and for much of the 1990s. By the mid 1990s, portable music had moved from cassettes to CDs. The digital technology used in music CDs reproduced sounds with higher quality at lower cost. As a result, Sony's competitors were able to introduce a large number of inexpensive portable CD players. Nevertheless, the Sony CD Walkman continued to enjoy strong market share.

When digital compression became popular in the late 1990s, Sony opted to promote its own proprietary ATRAC format over the more popular mp3 format. In early 2005, Ken Kutaragi, chairman and chief executive officer (CEO) of Sony Computer Entertainment, admitted that Sony employees were frustrated by the company's unwillingness to support other music compression formats. All the same, Sony continued to promote ATRAC for its Walkman and other Sony electronics products.

One way Sony tried to counter the threat of mp3s was through a software program named SonicStage that converted mp3 tracks to ATRAC. However, by doing so, Sony placed an unnecessary burden on consumers. The fact that users had mp3s to convert meant that they were already using mp3 music software to manage and play digital music. Sony's plan required them to install and learn another program simply to access the music already available to them. As if that were not enough to dissuade most consumers, SonicStage was difficult to use and was prone to bugs and security flaws. Finally, the program was not compatible with millions of Macintosh computers. For most customers, the simplest solution was to avoid the Walkman. And that is what they did.

Sony's decision to not support mp3 allowed rivals to capture most of the portable music market. The most successful of these was the iPod. Introduced by Apple in 2001, it became the fastest selling portable music player in history with 100 million units sold by 2007. The Walkman, by comparison, took a decade to reach the 100 million mark. The iPod's success can be attributed to both its design and features.

The iPod design was elegant in its simplicity. Users could interact with nearly all the functions of the iPod through a click wheel that responded to simple thumb gestures. Circular thumb gestures provided access to various menu options and volume control, while a press of the thumb turned the iPod on and off and controlled playback options. Apple also provided its easy-to-use iTunes music software as a free download for users of both Macintosh and Windows computers.

Whereas digital Walkmans initially only supported ATRAC, most of Sony's competitors took an agnostic approach. Creative Labs, SanDisk, Archos, and

Microsoft all offered popular music players that supported a variety of music formats, including mp3. The iPod supported at least seven different audio formats and various video and data files. Many models offered casual games, and synchronized contact and calendar data with Microsoft Outlook. Most recently, models such as the iPod Touch and iPhone turned portable music players into fully functional computers with Internet access and a large library of software applications.

PC users could use Apple's iTunes software to purchase, organize, and play music even if they did now own an iPod. It made upgrading to an iPod easier for consumers who did not own a music player. By early 2007, Apple had sold more than 2.5 billion songs, 50 million television shows and 1.3 million movies through its iTunes music store. Lastly, iTunes acted both as an interface for the free distribution of audio files, known as Podcasts, and as a conduit for online radio stations.

Sony viewed the mp3 revolution with caution. The company prided itself on making the best quality products on the market, and as such it saw lower fidelity digital music as a step backward. To counter this trend, Sony launched its Super Audio Compact Disk (SACD), an audio format that greatly improved sound fidelity of recorded music and, through proprietary copy protection technologies, prevented unauthorized copying of music content. However, Sony's copy protection schemes significantly added to manufacturing costs and made SACD systems incompatible with most stereos.

In the end, Sony found few electronics manufacturers willing to accept its restrictive licensing terms, and few consumers willing to invest in expensive proprietary stereo equipment. In 2004, after being on the market for four years, SACD had a market share of less than 0.5 percent of U.S. music sales. The following year, sales of lower quality digital music downloads more than tripled to $1.1 billion, representing a market share of 6 percent of total U.S. music sales.

What does any of this have to do with video games? Plenty, it turns out. When Sony launched the PlayStation 3, one of its key strategies was to provide an all-in-one entertainment console that would help launch another propriety standard, known as Blu-ray. And like Betamax, ATRAC, and SACD, Blu-ray was superior to other commonly available media formats. Sony's Blu-ray movie format was one of two competing technologies that offered a much higher definition than standard DVDs. The other was HD-DVD, a format developed by Toshiba.

Sony's Trojan Horse Strategy

The development and marketing of Blu-ray was the responsibility of the Blu-ray Disk Association (BDA), a partnership originally spearheaded by Sony, with Panasonic, Pioneer, Philips, Thomson, LG Electronics, Hitachi, Sharp, and Samsung as partners. As the lead developer, Sony spent an estimated $3 billion on Blu-ray, entitling the company to a third of royalties collected on Blu-ray drives and movies.

The PlayStation 3 was seen as the ideal catalyst for the universal adoption of Blu-ray as the next generation video standard. Sony expected to sell tens of millions of Blu-ray equipped PS3 consoles to gamers who would then purchase and rent large numbers of high-definition Blu-ray movies. As Blu-ray's share of the DVD market grew, late adopters would be more inclined to adopt Blu-ray when it came time to upgrade home entertainment centers to high definition. Some non-gamers might even be inclined to purchase PS3 consoles mainly for its non-gaming features. Once the console was in the home, owners would be persuaded to purchase games, thereby expanding the video game market.

The Xbox 360 was also capable of playing high-definition movies, but only with the purchase of an optional external HD-DVD drive priced at $249. Unlike the PS3 Blu-ray drive, the HD-DVD drive could not be used for playing games. That task was relegated to the Xbox 360's standard definition DVD drive, a design decision that would prove fatal for HD-DVD. However, because HD-DVD was primarily a Toshiba product, its success was never high on Microsoft's list of priorities.

HD-DVD offered several advantages over Blu-ray. Both the manufacturing cost and royalty scheme were lower for HD-DVD. Therefore, players could be produced more cheaply and the savings could be passed on to consumers. When both formats were launched in 2006, HD-DVD players were half the price of comparable Blu-ray players. Not surprisingly, HD-DVD players outsold Blu-ray players by a significant margin. In August 2007, Jodi Sally, Toshiba's VP of Marketing, declared that "with a majority market share in unit sales of next generation DVD players, consumers are speaking loud and clear, and they are adopting HD DVD as their HD movie format of choice." Sally, however, did not count PlayStation 3 consoles, which were arguably the most capable Blu-ray players on the market.

Initially, Sony's decision to bundle Blu-ray into every PlayStation 3 console appeared to give it the upper hand in the movie format war. Most major movie studios supported either Blu-ray or both formats. Few backed HD-DVD exclusively.

Even though most PS3 owners did not purchase a console for playing movies, the advantages of the PS3's movie player were clear. Even standard definition movies looked better in the PS3 because of the console's powerful upscaling technology. Using complex algorithms, the PS3 guessed what a picture should look like and then upscaled it by filling in missing details. In some instances, upscaling made standard definition DVDs look almost as good as high definition.

Companies have long used Trojan horse strategies to sell additional products and services. For example, cellular phone operators subsidized smartphone purchases in exchange for lengthy service contracts. They then used the phones to sell add-on services, like Wi-Fi (T-Mobile Hotspots), email, and texting. Apple used a Trojan horse strategy to sell computer applications for the iPhone, such as games, music programs, GPS maps, social networking tools, and more. Another good example that we discussed earlier in the book was how Nintendo tried (and failed) to use its NES console as a Trojan horse to gain control over global online services.

Right from the start, it seemed that Sony's Trojan horse strategy would give it a significant advantage over Toshiba. In comparison, Toshiba's Xbox strategy was bound to fail. After spending $400 on a console, few Xbox 360 owners could justify an additional expense of $249 for the sole purpose of playing high-definition movies. To make matters worse, many did not own a television capable of displaying high-definition images and only 30 percent were even aware of the console's HD capabilities. Even when they were aware of the console's HD features, most were content with the standard DVD drive, which, like the PS3, could upscale regular DVDs to near HD resolution.

Warner Bros. was the largest and most important movie studio to support HD-DVD. When it announced in January 2008 that the company would move exclusively to Blu-ray, HD-DVD's fate was sealed. "A two-format landscape has led to consumer confusion and indifference toward high definition, which has kept the technology from reaching mass adoption and becoming the important revenue stream that it can be for the industry," announced Kevin Tsujihara, President of Warner Bros. Home Entertainment Group. "Consumers have clearly chosen Blu-ray," he added, "and we believe that recognizing this preference is the right step in making this great home entertainment experience accessible to the widest possible audience" (Warner Bros. 2008).

With the loss of the last major studio to support HD-DVD, it was only a matter of time before HD-DVD would be discontinued. A month after the Warner Bros. announcement, Toshiba announced its withdrawal from the market. Nevertheless, Tsujihara's prediction of "mass adoption" and increased industry revenue never materialized.

Blu-ray advocates claimed that the format was a resounding success, as movie sales more than doubled in 2009. However, the growth in sales belied the fact that only 8 million Blu-ray movies were sold in 2008 and that the rate of growth had declined significantly from the nearly 400 percent increase that occurred the previous year. Even less impressive was the fact that in 2008 cumulative sales of Blu-ray players and PS3s were nearly equivalent to the annual unit sales of Blu-ray movies. Since purchasers of standalone Blu-ray players were likely to purchase several movies, it meant that a large percentage of PS3 owners chose not to purchase any Blu-ray movies. Clearly, Sony's Trojan horse strategy wasn't working.

Blu-ray was not alone. Between 2005 and 2008, U.S. per capita annual spending on DVDs fell from $60 to $43, as consumers increasingly turned to download services like Netflix and illegal file sharing services such as The Pirate Bay. Many did not seem to mind that video quality was often inferior to Blu-ray and (in many cases) standard definition DVDs.

Netflix: HD on Demand

Toshiba's decision to abandon HD-DVD caused many to speculate that Microsoft would replace its add-on drive with Blu-ray technology. However, according to Microsoft's Robbie Bach, a Blu-ray add-on would not offer value to Xbox 360 owners. "It's not a feature we get a ton of requests for," he replied when asked about the rumors.

When you ask people the list of things they want to see us spending time creating in Xbox, Blu-ray is way, way down on the list. The second thing is, from a technical perspective, it doesn't help us in the core of what Xbox does, which is in gaming. We can't have publishers produce games on Blu-ray disk, because then they won't play on the 28 million Xboxes we've already shipped. So it doesn't help us in the core gaming space. The third thing is that it costs a lot of money. And so the scenario is [that] I'm going to add something to the product that's going to raise the cost, which means the price goes up, consumers aren't asking for it, and by the way, my game developers can't use it. (Bishop 2009)

After Microsoft's annual strategy meeting Bach declared that the "Xbox Live solution," namely online content delivery, would remain the company's primary focus—and for good reason. Behind the scenes, Bach was negotiating a partnership with Netflix, "the world's largest online movie rental service." Netflix had begun experimenting with movie downloads on PCs with mixed success, and the on-demand service fit well with Microsoft's market position as the leader in online services. Under the terms of the partnership, Xbox 360 owners who were members of both Xbox Live Gold and Netflix could download any movie from Netflix's library of more than 10,000 online titles at no extra cost.

Both Netflix and Microsoft were primed to take full advantage of their new partnership. When the partnership was announced in July 2008, Xbox Live had 17 million subscribers, and Netflix had 10 million subscribers. Undoubtedly, some of those were already members of both services, but many more were not. Xbox Live subscribers were in the best position to benefit. They had already invested in the hardware and would only need to pay the additional monthly fee.

Netflix subscribers could download as much content as they wished for a flat monthly fee which started at $10 per month. Not only was it more economical, but it allowed users to try content that they were unsure they would like. If the film was not particularly good, the subscriber could just delete it and download something different. Only two months after the service became available, more than one million Xbox 360 owners had signed up for Netflix. The partnership also proved to be a boon to Netflix which posted higher than expected earnings during the first quarter the service was available.

Netflix downloads were previously only offered on personal computers, most of which had small screens that were poorly suited to home viewing. To take advantage of big screen televisions, users either had to hook their computers up to their television, obtain a physical disk through Netflix mail-in service, or acquire a specialized device such as a TiVo. With an entry level price below $200, the Xbox 360 compared favorably to standalone viewing devices like TiVo. Suddenly the Xbox 360 was a viable alternative for non-gamers to store and access multimedia content, one that drew comparisons to Apple TV. Film journalist M. G. Siegler (2008) "long thought the Xbox 360 was superior to the Apple TV as a living room digital entertainment device—and not just because of the gaming factor." Apple TV changed his perception with the ability to rent movies, he said, "but now the 360 is back with a vengeance."

Although it was impossible to be certain how many Netflix subscribers would purchase an Xbox 360 as a way to manage and consume downloadable content, those that did became prime candidates for purchasing other Microsoft products, such as music, games and other content.

Much has been written about the pros and cons of subscriptions and pay per use services. Mohr and Slater (2004) note that "if the technology is new and unfamiliar to consumers, pay-per-use (also called micropayment) encourages trial at lower risk. However, as consumers become familiar with the technology, beyond a certain usage volume, the subscription plan will offer more value to consumers." For example, cell phone providers win customers by offering unlimited text messages, or free calls on nights and weekends. These services place minimal demands on the network (text messaging requires minimal bandwidth and nights and weekends are times of low demand for voice calls), but attract heavy users who consume other products, such as music, ring tones, and wallpapers.

Americans consumed an average of approximately four hours of television per day. As such, online movie rentals were ideal for a subscription model, and Microsoft knew this. When it initially developed the Xbox 360, it deliberately left out a high-definition optical drive to focus on downloadable content. Xbox Live was the centerpiece of Microsoft's strategy, and movie downloads were seen as an enhancement of that service.

In the long run, the failure of HD-DVD may prove a godsend to Microsoft. Its partnership with Netflix demonstrates the company's commitment to Xbox Live, the one service that sets Microsoft apart from its competitors. For Microsoft, the challenge will be to remain competitive against the ever widening array of products aimed at delivering content through the Internet. At the present time, TiVo, Sling Media, Apple, and others offer devices that can be used to download video content directly to televisions. In addition, more people are watching movies and videos on their cellular phones and computers.

Sony, Amazon, Apple, and Blockbuster also participated in online movie rentals and sales. However, they followed a traditional model of charging a fee for each rental. The cost to download a television episode or movie ranged from $2.00 to $6.00 depending on the length, quality, and release date of the program. For example, high-definition content downloaded from the PlayStation Network was priced higher than standard definition content. Sony's online movie service proved far less popular than the Xbox Live—Netflix service. High rental costs, long download times, and limited viewing options were cited as some of the reasons behind the lack of interest shown by PS3 owners.

Blockbuster was one of the first companies to provide on-demand movie rentals, but its service never caught on with most consumers. Pricing was a major issue, since Blockbuster required subscribers to pay for each movie download. Customers who did not have access to personal computers or who wanted to view content on a big screen TV had to purchase a $100 download module that could be attached to a television. Apple offered a similar service, known as Apple TV, which could be integrated with iTunes for an upfront cost of $229.

Most viewers seemed to prefer the convenience and affordability of Netfix's fixed-fee monthly plans. During the economic crisis of 2008, Netflix stock price surged 25 percent even as the stock market as a whole fell by half. Apple shares outperformed the market on the strength of the iPhone, but its shares still experienced an overall decline of nearly 20 percent. Over the same period, shares in Blockbuster fell by a spectacular 95 percent on speculation that the company could file for bankruptcy protection.

Sony seemed to realize that the shift to on-demand content was unstoppable when it began to offer more exclusive content through its online PlayStation Store. In May 2009, Sony revealed the PSP Go, a portable gaming device that was unable to play disk-based media.

Digital distribution offered advantages to both customers and developers. Customers received products more quickly from the comfort of their homes.

In addition they were able to access less popular or hard-to-find out-of-print games. Developers benefited by interacting directly with customers, by developing new revenue streams for older titles and by eliminating much of the cost of packaging and distribution (Harding-Rolls and Keen 2005).

However, the biggest surprise came in July 2009, when Sony announced its own agreement with Netflix to deliver content directly to Internet-equipped Sony television sets. Although the Sony—Netflix partnership seemed to directly contradict the company's Blu-ray strategy, in the end, it may have been the more prudent decision. For most of its history, Sony has refused to accept competitor media formats, such as VHS and mp3, even when it was clear that they had become industry standards. As a result, the once mighty Walkman brand was relegated to a historical footnote. Perhaps Sony has learned from its past mistakes by embracing a competitor's rapidly growing media delivery system. Only time will tell.

Ever since the days of Betamax, Sony has sought to dominate the distribution of media with high quality, high performance products. Yet time and again, it failed to make significant inroads into markets dominated by cheaper, lower quality, but more convenient technologies. In their book, *Relentless: The Japanese Way of Marketing*, Johansson and Nonaka (1996) argue that Japanese companies tend to pursue marketing effectiveness rather than marketing efficiencies. Such a goal requires significant investments and a long-term perspective. This may be one reason why Sony has been reluctant to change its focus on performance. No one can be certain if Blu-ray will survive the shift to online content delivery or if it will follow the path of Betamax, ATRAC, and SACD. It is also too early to tell if the Netflix partnership will help Microsoft turn around its flagging Xbox brand. One thing is certain; with so many technologies competing to become the next dominant design in video content delivery, Blu-Ray will never dominate movie sales in the same way that DVDs and VHS tapes once did.

9

The Wii Revolution

Conventional wisdom held that success within the video game industry was largely dependent on graphics and speed. Prior to the launch of the Wii, Nintendo had become a marginal player in game consoles. Developers primarily focused their efforts on creating titles for the PlayStation 3 and Xbox 360, which they viewed as the probable market winners. Yet as we saw in previous chapters, technically superior game consoles do not always achieve market acceptance. Examples include the Atari Jaguar, the 3DO Multiplayer, and the Sega Dreamcast.

The success of the Wii took everyone by surprise, including Nintendo. In this chapter we consider how this relatively primitive console was able to capture more than 50 percent of the market for home consoles, despite the fact that it underperforms its competitors in almost every standard measure.

Revolutionary Simplicity

In 2003, Nintendo was in dire straits. Its GameCube console stumbled badly against competing consoles like the Xbox and PlayStation 2. Analysts began to wonder if Nintendo could ever hope "to recover from what appears to be a withering defeat at the hands of Sony." (*Electronic Gaming Business* 2003). Nintendo president Satoru Iwata remained unfazed by the criticism. "We are preparing a new product which will give a fresh surprise to consumers," he explained in a 2003 conference. That "surprise" was an early prototype of the Wii, codenamed Revolution.

Nintendo executives already realized that they could not hope to win back market share with faster processors and better graphics while continuing to make a profit on consoles. They also knew that lower prices could not sustain sales if consoles continued to perform poorly relative to competitors. Customers, it appeared, were willing to pay a slight premium for better performance. Nintendo's dilemma was how to increase performance while keeping costs low. Iwata and Director of Development Shigeru Miyamoto decided to focus the company's design efforts on one of the console's least expensive components, the controller.

The basic design of a video game controller had not changed in nearly two decades. However, as games became more complicated, console makers added more buttons to give players access to advanced controls. Iwata and Miyamoto believed that current game pads with their arrays of buttons were intimidating to most non-gamers. "As video games evolved, the video game experience became more complicated," explained Miyamoto.

> In order to control the more complicated experience, that resulted in more complicated controllers. So what we've been trying to do over the last few years is find ways to take advantage of technology to essentially create an interface that has a broader appeal and that's more approachable to the average consumer. (Kohler 2008)

If Nintendo could design a controller that looked more like a television remote, Miyamoto reasoned, the company might be able to attract new customers who might feel intimidated by a traditional controller. Rather than compete directly with Sony and Microsoft for the core 18- to 35-year-old male gamer, the Nintendo Revolution would be targeted to a broader audience that included young children, parents, and even senior citizens. Noted Iwata,

> We decided that Nintendo was going to take another route—game expansion. We are not competing against Sony or Microsoft. We are battling the indifference of people who have no interest in video games. (O'Brian 2007)

Robert Kotick, CEO of Activision, a leading game publisher, was one of several industry leaders to support Nintendo's new approach. "In the past I would have said that the 360 and the PlayStation 3 are likely to take leading market share and that Nintendo would have a very tough time competing," he said.

> But we've grown increasingly excited about Revolution and we do think that it will present some interesting opportunities for the future. The controller is so innovative that I actually think you'll see the potential for application development and genre development that is markedly different and will be a good point of differentiation. (O'Brian 2007)

The Nintendo Revolution was much simpler than other current generation game consoles. It used an IBM PowerPC "Broadway" microprocessor derived from the G3 microprocessor originally developed in the late 1990s for Apple computers. Broadway was an incremental improvement over the "Gekko" processor used in the Nintendo GameCube, which was also based on the G3.

Correspondingly, the development cost for a Nintendo game ranged from 25 to 50 percent of the cost of a similar Xbox 360 or PlayStation 3 title. Development cycles were significantly shorter, allowing publishers to produce more games in the same amount of time. That was "good news for Nintendo," noted one video games analyst. "Top game publishers are already developing content for the Revolution, and it's ultimately the software that drives hardware sales" (*Consumer Electronics Daily* 2006).

Although many game developers welcomed the simplicity of the Revolution relative to other consoles, some felt limited by the console's anemic processor and graphics capability. Julian Eggebrecht, president of Factor 5 (one of the leading studios producing titles for GameCube) said he felt let down by the Wii's limited potential. "When I heard what was going on at Nintendo, I cringed. Its audio is relatively mediocre. It's essentially Gamecube 1.5" (Radd 2006).

However, the decision to use inexpensive components reduced the cost to consumers, while still allowing Nintendo to make money on each unit sold. Finally, the decision to stay out of high-definition gaming meant that Nintendo could concentrate its R&D on other areas, such as motion control.

E3 Unveiling

Introducing ... Wii. As in "we."

While the code-name "Revolution" expressed our direction, Wii represents the answer. Wii will break down that wall that separates video game players from everybody else. Wii will put people more in touch with their games ... and each other.

But you're probably asking: What does the name mean? Wii sounds like "we," which emphasizes this console is for everyone. Wii can easily be remembered by people around the world, no matter what language they speak. No confusion. No need to abbreviate. Just Wii. Wii has a distinctive "ii" spelling that symbolizes both the unique controllers and the image of people gathering to play. And Wii, as a name and a console, brings something revolutionary to the world of video games that sets it apart from the crowd.

So that's Wii. But now Nintendo needs you. Because, it's really not about you or me. It's about Wii. And together, Wii will change everything. (Klepek 2006)

The Nintendo Wii was first unveiled on May 9, 2006, at the Electronic Entertainment Expo (E3), an annual video game trade show. Gamers scoffed at the name chosen by Nintendo, which seemed unusual and less aggressive than "Revolution." "Months of positive hype, a genuine competitive advantage, and they named the thing Wii?" complained one gamer. "If consumers don't even want to say the name of the product, they're not going to buy it" (Totilo 2006).

In reply to the flurry of criticism, Matt Atwood, Nintendo of America's public relations manager observed, "Anytime you announce a new name you're going to get a lot of questions."

We wanted a name that represented the fact that this system was really for everyone to play. There were thoughts of sticking with Revolution, then there were thoughts of a completely different name, but once everything came together this was the name decided. I think Nintendo wanted a name that was very unique, because this system is about an entirely new way to play, an entirely new type of system. (Berghammer 2006)

Unlike gamers, analysts attending E3 focused more on the Wii's new motion-sensing controller that redefined the way people played games. Unlike traditional controllers, which required players to manipulate an array of buttons and sticks, the Wii controller often required no button pushing at all. The Wii controller was "a multifunctional device, limited only by the game designer's imagination," Nintendo announced.

In a tennis game, it serves as a racket you swing with your arm. In a driving game, it serves as your steering wheel. For first-person shooters, the Wii Remote acts as a weapon that you point at an enemy. The list of potential uses goes on and on. In addition to its pointing and motion-sensing abilities, the Wii Remote also includes a speaker,

a rumble feature[1] and an expansion port for additional input devices.
(Nintendo of America 2006)

The Wii Remote was originally developed as an accessory for the GameCube, but Nintendo decided to withhold the technology until the release of its next generation console. Since the Wii offered only slight performance improvements over the GameCube, the company would use the controller as the new console's unique selling proposition. The plan proved to be one of the most astute marketing decisions in history, as trade show attendees, enamored with Nintendo's new device, queued for up to three hours for hands-on demonstrations at one of the company's 75 console booths.

E3 2006 was also Sony's opportunity to display its new PlayStation 3 console, which, like the Nintendo Wii, was to be released in November 2006. In the months leading up to the trade show, Sony publicized the PlayStation 3 as the only console offering "supercomputer-like power and performance." Yet when Sony revealed its pricing strategy, analysts were dismayed. At $599, it was higher than an Xbox 360 and Wii combined, they observed. At Sony's news conference, Ken Kutaragi, president of Sony Computer Entertainment, became an object of ridicule for suggesting that the PS3 was "probably too cheap." "Although the PS3 does have better graphics," wrote one gaming analyst, "we're really looking forward to the Nintendo Wii and all its titles."

> *We feel the fun aspect the Wii will deliver is going to be difficult to beat with better graphics alone. Of course, this is solely based on personal opinion, so we would like to see how far both the Xbox 360 and PS3 can push the limits of console gaming. (Farhan 2006)*

The Wii also impressed investment analysts. Noted one:

> *Nintendo accomplished the task of convincing publishers, developers, retailers, and the investment community that they have a compelling system. While some critics might say the Wii is a GameCube with a motion-sensing controller and not much in addition to that, the fact is the other hardware manufacturers are moving toward much more costly platforms—development costs are doubling for the PS3 and Xbox. Nintendo has something that is differentiated, and people are going to like that. (Feldman 2006)*

---

1   Rumble was a feedback mechanism within the controller that caused it to vibrate in response to certain game actions, such as weapons fire, crashes, road vibrations, etc.

By the end of E3 2006, Nintendo had won more awards than any other company, including the coveted "Best of Show" award, and "Best Hardware" award. Reginald Fils-Aime, president and COO for Nintendo of America, went away from the show with renewed confidence in his company's strategy. "Our competitors are both going down the same path," he observed.

> Both believe that more and more performance with higher and higher price tags are their keys to success. So what do I see? I think our two competitors will trade share between them, while we go off and grab share in a completely different way. (Acohido 2006)

The Viral Campaign

Instead of following a traditional print and television campaign, Nintendo initially supported the Wii with viral marketing efforts. It set up consoles in shopping malls and other venues, where people could try the console and then talk about their experiences with friends, acquaintances, and family members. "There is going to be massive amounts of hands-on activity," explained Fils-Aime, "as well as showcasing exactly how Wii games are different."

> We are going to create advocacy. We are going to make it so that everyone who tries the Wii experience talks to their friends and neighbors. It is going to be a really provocative sight to be seeing teens and 20-year-olds and 40-year-olds and 50-year-olds talking about how different this experience is. (Acohido 2006)

In an effort to expand beyond its traditional target market of 9- to 24-year-old males, Nintendo identified key community influencers in major U.S. cities, including gamers, mothers, and multi-generational families, and invited them to company-hosted events. These opinion leaders, from children to grandparents, were asked to take turns with the console. Afterwards, attendees were to go to their communities and talk about their experiences.

Nintendo's approach of soliciting opinion leaders to share their impressions of the Wii with others follows classic diffusion theory. As noted previously, diffusion theory states that certain customers are the first to try new products. Once they do, they communicate their opinions (either positive or negative) with other customers who are later adopters. Later adopters rely extensively on word-of-mouth to help make decisions about new products. Nintendo recognized that customers have perceptions about the characteristics of a product which can act as enablers or barriers to adoption. As defined by Everett Rogers (2003), these five characteristics are: relative advantage, compatibility, complexity, trialability, and observability.

Relative advantage refers to the extent to which the new product offers improvements over existing products. In the case of the Wii, the motion controller offers simplicity and ease-of-use over other controllers, thereby eliminating potential barriers for non-gamers.

Compatibility should not be confused with backward compatibility. Although backward compatibility is certainly a key success factor in the video game industry, Rogers uses the term in a sociological sense to refer to the extent to which the new product fits with existing values, social practices, and user needs. For example, video game critics raised concerns about violence and obesity. Both of these concerns are addressed by Nintendo's more family friendly content and its focus on fitness and sports titles, like *Wii Fit* and *Wii Sports*.

Complexity focuses on the degree to which a product is easy to use and understand. For Nintendo to achieve its goal of expanding the reach of video games to new audiences it needed to make the Wii intuitive to non-gamers. Then it needed to communicate the console's ease-of-use to potential customers by enlisting the support of non-gamer opinion leaders who could influence purchasing behavior.

Trialability is the extent to which customers can try the new product before buying. Once they had hands-on experience, they would be more likely to purchase a console for themselves. For this reason, Nintendo set up demonstration booths in malls and other venues frequented by the general population. "Our core presumption is if we could get someone to put their hands on the controller, they would be hooked," explained Nintendo Senior Vice President George Harrison.

> *Most were not video game players, or had potentially a negative attitude about video games, but we identified them as people who were influential in their community. One of the things we were concerned about was if we started advertising on television to this audience, they wouldn't pay attention. We felt like we had to open up the audience's willingness to hear from us before we started the TV advertising. (Chmielewski 2006)*

Finally, *observability* refers to the degree to which the benefits of the product are visible. For example, Nintendo television commercials centered on the user experience rather than the product. They showed people from all walks of life enjoying the Wii in group settings. Traditionally, many non-gamers viewed video games as antisocial. Nintendo demonstrated that the Wii could be the center of enhanced social experiences between friends and family members. Also, by having consumers try the Wii remote in shopping centers, passersby would see how the console was different. Normally, watching others play video games is a tedious endeavor, even for gamers. Consider G4, a television channel devoted to video games. It had to shift its programming to general interest content after it discovered that viewers were not interested in watching others play games. In contrast, the Wii somehow draws people in after they see players swinging their arms in gameplay.

The company also showed up at non-traditional venues. One that caught the attention of the media was the American Association of Retired Persons Annual Meeting. Nintendo was the first video games company to participate in the conference. Articles about Nintendo's courting of "grey gamers" appeared in dozens of newspapers, including the front page of the *New York Times*.

Nintendo benefited from the media's extensive coverage of the Wii, which was invariably positive. The majority of the more than 300 newspaper articles published each month about the Wii focused mainly on the console's motion controller, its ability to help tackle obesity and improve fitness, and its success against the Xbox 360 and PlayStation 3, while the relatively few negative articles centered on sports injury cases and property damage caused by controllers flying out of users' hands.

Traditional game advertising typically emphasized the technical qualities of a console. Television commercials displayed scenes from games that demonstrated the more advanced qualities of the system. Sony, for example, demonstrated the advanced graphical capabilities of the PlayStation 3 through a combination of game play scenes and narration (Figure 9.1).

For the Wii, Nintendo took a decidedly different path. Instead of showing games, commercials focused on users. In one television spot, titled "Wii for all," two Japanese Nintendo representatives dressed in black suits arrived at American homes (Figure 9.2). After bowing to their hosts, they announced, "Wii would like to play." These were the only words spoken during the commercial, followed by scenes of regular people swinging their arms, jumping, and running as the two Nintendo representatives watched quietly from the back of the room. "One thing that is very important in entertainment," explained Miyamoto, "is that when one person is doing something, it has to be entertaining in a way that when other people see that person playing a game, they want to play it too. That was one of the concepts of the Wii. We not only wanted it to be fun, we wanted it to look fun so that it would be inviting to other people, who would then want to pick it up and play it" (*GameSpot* 2007).

Scene 1: Opening Scene

Scene 5: "Every vivid detail is rendered"

Scene 2: "This is a pixel"

Scene 6: RSX "100 billion operations a second"

Scene 3: "Image that is 10× the quality"

Scene 7: HDMI "highest quality video and audio"

Scene 4: Blu-ray—50GB High Definition

Scene 8: Closing Scene

Figure 9.1   "Higher Definition: Play Beyond" PS3 Trailer
Source: Playb3yond.com

Scene 1: "Wii Would like to Play"

Scene 5: Urban Professionals—Adventure Game

Scene 2: Surburban Family—Wii Sports

Scene 6: Farmers—Football and Action Games

Scene 3: Mexican American Family—Fitness

Scene 7: Farmer Shows his Gratitude

Scene 4: Mexican American Family—Boxing

Scene 8: Wii Ambassadors Drive into Sunset

Figure 9.2   Nintendo "Wii for All" Trailer

Source: wii.nintendo.com

Pricing

Nintendo approached its business very conservatively. When it launched the NES in the 1980s, the company was debt-free. This helped Nintendo thrive when other, more debt-laden, companies like Atari struggled. Unlike other console makers, Nintendo was unwilling to subsidize its consoles in order to win market share. Both Sony and Microsoft had diverse business interests that could be used to finance R&D and new product launches. If one area of the business temporarily lost money, they could make it up in other areas of the business. Nintendo did not have that luxury. Selling consoles at a loss could have a profound impact on the entire business. As a result, Nintendo had a strict policy of making a profit on every console it sold.

Despite Nintendo's conservative pricing policy, the Wii was the least expensive next generation console on the market at $249. Unlike the Xbox 360 and PS3, both of which required the purchase of additional content in order to play games, the Wii included a collection of five sports games in the standard retail package. The games were chosen carefully by Nintendo to demonstrate the motion-sensing capabilities of the Wii Remote. For example, in Wii Tennis, users used the controller as a tennis racket, while in Wii Baseball it was used as a bat.

Despite the Wii's lower price relative to competitors, Nintendo earned about $50 on each console sold. The acclaimed Wii Remote cost Nintendo approximately $10 to manufacture, including a motion sensing chip, rumble feature, and Bluetooth wireless communications.

Online Gaming

Although Microsoft was the undisputed leader in online gaming with more than 6 million subscribers to its Xbox Live service in 2006, Nintendo offered its own free service, known as the Wii Channel. As Nintendo extended its online service, it hoped to generate revenue from online advertising and from subscription fees for access to the site's advanced features.

One of the more popular features of Nintendo's online service was the Virtual Console (VC), a section of Nintendo's online store where Wii owners could purchase and download classic video games originally released for Nintendo 64, the Super Nintendo Entertainment System and the NES. Nintendo also struck deals with Sega Corporation and 24 other software developers to offer third party classic game titles, including many that had never before appeared on a Nintendo console. Titles were priced between $5.00 and $10.00 each.

Another popular feature was the Mii Channel, which included an art program for creating personalized avatars (digital representations of a player), known as Miis. Once players created their Miis, they could use them in multiplayer games such as *Wii Sports*.

Nevertheless, for a company that had once planned to dominate home-networking, Nintendo's online service was woefully primitive compared to services offered by Sony and Microsoft. "The current gold standard of online gaming services is Microsoft's Xbox Live," observed video game journalist Jack Rogers (2008).

> The Wii, by comparison, doesn't have a consistent online network, forcing each developer to devise its own solutions … What the Wii's online games all have in common is that they're shamefully primitive.

Part of the problem was the Wii's limited storage space for downloadable content. Another was the general lack of compelling content compared to what was available for competing systems. For example, *Guitar Hero* players could not download songs from their favorite artists, but instead had to be content with the prepackaged content distributed on the game disk.

Finally, the Nintendo service was criticized for not having a consistent interface for online games and for its lack of social networking functions. At a time when Facebook, Flickr, and Twitter were all the rage, Nintendo implemented draconian restrictions aimed at protecting children from coarse language and other adult content, but which made communicating with other players nearly impossible. According to Kombo.com editor Michael Kelly (2008), the problem was a system known as the friend code, which is "a string of numbers distinguishing each Wii, and yet another unique code for each game."

> Nintendo likely saw this system as a surefire way to identify friends and limit the potential harm that could come through as a result. However, the Friend Code system is needlessly restrictive. While there is an option to play anonymously, there is no way to make friends out of players that you meet online, as their identity is masked far too effectively. There is no opportunity to build community within the game itself. No opportunity to meet like-minded players who play at your level. This mode of interaction is part of the defining experience of playing online, and its absence is keenly felt.

Even in the few games that offered online capabilities, such as *Mario Kart*, players had no way to identify whom they were playing against. As such, forming online communities and teams was impossible.

Most Wii customers did not seem to be troubled by the console's primitive online capabilities. A quick scan of customer-review sites like Amazon revealed that online gaming was not as important to Wii owners as it was to traditional gamers. The reason was simple. Nintendo never focused on online gaming as an important aspect of the gaming experience. In addition, many Wii customers were first-time console owners, and therefore they lacked a point of reference.

Nintendo did an exceptional job of managing customer expectations. Unlike Sony, which advertised the PS3's supercomputing abilities and then delivered a console that was no better than the Xbox 360, Wii advertisements avoided discussions of online gaming altogether. Instead, television commercials focused on gatherings with friends and family and the enjoyment derived from person to person contact. They showed groups of people laughing, shouting, hugging, and dancing. Commercials for *Mario Kart*, arguably Nintendo's most capable online game, showed four players in a room competing against each other. Near the end of the commercial, the word "Wi-Fi" flashes on screen for less than a second. The commercial makes no other mention of *Mario Kart's* online features.

Third Party Support

The early success of the Wii caught many game studios off guard, as they scrambled to shift resources to Wii development. In particular, the popularity of sports games prompted some developers to announce new sports-related game titles exclusively for the Wii platform. For cash strapped studios, it was a godsend. The lower development costs and faster turnaround times meant that developers could produce new titles quickly and earn higher margins. David Zucker, president and CEO of Midway Games, explained,

> Since the typical development cost for a Wii title is significantly less than it is for a PS3 or Xbox 360, it allows you to continue to invest efficiently in that platform. We have plans to continue to pursue and support the Wii with three more titles this year. And we will have more next year. (Midway Games 2007)

Even games that were not exclusive to the platform often functioned differently on the Wii. For instance, THQ Inc., modified the controls on its popular wrestling game, *WWE SmackDown*, to take advantage of the Wii's motion controls. Specific motions with the Wii Remote controlled corresponding punches, throws, and slams against virtual opponents. On other platforms, users pressed buttons to control on-screen action.

Just as the success of the PlayStation and PlayStation 2 depended on the thousands of software titles available for those systems, a steady stream of new Nintendo titles ensured that interest in the Wii would remain strong. By the end of June 2007, the Wii had more than 400 available or announced game titles, compared to less than 300 for the PS3. Robust console sales and strong launch titles translated into healthy game sales. Seven of the top ten selling titles in 2007 were for Nintendo systems, including four for the Wii and three for the DS.

As more companies tried to capitalize on the popularity of the Wii, Nintendo was faced with the problem of assuring that consumers received quality products. The fact that the Wii was a relatively easy programming platform increased the likelihood that less skilled developers would produce mediocre games for the system. "By allowing developers the opportunity to create software easily we don't want them to release sub-standard titles," explained Nintendo managing director Hiroshi Imanishi. "Practices like that alienate users, and hurt the entire industry, we won't let it happen" (Shimbun 2000).

Despite Imanishi's assurances, numerous mediocre titles made it to the system. By early 2009, Gamespot listed 150 Wii titles that it considered to be, at best, "mediocre," and titles like *Anubis*, *China Warrior*, and *Double Dungeons* received the lowest ratings of any current generation games. "The Wii is a great platform, but there is some indication that the Wii is becoming polluted with crapware," cautioned Dave Roberts, CEO of PopCap Games (Takahashi 2008a).

Although new content was critical to a gaming console's success, too much new content could confuse customers and lead to poorer sales of key titles. With thousands of titles available for various gaming platforms, retail stores had a difficult time displaying games effectively. Often games had to be stacked together in such a way that only the spine of the display box was visible. Even then, only the most popular titles were stocked.

Sony and Microsoft Respond

Sony responded to the Nintendo juggernaut by lowering the price of its PlayStation 3 and PlayStation Portable consoles to $499 and $169, respectively. Microsoft followed Sony with price reductions of between $20 and $50 for its Xbox 360 systems. This placed the base Xbox 360 within the same price range as the Nintendo Wii, with base Xbox 360 systems selling for as little as $199.

Both companies tried to put a bold face on the situation by emphasizing the value added features of their consoles. Compared to the Wii, they offered significantly better graphics and a consistently better online experience. In addition, the PS3 included a Blu-Ray DVD drive for watching high-definition movies, while Xbox 360 owners could download movies directly by subscribing to Netflix for a low monthly fee. To take full advantage of these features, users needed to connect their consoles to high-definition television (HDTV) sets and to broadband Internet. Although HDTV penetration rates remained low at 30 percent of U.S. homes, that number was set to increase substantially with average annual growth of more than 50 percent. Broadband penetration was considerably higher at 53 percent of U.S. households and more than 70 percent of Internet subscribers.

Sony and Microsoft also took direct aim at Nintendo by introducing new games for casual gamers. *"Scene-It?"* for the Xbox 360 required players to respond to trivia questions and puzzle challenges. The retail package also included a simplified controller designed to imitate a game show buzzer. Sony offered *Echochrome* for the PlayStation 3 and PSP, a downloadable puzzle game in which a stick figure tries to cross a rotating 3D platform.

Managing Supply Shortages

In the United States, the holiday season was critical to the success of a new game system. Although console sales invariably declined after the holidays, demand for the Wii unexpectedly accelerated in the early months of 2007, leaving Nintendo scrambling to increase production. When new stock arrived at retail stores, it sold out within a few hours. By the summer, Nintendo was still struggling to make enough units to meet demand. At the Nintendo store in New York City, approximately 100 customers stood in line every morning hoping to obtain one of the consoles that arrived nightly, something normally seen during the first few days after a popular product launch.

Many new Wii owners became advocates, spreading the word through social networking and blog websites. Even Nintendo was unprepared for such a response. "We have no recollection of a time when our products were being talked about this much in non-business situations," Nintendo of America executives told Iwata.

Although Nintendo admitted that it was unprepared for the popularity of the Wii, some accused the company of deliberately withholding stock. Dan DeMatteo, COO of GameStop, a leading video game retailer, believed that "Nintendo intentionally dried up their supply," to meet certain financial objectives. Mike Wolf, research director for Digital Home magazine, felt the shortage was an attempt to create demand for the Wii. "Intentional scarcity is nothing new," he explained.

> It can be a great demand-creation tool as the buzz builds for consumers who hear great things about a new product and yet, cannot get one themselves. Whether or not this shortage of Wiis in the market was happenstance or calculated, Nintendo needs to realize that consumers are fickle and the well of Wii-mania they are drinking from may not be entirely bottomless. (Wolf 2007)

If the accusations were true, it would not be the first time that Nintendo had held back stock in order to increase demand. During the height of the Nintendo craze of the late 1980s and early 1990s, the company implemented a policy that it referred to as "inventory management." Whenever it released a popular title like *Super Mario Bros. 3* or *Zelda 2*, it deliberately withheld as much as half of the inventory. This created a frenzy of demand as kids lined up to get newly released titles. If they failed to get the title they wanted, they often returned home with other Nintendo products that were less popular. Harrison, however, was adamant that this time the shortages were unintentional.

> We have worldwide territories that are all competing over the available production. The Japan and European markets are doing extremely well with the Wii. People in Nintendo Japan are making the best decisions that they can about which products get shipped to which market and when. (Next Generation 2007)

One way retailers attempted to manage demand was to bundle accessories and games with the console. Many retailers offered Wii packages for between $350 and $600, depending on the number of included accessories. Miyamoto was concerned that expensive bundles would place the Wii out of reach of many families. "When the peripheral is bundled together, it makes it all more expensive and people aren't willing to spend the money on it," he explained. Nevertheless, retail bundles appeared to do little to soften demand, with most packages going out-of-stock within hours.

Simplicity vs. Performance

Although one might attribute the Wii's success to its ability to simulate activities more realistically, Nintendo was not the first to create virtual reality interfaces. However, past attempts had limited success. They included dance pads, light guns, and a device called Gametrak that tracked player movements in 3-D. Gametrak offered many of the same benefits as the Wii Remote, but the controller itself was relatively unwieldy. After installing special software on their game console, Gametrak players had to strap on a pair of gloves that were attached by wires to an external interface device. The limitations of Gametrak are discussed in a review of the PS2 game *Real World Golf*, one of the few titles specifically designed for Gametrak.

> Once you've connected everything and you're standing in front of the device with your hands up, you'll see the shock cord-like cables that come out of the Gametrak. The game comes with a plastic "miniature golf club" for you to swing around so that you don't destroy anything and actually have something to grip. As you're picturing all of this, keep in mind that this is not a good thing to have around small children or animals, as they can run into the cables and get tangled up pretty quickly. (Ayers 2006)

The key differentiator that separated the Wii Remote from previous virtual reality controllers was simplicity. The Wii eliminated barriers for less tech savvy players. For the average non-gamer to attempt to learn even one game on the PlayStation 3 required a significant amount of time and determination. The remote alone had 15 buttons and two control sticks. If that was not enough, most of the buttons had different purposes in different games, which meant that learning a second game was almost like starting over from the beginning. The more games players learned, the easier it became. However, even experienced gamers had to learn the control schemes for any new titles they acquired.

One difference between an experienced gamer and a non-gamer was the adeptness with which new games were learned. Just as a person who learns multiple languages develops an aptitude for learning languages, experienced gamers are able to learn new games quickly. Imagine the difficulty experienced by adults who have never been exposed to a foreign language when they suddenly find themselves in a foreign country without a translator to guide them. Even the thought of such a situation can instill fear in people who have never traveled outside their home countries. When they do travel, they are more likely to choose organized tours where they are protected from uncomfortable situations.

Nintendo eliminated this barrier by making the Wii Remote feel intuitive. Gone were arrays of buttons and control sticks that were so intimidating to non-gamers, replaced by a couple of well-placed buttons combined with simple motion control. Although the control schemes varied slightly from one game to the next, most often they corresponded to real-life movements. In games that involved swordplay, controlling an in-game sword was as easy as swinging the Wii remote.

The Paradox of Choice

Both the Xbox 360 and PlayStation 3 offered a variety of options and configurations. At launch, the PlayStation 3 could be purchased in a 20 gigabyte or 60 gigabyte option. The 60GB console included Super Audio CD playback, wireless, and backward compatibility. The 20GB version was also backward compatible but could not connect to a wireless network. Later Sony introduced a 40GB version with no backward compatibility and an 80GB version with limited backward compatibility. Special editions were released in a variety of colors. Some accepted multimedia memory cards and some did not. Microsoft took the same approach as Sony, offering the Xbox 360 in a variety of colors and configurations.

Too much choice can often lead customers to regret their decisions. For the PlayStation 3, this was most evident in the debate over backwards compatibility. The model without it was priced $100 lower and had a more efficient processor, which meant the console was quieter and used less electricity. For most people, the decision should be simple. If a person already had PlayStation 2 games, then the customer most likely had a PS2 console as well, thereby negating the need for backward compatibility. Yet many customers seemed to struggle in their decision over which model to buy.

Consider what happens when one potential Sony customer goes to an online gaming forum for advice on which PS3 to buy. This person is a parent and knows little about video games, but his son has a PlayStation 2 that he "wants to upgrade to the PS3 for Christmas." Hoping for a clear answer on which model to buy, he asks if the 40GB, 60GB or 80GB is better, and "is one version more compatible than the other with PS2 games?"

"The 40GB is the best for those on a budget," responds a well-meaning video game enthusiast, but another gamer thinks he should get the 60GB "because it can play any PS2 game through direct hardware emulation." When someone suggests getting an 80GB model for the larger disk space, a fourth person responds that it is a "waste of money," since it "uses software emulation for backward compatibility" and the hard drive can be upgraded cheaply at a later time. In the end, these well-meaning PlayStation 3 owners probably caused the potential buyer to be even more confused than before. One thing the parent has learned is that no matter which model he chooses, he is going to be faced with trade-offs. And the last thing he wants to do is spend hundreds of dollars on the wrong console.

In *The Paradox of Choice*, Barry Schwartz (2004) observes that, when faced with trade-offs, people tend to avoid decisions. He cites several examples ranging from buying a new CD-player to closing a public hospital. In each case, when the subject was given one choice, the decision was easier. When more options were added, subjects were more likely to avoid the decision altogether. For example, when given the option of closing a poorly performing hospital or keeping it open, most legislators chose to close the hospital. However, when faced with the choice of closing one of two poorly performing hospitals, legislators tried to avoid making a decision. The same was true for shoppers who were given the option of buying a Sony CD player in a limited time sale. Most people chose to purchase the CD player. Yet when customers were given the choice between two different CD players, both priced very low, more people walked away with nothing.

The problem with too many choices is that people are faced with opportunity costs. In order to select one option, they must give up something else, and the trade-offs associated with that decision can cause most people to feel remorseful and unhappy. Schwartz points out that "the cumulative cost of adding options to one's choice set can reduce satisfaction. It may even make a person miserable."

For some, the solution to this dilemma is easy: choose the "best" option. However, exactly what is "best"? It will depend on the customer and his/her needs. For those with financial constraints who are concerned about cost, the extra money spent buying the best options available for a particular console could be spent on games, accessories, or even groceries and other necessities.

Even when price is not an issue, the definition of a top-of-the-line gaming console is not always clear. For example, is a PlayStation 3 with a 60GB hard drive and nearly 100 percent backward compatibility for PS2 games the best console, or the 80GB console that comes with a free game and 90 percent backward compatibility? Even though few customers were in a position to benefit from the backward compatibility offered on some PS3s, by forcing customers to choose between backward compatibility and a lower price, Sony was encouraging customers to postpone their decision until they could better evaluate the trade-offs.

Sony tried its best to avoid dropping the price of the PS3, but instead offered upgraded models for the same price. The 60GB launch version was replaced with an 80GB model that included a free game. Later, the 80GB version was replaced with a 160GB version that also included a free game. Clearly, by waiting, customers were rewarded with more disk space and free games. Wait long enough, however, and potential customers could be persuaded to purchase a competing console. By the time the 160GB PS3 was released, Microsoft had rectified a number of the hardware issues that plagued early Xbox 360 consoles. At this point, a late adopter who was leaning toward the PS3 for its greater reliability might be persuaded to purchase an Xbox 360 instead.

Eventually, Sony was persuaded to develop a less costly console for budget conscious consumers. By eliminating some less used features that added to the cost, Sony was able to bring the price down by $100. The decision was clearly the right one, as sales immediately began to improve. However, the lower price was not all that attracted customers to the 40GB console. Even though it lacked PS2 compatibility and SACD playback, some people argued that it was the best console, because it was quieter and more energy efficient, and because its wireless controllers offered greater range. For movie enthusiasts, noise is an important consideration, but what if you are a movie enthusiast who also enjoys listening to high-definition SACD audio disks? Suddenly you are faced with new trade-offs between a quieter console and one with SACD playback.

Nintendo customers faced no such dilemmas. Every console was the same and every console was fully backward compatible with GameCube games. Even the packaging was minimalist in its lack of pictures and words. From a distance, "Wii" appeared to be the only word displayed over a Spartan white background. Upon closer inspection, an inconspicuous blue label in the upper right corner announced, "Wii Sports Game Included."

The price remained consistent at $249 for the first three years the Wii was on the market. A Wii customer in 2009 essentially received the exact same console as a Wii customer in 2006, for the exact same price, and with the exact same features and free games. Henry Ford once famously said about his highly successful Model-T motor car, "The customer can have any color he wants so long as it's black." Likewise, Wii owners can have any color they want as long as it is white. Of course, limiting the number of choices also helps keep manufacturing costs low.

The Need for Compelling Games

One way to extend the life of a console is to continue offering compelling games and game peripherals. So far, Nintendo has demonstrated its talent for doing just that.

For years, dance mats gave players the option of using their feet to play games. When Nintendo introduced *Wii Fit*, critics assailed it for its limited controls and resemblance to a bathroom scale. Yet once again Nintendo proved the naysayers wrong. In its first year on the market, *Wii Fit* sold more than 14 million units and generated $1.2 billion in revenues, outselling *Halo 3* (8.1 million copies), *Gears of War* (5 million copies), and *Grand Theft Auto IV* (4 million copies).[2] More importantly, it helped maintain the sales momentum for the Wii. In Japan, "40 percent of the people that [Nintendo] surveyed said that they bought a Wii in order to play Wii Fit" (Kohler 2008).

On the surface, the *Wii Fit* Balance Board was simpler than dance pads used in *Dance Dance Revolution*. For instance, all the arrows and buttons were gone. Inside, however, the balance board had sensors that measured shifts in weight,

---

2   Figures represent total sales up to January 15, 2009

centers of gravity, and movement. As a result, the balance board provided a much more versatile experience than could be achieved with a dance mat.

Early television commercials emphasized the basic fitness functions of *Wii Fit*. By stepping on and off the controller or by swaying from side to side, users could perform a number of exercises similar to those commonly found on television aerobics programs. However, unlike dance mats that had very limited use outside dancing games, the *Wii Fit* Balance Board could be adapted for use in sports games, puzzle games, and first person shooters. Marketing studies conducted by Nintendo in Japan found that 60 percent of *Wii Fit* purchasers were males in their 30s. More importantly, actual usage mirrored the demographics of Japan as a whole. "Everyone in the family is playing it," observed *Wii Fit* creator Shigeru Miyamoto (Kohler 2008).

One of the first standalone games to take advantage of the balance board was *Shaun White Snowboarding: Road Trip*. Gamers extolled the realism of snowboarding on the Wii, not for the visual details, which were reminiscent of games developed for the original PlayStation more than a decade ago, but for the system's ability to interpret the user's full body movements. On Amazon. com (2009) *Shaun White Snowboarding* for the Wii earned a user rating of 4.5 stars out of five, compared to only three stars for the Xbox 360 and PlayStation 3 versions. One Wii owner expressed her enthusiasm for the game. "I'm in my 50s, and I absolutely love this game," she noted.

> When you lean to the side, you go in that direction. When you lower yourself and then quickly straighten your legs, shifting your weight to the balls of your feet, your character jumps. You are in constant motion, using the board and the Wiimote to help with some of the more complex movements and tricks. Using the balance board you can just get onboard and play right away, without a big learning curve. It gets more difficult and there are tricks to be learned as you progress through the slopes, but you can have fun right from the start.

Once again, what set the Wii version of the game apart from its high-definition cousins was its intuitive ease of use. Consider for a moment the control scheme used for the PlayStation 3 version. There was a total of 74 button combinations that controlled movements and tricks for *Shaun White Snowboarding*. For example, depending on where the player was in the game, pressing the R2 button could mean any one of the following: jump, pump, tweak, time forward, time back, or big air. In contrast, the Wii version was controlled by seven different body movements on the balance board. To jump, the player simply crouched down. Turning was achieved by leaning back or forward. Advanced tricks were achieved through a combination of movement and pressing one of two buttons on the Wii Remote, and because the movements were based on real life experience, they were both intuitive and easier to remember.

For most users, the fact that the Xbox 360 and PlayStation 3 versions offered stunning photorealistic imagery of exotic locations, such as Switzerland, Japan, Chile and Park City, Utah didn't matter. Owners of the game derided it for its lack of story and poor controls. "The graphics are terrific in most areas," explained an Xbox 360 owner. "The mountains look great from afar and whether you're heading down the mountain or looking up, it all looks terrific." However, when it came to game play, he was less impressed.

> *My biggest complaint with this game is the controls. As an avid gamer, I can quickly adjust to almost any control setup, but this was really bad. The controls are not set up well for doing tricks, which is why most people tend to just rotate, or do flips.*

Professional reviewers likewise extolled the virtues of the Wii version over its Xbox 360 and PS3 cousins. "*Shaun White Snowboarding: Road Trip* nails the controls, taking full advantage of the unique opportunities offered by the Wii." wrote Gamespot reviewer Tom McShea (2008). "… movement is so enjoyable that you'll gladly replay the same goals over again just to tilt and twist your way back down the slopes."

McShea was not so kind in his review of the Xbox 360 and PS3 versions. "Even as a pure snowboarding game, Shaun White comes up way short. Mindlessly performing tricks either by yourself or with friends can be enjoyable for a while, but the lack of depth ensures your attention won't be grabbed for long."

Not only did the Xbox 360 and PS3 versions fall short, they were so similar to each other that McShea decided to use the same review for both versions. "The Xbox 360 and PlayStation 3 offered an unfocused and often boring rendition of the popular winter sport," he concluded. "Thankfully, the Wii version is a completely different experience." Moreover, with the focus squarely on the intuitive use of the balance board, McShea was willing to overlook the Wii version's lower quality graphics, describing "the cartoony aesthetics" as "vivid and eye-catching." The key differentiator that made *Shaun White Snowboarding* so enjoyable was the balance board.

The Complacency Trap

At E3 2009, representatives of the media seemed underwhelmed by Nintendo's offering relative to competitors. The most innovative product it offered was the *Wii Vitality Sensor*, a heart rate monitor that could be connected to the Wii remote to measure fitness and promote relaxation. "Nintendo seems to be getting just the slightest bit smug," complained Troy Wolverton (2009) of the *San Jose Mercury News*. "The company's presentation included no celebrities, few real surprises in terms of games or new accessories and was kept to a relatively curt 72 minutes."

Many of the new products showcased at E3 looked identical to products revealed at previous E3 events. Take *Wii Sports Resort*, a game that looked almost identical to *Wii Sports*. Its only advantage was its ability to use Wii MotionPlus, an extension to the Wii remote that increased the controller's sensitivity. Mini games like table tennis and golf were "retreads" of previously released games, complained JC Fletcher of Joystiq, an online gaming magazine. "Nintendo must be very confident that MotionPlus improves these games significantly." Developers were skeptical, however. "[MotionPlus] didn't offer a notable improvement to the input mechanisms of our primarily ranged combat game," noted Eric Nofsinger, Sega's chief creative officer (Fletcher 2009).

Could the success of the Wii and *Wii Fit* eventually cause a repeat of the 1990s, when Nintendo was the undisputed leader in video game entertainment, but saw its lead slip quickly slip away when it failed to keep up with competitors? As we saw in earlier chapters, Nintendo's success blinded it to the fact that its products no longer fulfilled the changing needs of consumers. For example, it took several years for Nintendo to finally abandon cartridge-based gaming, but by then Sony had a significant lead.

Nintendo is once again falling into the trap of complacency. In the 1990s, the company overextended the Mario franchise with poorly thought out educational games. Over time, one game began to look like another. Products that were revolutionary in the 1980s seemed tedious and repetitive in the 1990s. The same holds true for *Wii Sports Resort* and other avatar sports games. Increasingly, the games of 2009 are looking like the games of 2006. With fewer of the innovations needed to keep its sales momentum, Nintendo could quickly lose market share to Sony and Microsoft. Both companies were caught off guard by Nintendo's success, and have been scrambling to find new ways to win back customers.

Successful companies are often the last to respond to changes in the business environment. "Competency dependence becomes a self-destructive habit when it limits your vision and blinds you to other opportunities," notes Emory University's Jagdish Sheth (2007). A classic example is the U.S. auto industry. In the 1990s, Detroit developed the most fuel efficient commercially viable automobiles in the world, mid sized sedans that achieved more than 65 miles per gallon. Yet they failed to bring the cars to market, because of the success of SUVs, trucks, and large cars. Instead, Toyota became the industry leader in fuel efficiency, despite the fact that its cars were smaller and less advanced than Detroit's.

Detroit had good reason to abandon its fuel efficient "supercars." Adjusting for inflation, gasoline was cheaper than at any time in history. Gas-guzzling SUVs, like the Ford Explorer, GM Hummer, and Dodge Durango accounted for more than 35 percent of new car sales. Moreover, introducing new cars can be a costly affair as companies retool factories and line up new suppliers. At the time, many thought Toyota was foolish to release the Prius. Yet Toyota believed that rising automobile ownership in developing countries, such as India and China, would eventually strain world oil supplies, resulting in rising fuel prices.

Despite the availability of cheap fuel, the Prius was an immediate success. It was particularly popular with environmentally conscious consumers who were more concerned about global warming than gas prices. The initial success of the Prius caught Toyota by surprise in much the same way as the Wii's success surprised Nintendo. "I did not envisage such a major success at that time," admitted Toyota president Katsuaki Watanabe (Taylor 2006). After initially projecting sales of 1,000 vehicles per month, the company had to quickly ramp up production to twice that number. Like Nintendo, Toyota's products appealed to a segment of the market that was previously ignored. In Nintendo's case it was casual gamers, in Toyota's it was environmentalists.

A decade later, the picture has changed. After a rapid run-up in oil prices that reached $150 a barrel in 2008, GM and Chrysler were forced into bankruptcy and, for a time, Toyota became the world's largest carmaker. Ford avoided bankruptcy by leveraging its assets and by offering some of the most fuel efficient cars in Europe. The company used its international success to subsidize its U.S. losses.

The picture is also changing for the video game industry. The wide availability of broadband Internet has increased the value of online services, including online games, movies, music, and social networking. In addition, more people are buying high-definition televisions. In both online services and graphics, the Wii is woefully behind the competition.

Nintendo has not revealed any significant innovations in the last year. And why should it? Like Detroit in the 1990s, it can't keep up with current demand. Rather than improve in areas that currently have little value to consumers, it has decided to produce more of the same types of products that have been the mainstay of its success for the past few years, namely sports games and peripherals. In a 2007 conference call with investors, Iwata seemed indifferent when asked about Nintendo's plans for the next generation. Console innovation is a "new weapon in the fight against other consoles," he said, "but today's situation is such that we are not desperate for any new weapons at all" (Hinkle 2007). ·

However, innovation is critical to all firms' success, including Nintendo's. Nintendo needs to keep moving forward with both incremental and radical innovations that provide value to casual gamers. Their biggest challenge is to maintain the momentum created by the early success of the Wii. There are already signs that the market for new Wii consoles is slowing down. Eventually, it will reach a point when most potential Wii owners will have purchased a console, and sales will be driven by the need for replacements and upgrades. Nintendo has a reputation for building durable consoles that last far beyond the product life cycle. The fact that the Wii has no internal hard drive and runs on relatively low power processors means there is less that can go wrong.

In the future, Nintendo could offer a high-definition Wii as a way to attract new buyers and encourage existing owners to trade up. Yet as we have seen, performance seems to have little impact on the purchasing behavior of casual gamers. Since consumers already have a wide variety of alternatives to fill their high-definition needs, the only way Nintendo can continue to compete against more technically advanced opponents is to continue offering better content and controls. By itself, Wii HD will not be enough to win the next generation race.

Recently, the Wii has begun to lose momentum. In June 2009, the Wii's market share was 47.2 percent, down from 65.6 percent in April 2008. Early 2009 sales saw declines for both Nintendo and Sony. Meanwhile, Microsoft saw a year over year increase, despite the economic recession. In the end, Iwata may wish he had been developing "new weapons" to prepare for the next battle in the ongoing console wars.

10

Game Development and the Rise of Casual Games

In recent years there has been a transformation in the way people think about games. In the past, gaming was the domain of young males, and game studios devoted considerable resources to titles that appealed almost exclusively to this demographic. Today, as development costs skyrocket and video game companies compete for the same customers, more studios are finding success in markets that traditionally have not been well served by the video game industry. Today's gamers include women, parents, and even senior citizens who enjoy playing puzzle games, arcade games, and sports games. Among 25–34 year olds, women gamers now outnumber men by a considerable margin.

Casual gaming comes in different forms. Some companies are reviving classic arcade games from the 1970s and 1980s that have nostalgic appeal for audiences that grew up during the era of Atari and the NES. Other companies specialize in puzzle games like *Tetris* and *Bejeweled* that are distributed on handheld devices, on Internet websites, or on low-cost CD-ROM packages. And as we saw in an earlier chapter, Nintendo created a new genre of fitness titles by combining simple sports games with its Wiimote controller.

In this chapter we will look at how game development has changed and why the traditional approach to video game marketing is no longer working. Under the new paradigm, large game companies have had to rethink the way they do business. The most successful ones are partnering with small innovative studios, creating tools that help facilitate community-based development, and focusing big-budget resources on their most successful franchises.

As we consider each of these approaches, we will show that development practices need to match the strategic objectives of each company. In the future, there will still be a market for big budget games that appeal mainly to young men, but as costs skyrocket, companies in that segment need to use their intellectual and financial resources in smarter, more focused, ways.

The Challenge of Complexity

By definition, something that is complex is difficult to understand. The complexity of the advanced graphics engines and processors utilized in the Xbox 360 and PS3 significantly increased the burden on software developers who sought to take advantage of these features. Development cycles stretched from 12 months for the previous generation consoles to up to 36 months for Xbox 360 and PS3 titles. As a result, fewer game developers were willing to stake their future on a single platform, preferring instead to spread their development costs over several platforms. For some developers, there was no other option. "When companies try to create these vast games that consumers really want," explained Shigeru Miyamoto, director and general manager of Nintendo Entertainment Analysis and Development, "they try and use every last bit of technology to create really incredible games" (Jones 2007). Miyamoto, an industry veteran who famously developed the original *Donkey Kong*, *Mario Brothers* and *Zelda* games, believed that "the development cost is going to be so high that they'll never be able to recoup it from sales." Cross-platform licensing was one way to reduce that risk.

Microsoft tried to facilitate development by creating a core set of developer tools, known as XNA, which allowed code to be shared across different Microsoft platforms. As a result, games developed for personal computers, such as *Final Fantasy XI* by Square Enix, could be more easily ported to the Xbox 360. Whereas *Final Fantasy* took about six months to port to the Xbox 360, Square Enix estimated that it could take up to three years and cost several million dollars to completely rewrite the code for the PS3.

In Table 10.1, the average unit game costs have been broken into several categories. Art, design and programming accounted for nearly half of the total retail cost of a next generation video game, while the remainder went to marketing, distribution and retail markup. Increasingly detailed computer-generated graphics and animation, much of which mirrored the special effects work normally associated with Hollywood studios, had the most impact on development costs. Programming costs, which included basic game play, artificial intelligence and online services, also increased.

Table 10.1   Video Game per Unit Cost: Next Generation Console Estimates

Item	Cost (S)	% of Total Cost
Art and design	15	25
Programming and engineering	12	20
Retail markup	12	20
Console license fee	7	12
Marketing	4	7
Market development fund	3	5
Manufacturing and packaging	3	5
Third-party licensing	3	5
Publisher profit	1	2
Total retail cost	60	100

Source: Forbes 2006.

Retail markup on a $60 title was about $12. Of this, *Forbes* estimated a net earnings contribution of only one dollar per title sold by large retailers, such as Best Buy and Wal-Mart (Rosmarin 2006).

The Nintendo Wii, on the other hand, was a much simpler system, which in turn helped reduce development costs. Brian Farrell, CEO of THQ Inc., one of the world's leading game developers, noted:

> *One of the things we like about the Wii is that development costs are nowhere near what they are on the PS3 and Xbox 360. It wasn't a whole new programming environment. So we had a lot of tools and tech that work in that environment. Costs could be as little as a third of the high-end next-generation titles. Maybe the range is a quarter to a half. (Sinclair 2006)*

As a result, Nintendo was able to boast a number of exclusive titles for the launch of the Wii, including highly rated games, such as *Zelda: Twilight Princess* and *WarioWare: Smooth Moves*. It also allowed Nintendo to include its popular *Wii Sports* title free with each console.

The Wii also had its drawbacks. For one, its relatively anemic processors limited the ability of developers to push the limits the way they could with leading edge hardware. Also, the lack of a hard drive made the Wii ill-suited for Internet-based game distribution. Both Microsoft's Xbox Live and Sony's PlayStation Network were significant distribution conduits for add-ons and new games that provided valuable ongoing revenue streams for game publishers.

Build or Buy

Video game development did not always require the creation of completely new software. Frequently, developers built upon existing software systems known as game engines. Game engines provided platforms that developers could reuse for different titles. They included systems for graphics, physics, artificial intelligence, and other functions. Engines provided developers with the tools needed to speed up development and reduce costs. Some studios created their own engines that could be used across multiple titles, while others purchased them from third party studios that specialized in these programs.

Game engines provided a way to limit costs by supplying a software system that provides the core functionality, around which developers build the storyline, artwork, and other frontend features. A well-known example was the Unreal Engine developed by Epic Games in the late 1990s. Unreal provides the game mechanics behind hundreds of first person shooters (FPS) on every major game platform, including best-sellers such as *Gears of War, Splinter Cell,* and *Unreal Tournament.* Since game engines could cost as much as $100 million to develop, it made sense to spread those costs over as many titles as possible. Using a proven engine also limited the risk of unforeseen software problems that could increase development and support costs.

Although the benefits of off-the-shelf game engines are clear, their increased use made it more difficult to distinguish one product from another. Nevertheless, big budget games have failed because of poorly developed engines. When UK developer Free Radical Design created its own artificial intelligence engine for the game *Haze,* it fell so short of expectations that the company was forced into administration (a form of bankruptcy protection). It wasn't that *Haze* was a bad game. It simply didn't measure up to the hundreds of other first-person shooters on the market. "I don't think we'd be in a big rush to build engine technology from the ground up again," noted *Haze* designer David Doak. "It's just a massive expense" (Boyes 2009).

With examples like Free Radical, it is not surprising that developers are shifting resources away from unproven concepts to focus on proven formulas. Four genres—sports, first-person shooters, racing, and crime-based action—already make up approximately three-quarters of all game sales, and their market share continues to grow.

Back to Basics: The Rise of Casual Games

The first games ever to appear on home consoles were casual games. Titles like *Pong, Frogger,* and *Pac-Man* could be played for a few minutes or a few hours. They did not require significant time commitments to learn how to play, they did not revolve around complex storylines and plot development, and in most cases they did not require strategic thinking. However, these games were simple for a reason; the hardware they were played on was not powerful enough to support more complex software.

Such simple products are the mainstay of the introductory phase of a product's life cycle, particularly for radical types of innovations. Because such innovations involve emerging technologies aimed at new markets, the introductory form of the product tends to be crude and simple relative to later generations of the product and appeals primarily to innovators and early adopters.

As the technology developed and consoles became more powerful, developers learned to tap into that power to offer more challenging titles. Nintendo was the first company to introduce story-based console games that had to be played through multiple stages. Most of these games followed a similar pattern. A hero sets out on a quest and encounters various enemies along the way. At the end of each level, the player must defeat a much stronger enemy, known as a boss. Each level becomes successively harder until the player reaches a climactic final boss and defeats the game.

This progression is typical of the growth stage of technology products. As more is learned about the technology and how to apply it, more features are added to the product making it more complex, but also providing more benefits. These attributes help to attract more customers who are usually referred to in marketing literature as the "early majority" of the adopter categories.

Over the years, the tried and true formula of multistage story-based games became the mainstay of the video game industry and casual games were relegated to the dustbin. Only on the PC did casual gaming still find an audience with titles like solitaire and minesweeper, which came included with every copy of the Microsoft Windows operating system. Solitaire was a particular favorite of executives who needed to kill time on long flights.

With the rise of the Internet in the late 1990s, more people began to play casual games online. However, it wasn't until the release of the Nintendo DS and Nintendo Wii that the casual gaming segment began to be taken seriously by large game publishers. Today, more companies are shifting resources away from hyper realism and focusing on alternative interfaces (like the Wiimote and Rock Band drum set), simple puzzle games, classic arcade games, and experimental games.

The lower cost of these games means that developers can afford to take greater risks. As a result, many of the most innovative titles are no longer coming from big budget studios, but from small developers who are producing inexpensive casual and party games. "Large developers have a tendency, in order to try to support future development, to make more conservative games and try to essentially find a way to make those games profitable," observed Shigeru Miyamoto. Whereas, independent developers "are able to let their own personality and their own kind of unique interests really flourish in the games that they are creating" (Kohler 2008).

This phenomenon was not unique to the video game industry. Once an industry has matured, major players commonly develop what Dorothy Leonard-Barton (1998) described as "core rigidities".

> That is, a firm's strengths are also—simultaneously—its weaknesses. The dimensions that distinguish a company competitively have grown up over time as an accumulation of activities and decisions that focus on one kind of knowledge at the expense of others. Companies, like people, cannot be skillful at everything.

In this case, video game companies have developed competencies in particular genres and styles of gameplay that have become so ingrained that it is difficult to develop new competencies. As a result, new firms, sometimes from outside the industry, become the innovators as they strive to enter new markets. Many of these companies are behind the renaissance in casual gaming. Some revived older gaming styles, while others have introduced radically new ways of playing games.

Casual games appealed to demographic segments not normally viewed as "gamers." According to the Casual Gaming Association, women made up 75 percent of the audience for casual games and more than 72 percent of casual gamers were over the age of 35. However, even core gamers turned to casual games for respite from the intensity of first-person shooters and time demands of adventure games. In fact, a significant part of their appeal came from the fact that players did not need to invest considerable time and effort to play them. Thus, they were ideal for situations when time was short, such as at train stops, on lunch breaks or between business meetings. And because most casual games did not require significant computing power, they were popular on handheld devices ranging from portable consoles to cell phones and mp3 players. Finally, the wide appeal of casual games made them popular at parties and family gatherings.

Retrogaming: Selling Nostalgia

There were two general categories of casual games: arcade-style games, and experimental games that explored new concepts, interfaces, and stories. The terms "retrogaming" and "old school gaming" usually referred to classic arcade games, such as *Pac-Man, Mario Brothers,* and *Tetris,* but could also include older role-playing games (RPG), strategy games, and first-person shooters. Some retrogamers collected obsolete hardware that allowed them to play classic games on the original platforms they were designed for. However, most titles were recompiled to run on modern systems or relied on emulation software.

Retrogamers had various motivations for playing classic games. Parents and older gamers felt nostalgia for the games that they played as children. They wanted to recreate that experience or share it with their children. Marketers of a wide range of goods recognized the importance nostalgia played in consumer purchasing behavior. Companies like Coca-Cola, General Mills, McDonald's, MillerCoors, Target and Unilever recently revived classic brands or used classic advertisements to appeal to an aging population. Classic products and brands provide consumers with a sense of comfort and security, according to Ric Hendee, marketing VP for Cotton Incorporated. "In a time of anxiety, people are seeking out brands they're comfortable with and they can trust."

In *The Past as Future: Nostalgia and Retrogaming in Digital Culture,* Jaakko Suominen (2007) of the University of Turku (Finland) explains that retrogaming has a social importance that helps define collective social experiences.

> In addition to the psychological level of an individual, the term contains
> a strong collective—if not even collectivising—dimension. In media
> culture, longing for something old is a mutual event, when referred to

> *such old moments, situations and experiences, which have been shared*
> *with friends and family or even with the nation or "the whole world".*

Suominen notes that nostalgia was particularly important to video game marketing in Japan, where video game companies "with the aid of quite clever pastiche and a slightly increased degree of difficulty attract those parents who play games with their children and who have played similar games already in the 80s."

Retrogaming not only appealed to the nostalgic sensibilities of older gamers. Younger gamers, many of whom were experiencing classic titles for the first time, turned to older titles from franchise games like *Zelda*, *Final Fantasy*, and *Metal Gear Solid* as a way to experience earlier episodes from their favorite stories. Interest in older titles paralleled the behavior of fans of television remakes like *Star Trek* and *Battlestar Galactica* who sought out the original series from decades past. For example, the highly successful reimaging of *Battlestar Galactica* beginning in 2003 resulted in a surge in DVD sales for the classic series from the late 1970s. Younger gamers may also have heard about great classic games from friends, online discussions, or news articles and simply wanted to experience these titles for themselves.

In many cases, classic games appealed to price-conscious gamers. For example, Sega offered 40 of its Genesis titles on a single PS3 or Xbox 360 disk for $30, Namco offered 8 of its classic titles for the PS2 and DS for $20, and Atari offered 80 classic games on one PC disk for $10. On Amazon, these value packages were consistently ranked among the top 10 best sellers for their respective publishers. The PS3 version of the *Sega Genesis Collection*, which featured classic games from the late 1980s and early 1990s, was Sega's fourth best-selling title on Amazon in May 2009.

Puzzle Games

The leading publisher of casual games was Seattle-based PopCap Games. PopCap was founded in 2000 by three developers who created a web-based puzzle game called *Bejeweled*. It was the height of the dotcom bubble and PopCap licensed its game to Microsoft for $1,500 per month. Within a few months, the NASDAQ crashed and nobody was investing in Internet companies. PopCap tried to sell *Bejeweled* for $65,000, but nobody was interested.

At the time, most Internet users still used dial-up telephone lines to connect to the web. *Bejeweled* fans petitioned PopCap for a downloadable version that could be played offline. Company founder John Vechey then realized that he could make more money selling the game directly to consumers than by licensing it to third-party web sites. People could still play these games online for free, but they could also pay a fee to download a copy to their personal computer for offline use. Downloadable games also typically came with "premium" content that was not available in the free version.

> *In the first month, we made $35,000, which was amazing for three guys. The next month we made $35,000. So we went to bigger companies like Yahoo Games and MSN Games. We said we can give you the web version now. We won't charge you that $1,500 a month anymore. And we asked them to put this downloadable version up. We could share revenues when people purchased the downloadable version. That created a casual games industry that became the start of the business model. (Takahashi 2008)*

According to Vechey, what made puzzle games so successful was that they never became outdated. As technology improved, big budget FPS and fantasy games quickly became dated as gamers turned their attention to the next big title. Therefore, the shelf life of these games was often short and publishers expected to make most of their money in the first year or two on the market. After that, all but the most successful big budget titles were relegated to the remainder bins at retailers and discount outlets. Games like *Bejeweled* and *Tetris* never became outdated because they did not depend on leading-edge technology to entice customers.

Once titles could be purchased for offline use, PopCap Games revenue took off. By 2008, the *Bejeweled* franchise sold more copies than leading FPS franchises like *Halo*. Yet the cost to develop casual games was insignificant compared with core gaming titles. Most of PopCap's titles, which in 2009 numbered about 35, cost between $200,000 and $1 million to develop.

In 2005, PopCap created its own open-source development kit for Windows XP to encourage programmers to produce casual games. The wide availability of free and inexpensive development kits contributed to an explosion in casual game development by hobbyists. Most part-time developers had limited resources and created games for personal enjoyment rather than financial gain. Given these limitations, it was not surprising that most casual games were written for PCs, handhelds, and web-based applets, such as Adobe Flash, Shockwave, and Java.

For sites that hosted these games, community-based development was a boon. Advertising supported online gaming sites like Yahoo! Games, Miniclips, and MSN Games had a nearly unlimited ability to host free games, and the steady stream of new content enticed users to repeatedly visit the most proactive of these sites. In 2008, traffic on advertising supported casual games sites increased by 42 percent, while total Internet traffic increased by only 4 percent.

Online Distribution: Opportunities and Challenges

Even as revenue from casual games and console games continued to hit record numbers, sales of traditional CD-ROM based PC games declined for four years in a row. In 2008, despite the popularity of massively multiplayer online role-playing games like *World of Warcraft*, PC game sales declined 21 percent in North America to just over $700 million.

Game distributors attempted to slow the decline in PC game sales by distributing games online. The most popular of these was Steam, the online distribution arm of Valve Corporation, a major developer of big budget PC games. However, even Steam derived a significant portion of its revenue from casual games. In May 2009, one of Steam's top 10 best-selling titles was a PopCap game called *Plants vs. Zombies*, an arcade style action-strategy game in which players had to use plants to defend their homes from attacking hordes of zombies. *Plants vs. Zombies* could be downloaded as a standalone title from Steam for $10 or as part of a $99 PopCap bundle that included 30 casual game titles.

One of the benefits of Internet distributors was their ability to offer online game play. In 2009, Steam registered between 1 million and 2 million concurrent online players of its Internet based games. The main cost was in providing the bandwidth and servers needed to support sudden surges in game play. This could result when new games were released or for special events, such as free gameplay weekends occasionally offered by Steam to promote its service. The popularity of sites like Steam, Xbox Live, and PopCap Games gave independent studios the opportunity for wide exposure, and because these services cut out the retailer, most of the revenue went directly to the developers.

Garry's Mod was an example of an independently developed program sold directly on Steam. *Garry's Mod* was created in 2005 by Garry Newman using Steam's software development kit. It allowed users to manipulate and customize objects for other games offered on Steam. By the end of 2008, *Gary's Mod* posted cumulative revenues of $3 million of which 60 percent went directly to the developer. However, few independent developers on Steam were as successful as Garry Newman. John Warner, for example, developed a small game titled *Raycatcher*, a music pattern matching game that sold for $5. "The money we're making off *Raycatcher* doesn't justify working on a project for a long period of time," Warner complained.

> *I can't support myself on it. Especially when you release a game and it has bugs, and you have to fix them. In a certain sense, when you release something for money, it's almost like you create a liability for yourself. (Good 2009)*

Although the Internet allowed games to be distributed as never before, it also posed new challenges. Chief among them was piracy. On the day it was released, *Raycatcher* sold 1,000 copies on Steam. However, another 35,000 pirated copies were distributed through illegal file-sharing sites. Warner hoped to circumvent pirates by using in-game advertising instead of game purchases to generate revenue. The challenge was finding sponsors to support the game.

For developers like John Warner, the casual game market may not be the profit machine that they had hoped for. As new development tools continue to drive down costs, more casual games will be offered by independent developers and small-game studios. As the market becomes increasingly saturated with amateur titles, better titles can become lost in the noise. Satoru Iwata, president and CEO of Nintendo, was concerned that many of those titles did not represent the best gaming experiences. Instead, low quality games could give casual gamers the wrong impression. "If a person is disappointed by the software he or she has chosen," Iwata explained, "they may say, 'I won't play games anymore.'"

> *The increase in software titles per se is good, but we cannot be content with the situation. We have to recognize that our customers have a limited amount of attention, we have to struggle to find out a way to communicate what they really want to know and we have to be considerate so that we will not betray our customers' expectations. This*

is going to be an increasingly important mission for us. (Nintendo of America 2007)

As casual gaming increased in popularity, Microsoft created a programming kit to encourage casual game development for the Xbox 360 console. The framework, known as XNA, allowed anyone with a PC to create games for the Xbox 360.

In 2008, Microsoft created its own online XNA development community. For a nominal fee, XNA members could submit their work to peer review, and those games that passed scrutiny could then be sold on the Xbox Live marketplace. Microsoft's publishing terms were generous, with 70 percent of any revenue generated going directly to the developer. In addition, no deductions were made for Microsoft-initiated advertising and promotion. In an announcement to community members, Microsoft hailed the success of its developer program.

You have been producing games at an incredible rate. On average, 10 games are added to the channel every week totaling more than 200 unique titles in only four months. This has never been done before on any console, so when we started this program we weren't sure how large the demand would be. In just four short months, you've shown us the incredible growth potential for community-generated content on Xbox 360. (XNA Creators Club 2009)

Microsoft found other ways to tap into the casual gaming phenomenon. For example, it created the Xbox 360 Arcade to specifically appeal to casual gamers by including five arcade titles, *Boom-Boom Rocket, Feeding Frenzy, Luxor 2, Pac-Man Championship Edition,* and *Uno.* Microsoft also offered Xbox Live Arcade (XLA), an online download service integrated into Xbox Live. More than 200 titles were available for purchase on XLA. Prices ranged from $3 to $15 per title and included classics, like *Chess* and *Frogger,* and newer titles, like PopCap's *Peggle* and *Bejeweled 2.*

Nintendo realized early on that impressive graphics were not the main selling point of most games. The Wii, for example, had severely limited graphical capabilities, and yet it led the market in console sales consistently year after year. Unlike Sony, which offered a limited number of PS1 and PS2 titles in its online store, Nintendo offered Wii owners the opportunity to play a large number of titles originally designed for previous generation consoles. In

North America, Nintendo made available more than 300 previous-generation titles in its "virtual console" library. Most titles cost between $5 and $12 each, and included games originally developed for NEC, Sega, Commodore, and Nintendo consoles.

One constantly complained-about limitation on the Wii was the lack of an internal hard drive. With only 512MB of flash storage, the Wii was ill-suited for downloading and storing games. Owners had to use external memory cards to store more than a few purchased games, and any games stored on external devices had to be moved back to the Wii's internal memory before they could be played. Purchased games were also restricted to the system that was originally used to download the game. Therefore, a Wii owner could not play downloaded games on a friend's system. In order to enjoy games while away from home, Wii owners had to take their entire system with them. To make matters worse, saved game data could not be stored on the same external memory card as the game. The combined result of these limitations made playing retro games unnecessarily complicated.

Sony took a less restrictive approach to online purchases. After all, since gamers who purchased titles on Blu-ray disks could play their games on any PS3 system, they should be able to do the same for downloaded titles. At a time when film studios, music labels, and software firms were finding new ways to prevent users from copying and sharing content, Sony encouraged gamers to share their downloaded games with friends. Once purchased, downloaded content could be played on up to five PS3 consoles. In the days leading up to the PS3's launch in 2006, Jack Tretton, President and CEO of Sony Computer Entertainment of America presented Sony's liberal file sharing policy as an important selling point. "You can send that content to four other friends for that initial investment. We want to get the game in as many hands as possible" (Kohler 2006).

Sony had its own list of casual games available on the PlayStation Network, including many of the same titles available on Xbox Live Arcade. The PlayStation 3 also had the ability to run PlayStation One titles, but few of the most popular titles were available for download. Nevertheless, fans sought out titles on the secondary market, often driving up prices in the process.

Lunar 2 was one such title. The RPG was originally released on the Sega Saturn system in 1998, followed by a Sony PlayStation port one year later. Game reviewers gave *Lunar 2* mixed reviews. A 2001 review on Gamespot, for example, gave it a modest 7.2 out of 10 rating. Even at that time, the reviewer felt the game was dated, noting that "forward-minded gamers will probably want to look toward newer games for their RPG fix" (Shoemaker 2001). Yet nearly a decade later, modern gamers looked beyond the dated graphics that placed it on par with a Nintendo DS or Game Boy title. Gamespot members gave the title an impressive 8.9 average score and praised its "superb story line and memorable characters." On eBay, used copies regular sold for more than $60, while new and mint copies sold for between $100 and $230.

Lunar 2 was not the only PlayStation One title that fetched premium prices on grey market sites. *Metal Gear Solid, Final Fantasy VII, Suikoden II,* and *Xenogears* were a few of the older PlayStation titles that sold for more than $100 each on eBay. Fans criticized Sony for not making classic PlayStation titles available for download. "There are a lot of people who can't afford eBay prices," observed one collector. They hoped that North America and Europe would eventually follow Japan, where the most popular PS1 games were available to purchase online.

The Role of Independent Developers in Video Game Innovation

Although Sony did not do as good a job as Microsoft and Nintendo in making classic games available on current generation consoles, it excelled at developing partnerships with small independent studios who were leading the way in innovative game design. The spectrum of games developed by these independent studios often pushed the boundaries of technology and redefined the way we think about games. And with virtually unlimited storage space, the PS3 had the ability to locally store hundreds of these titles on a single console.

Independent studios, like independent filmmakers, were typically more innovative than large studios. What they lacked was the funds to bring grand ideas to fruition. For Sony, the cost of supporting independent studios was relatively small. As a result, Sony had little to lose if a concept failed. If, on the other hand, a concept proved successful, Sony not only stood to gain from the revenues generated by the game, but from its ongoing exclusive relationship with some of the brightest minds in the video game industry.

Sony's use of "open innovation", a term coined by Henry Chesbrough (2006), suggests that it recognizes that it cannot conceive, design, develop and market new products and services all on its own. No firm has all the knowledge capabilities, money or time needed to do innovation alone in today's world. So, some firms are adopting an open innovation approach that "assumes that firms can and should use external ideas as well as internal ideas, and internal and external paths to market, as the firms look to advance their technology."

Flower is a good example of how independent studios were leading the way in video game innovation. Developed for the PS3 by Thatgamecompany, a seven person studio based in Los Angeles, California, it challenged the way people think about video games. *Flower* was the brainchild of Xinghan Chen, who immigrated to the U.S. in 2003 from Shanghai, China to pursue a master's degree at the University of Southern California. While at U.S.C., Chen was lead developer for an experimental game called *Cloud*, which used atmospheric modeling to tell the story of a seriously ill child whose only escape is to travel among the clouds. *Cloud* combined serene orchestral music with lush hand-painted visuals to create what could best described as interactive art.

The success of *Cloud* (available as a free download for Windows) prompted Chen to start his own game studio with fellow U.S.C. graduate student Kellee Santiago. At first, Thatgamecompany faced the same challenge as most innovation-based startups, namely finding investors to support an unproven concept. *Cloud*, after all, was an experimental game that was made free to the public. The fact that it had won several awards did not guarantee its commercial success. Chen and Santiago began to "pitch the grand idea" of a commercial version of *Cloud* to American game distributors.

> *Quickly, we realized that based on the experience we had fresh out of school and the ridiculous budget we asked, there was simply no one who would take the risk with us. (Dillon 2008)*

Eventually, they were able to win the support of Sony, which had been looking for exclusive content for PlayStation Network, particularly games that could take advantage of the unique features of the PS3. "They're made to show off a high-definition gaming experience that only the PS3 can offer," explained Peter Dille, senior vice president of marketing at Sony Computer Entertainment America.

> *They are not retreads; they are not experiences I've had before that are nostalgic—and again, there is a role for nostalgia in this category— but they are things that are new and imaginative and show off the*

technology under the hood in the PS3 in ways that other games just can't. (Nutt 2009)

Sony didn't just want a commercial version of *Cloud*, but a whole new game that would push the limits of high-definition video and sound, and it was willing to commit the entire development cost to see it happen. That provided the studio with the funds needed to push the limits of their creative ability, such as simultaneously rendering up to 200,000 individual blades of grass. Kellee Santiago explained that such a feat would have been impossible on any other system. "But, it's one of the pros of knowing your game is exclusive to a specific system—you can really design everything towards that one platform." *Flower* first became available on February 12, 2009 as a download on the PlayStation Network. *Flower* not only offered some of the most stunning visuals and music ever seen on a video game platform, it was, in the words of IGN reviewer Ryan Clements (2009), "one of the most elegantly crafted gaming experiences of all time."

Because of their small development budgets, high-quality downloadable games showed a profit much sooner than big budget games like *Metal Gear Solid 4*. More importantly, it provided console makers like Sony with an opportunity to build ties with talented developers. For Sony, games like *Flower* were part of a shift away from first-person shooters towards games with broad appeal. "Over time, we'll continue to build the install base against the core gamer … but we'll also be broadening the market to social gamers, casual gamers, A/V aficionados that we can get involved in gaming for the first time," noted Dille.

Independent studios that pushed the boundaries of game design were "not really necessarily looking to appeal to a mass market," noted Simon Carless, chairman of the Independent Games Festival.

> *They are really looking to appeal to certain people that like alternative games … they value design over profits, they create games as an exploration of a medium or as an expression, they take bigger risks in the process, and they work in small teams (VanBurkleo 2009).*

As such, the path is not as straightforward as a big budget first-person shooter that can build on proven concepts or use pre-built engines. Independent developers must deal with vague unproven concepts, such as the time when Chen arrived at his studio and declared that he wanted to do a game about flowers. He began by showing his team pictures of flowers he had downloaded from the Internet. He then told them to begin brainstorming. He offered no models, no outline, and no objectives, just the idea of making a game about flowers. "It definitely took a while to finalize the gameplay experience," recalled Santiago.

> *Developing* Flower *was not a straight-forward experience. We initially began with an extremely vague and difficult subject. It took us more than a dozen prototypes to settle on the gameplay. We went through so many different versions of stories and characters, and we ended up not using any of them. Because we are innovating on the experience, the process is very much like walking in the mist. Our destination is very exciting; however, the path leading to it is not clear. Nobody's left any footprints for us to follow. There is quite a bit of trial and error. But once someone sees the light-tower in the distance, we hack through bushes and jump over ditches to reach there. It's hard and painful, but the final view is worth the effort. (Steen 2009)*

As painful as the process of traveling into uncharted territory may be, it is also liberating, as independent developer Matt Gilgenbach explained.

> *The best part about being indie is that we have complete ownership of the product. We are making the game that we want to make the way we want to make it. We don't have to compromise our vision in order to make a game more marketable or to appeal to every demographic if we don't want to. We don't have to hit a specified release date, so we can take the time to make the game meet our high standards. (VanBurkleo 2009)*

LittleBigPlanet: User Generated Content for the YouTube Generation

One of Sony's more successful partnerships was with Media Molecule, a UK-based independent studio responsible for the hit platform game *LittleBigPlanet*. Platformers, games in which users must jump over objects to get from one platform to the next, were almost as old as the industry itself. The earliest platformers were developed by Nintendo in the early 1980s and included titles like *Mario Bros.* and *Donkey Kong*. Soon platformers became all the rage, spawning successful franchises like *Sonic the Hedgehog, Castlevania,* and *Prince of Persia.*

The introduction of the PlayStation in 1995 ushered in a new era of 3-D gaming and the beginning of the first-person shooter craze. Platformers continued to be developed, but mainly for handhelds like the Game Boy and DS. Some developers also built 3-D platform games for home consoles, but they were never as popular as their 2-D ancestors.

One of the most innovative platformers developed for home consoles was *Psychonauts*. First introduced in 2005, *Psychonauts* was about a summer camp for psychic children who used their powers to defeat evil. Critics praised the game for its unusual story and humor. Among its many awards and honors was the coveted E3 "Best Original Game" award for 2006. Nevertheless, *Psychonauts* sold fewer than 100,000 copies, eventually forcing its publisher, New Jersey-based Majesco, out of the home console business.

On the heels of *Psychonauts'* failure, Media Molecule founder Mark Healey went to Sony with the idea of building a 2-D platformer for the PS3. Healey was unfazed by the lack of interest in platformers, because he believed that his concept was somehow different. Unlike other platformers, *LittleBigPlanet* encouraged users to develop and modify game content, essentially creating their own customized games. Nevertheless, Healey was appropriately worried that Sony would "think we were a bunch of madmen." Sony quickly put those fears to rest.

> They immediately saw the potential, and at this stage we weren't showing much (a simple prototype of a character running around a physical 2d world and lots of arm waving and high concepts). It's a credit to Sony that they saw the concept, accepted our credentials, and just left us to run with the project without ever interfering. (Cornelisse 2008)

By this time, video sharing sites like YouTube and information sharing sites like Wikipedia had already demonstrated the concept of user-generated content. *LittleBigPlanet* extended this concept into the realm of video games. In a public announcement of the partnership, Michael Denny, Vice President for Sony Computer Entertainment Worldwide Studios Europe explained Sony's support for the concept.

> We were immediately struck by Media Molecule's ambitions for what a next-gen title could be. Innovation is the key to our shared vision

and everyone here at [Sony] is highly impressed by Media Molecule's ability to deliver on that vision. (Media Molecule 2006)

Sony's intuition was right. Gamers, who had for years been inundated with first-person shooters, were clamoring for something different. Just as the Wii changed the way gamers think about controllers, *LittleBigPlanet* changed the way people looked at games. Instead of being passive bystanders, gamers could now take the front seat and customize games to their own liking.

This phenomenon is illustrative of the broad trend towards customer co-creation of value. In an increasingly networked world, C.K. Prahalad and Venkatram Ramaswamy (2003) argue:

> *Neither value nor innovation can any longer be successfully and sustainably generated through a company-centric, product-and-service-focused prism. A new point of view is required, one that allows individual customers to actively co-construct their own consumption experiences through personalized interaction, thereby co-creating unique value for themselves.*

However, despite the success of games like *Flower*, *LittleBigPlanet*, and *Garry's Mod*, Simon Carless believed that exclusive partnerships with large distributors increased the risk for small studios.

> *As an indie, if you're putting all your eggs in one basket, that's actually kind of risky—especially as an indie when you're only making one game at a time. In some cases it makes sense to only put it on one medium, but what if you put your game on only one medium, then it's a massive flop and you can't make games for a living anymore? (VanBurkleo 2009)*

Mark Healey defended his company's exclusive relationship with Sony, which not only provided access to the advanced features only available with the Cell processor, but also provided the funding needed to fully tap into his team's creativity.

> *We don't have an awful lot of competition out there. It would feel far more risky to be making an FPS or a racing game knowing that you only have a window of a couple of weeks before 'the next big game' comes out and eclipses yours. Hopefully, LittleBigPlanet differentiates itself enough from the other games around at the moment that we'll be*

around a lot longer. And I think it shows a bit of vision on Sony's part to see the importance of a game like LBP in order to differentiate the PS3 even more from the competition and give more exclusive reasons to buy a PS3. (Cornelisse 2008)

The Future of Big Budget Titles

Although the explosion of inexpensive casual, experimental, and retro games posed a challenge for large publishers like EA and Square Enix that invest tens of millions of dollars in each title, there will always be a market for big budget blockbusters. However, publishers will need to be more selective about the titles they bring to market. They can no longer afford to have a large portfolio of titles. Instead, they will need to focus resources on games that stand out from the competition.

Electronic Arts (EA) was the world's largest game publisher, best known for popular sports games, such as *Madden Football* and *Tiger Woods Golf*. However, EA also published games in nearly every category and for every system, including First Person Shooters (*Half-Life*), life simulators (*Sims, Spore*), racing games (*Need for Speed*), film tie-ins (*Harry Potter, The Godfather*), music games (*Rock Band*), interactive fitness (*Sports Active*), and puzzles (*Scrabble*). A search of online retailer Amazon revealed more than 500 EA titles, including several educational and utility programs unrelated to video games.

The wide variety of titles reflected company founder William M. Hawkins' belief that EA should not rely too heavily on a few popular games. In its early years the company developed a policy that no single game could account for more than six percent of company revenue. When game development was relatively inexpensive, EA's strategy made sense. It ensured that the company could respond more quickly to changing tastes. However, as development costs rose, EA's large assortment of games became burdensome. How could a company, even one as large as EA, allocate development resources adequately and effectively to hundreds of projects?

Despite its large portfolio, Electronic Arts had only one title among the top 10 best sellers during the 2008 holiday season. Retailers criticized the company for producing too many mediocre titles. Unlike Amazon, most retailers had limited shelf space and, as such, constrained their offerings to top sellers. Yet even as the company's profit declined, it sought to further diversify its offerings by acquiring competitors, like *Grand Theft Auto* publisher Take-Two Interactive Software, which EA tried unsuccessfully to acquire in early 2008 for $2 billion.

Take-Two had a more focused approach than EA. It owned fewer studios and it developed fewer games. Take-Two's best known studio was Rockstar Games, developer of the best-selling *Grand Theft Auto* series. Take-Two invested unprecedented sums of money in games like *Grand Theft Auto* to ensure that players received the best quality and most value out of their titles. Therefore, even though *Grand Theft Auto IV* cost an estimated $100 million to develop, it posted industry record revenue in excess of $500 million in its first week on the market.

Despite the fact that Take-Two was the third largest video game publisher in the world, most of its revenue was generated by only 15 franchises. Some analysts criticized Take-Two for putting its eggs in too few baskets. That didn't bother CEO Ben Feder. "At the end of the day, I'm a businessman, and our profitability speaks for itself," he countered.

> We do have the kind of 'James Bond' of the video game business. By that, I mean hits that generate other hits and that every sequel does better than the previous release in that franchise. (Brightman 2008)

Take-Two's strategy was less about controlling costs than "consolidation in terms of costs," meaning that spending would be targeted on fewer blockbuster titles. In fact, Feder believed that skyrocketing development costs gave his company a competitive advantage over other publishers.

> I don't mind costs going up as long as the opportunity goes up. By spending more in a game, I get more market share or get to sell games to customers I wouldn't normally. If the market grows and you can justify spending more on a game, then it is fine. (Brightman 2008)

Extending existing franchises had other benefits. For one, publishers could build upon the intrinsic brand equity of popular franchises to reduce marketing costs. Video game analyst Jesse Divnich (2009) of Electronic Entertainment Design and Research noted,

> On average, to get a new IP in the same league as your *Grand Theft Autos, Pokémons,* and *Mario Bros., you need to spend almost 10 to 20 percent more in advertising, on top of having larger development*

costs—and trust me, these types of marketing budgets would make a Nike advertising manager cringe. Wii Fit *alone had a marketing expense that exceeded $50 million worldwide, 35 percent more than* Grand Theft Auto IV.

Divnich added that changing social trends made it difficult to predict the popularity of a new title two years into the future, which is the average time it takes to develop a game and bring it to market. On the other hand, the proven staying power of franchises allowed companies to make accurate sales projections and reduce perceived risk.

Square Enix took a slightly different approach. Like Take-Two, Square Enix developed franchise games that helped establish customer loyalty. However, it specialized in one gaming genre, fantasy role playing games. This allowed it to develop its own game engines that could be shared across several game titles.

As we saw in earlier chapters, most gamers are console agnostic. They will switch brands from one generation to the next. Despite industry efforts to build brand loyalty, gamers were not sufficiently attached to gaming hardware. Games were different. Software offered emotional rewards in ways that hardware could not. Ever since Shigeru Miyamoto redefined gaming by focusing on mythical characters and heroes, people have been able to relate to games in a more emotional way. Films and novels offered similar emotional rewards, but they were passive media. Games allowed players to accompany their heroes on their journeys in ways that film and books never could.

Square Enix built upon those relationships to not only establish successful game franchises, but to sell tie-in products ranging from movies and soundtracks to memorabilia. The company's most successful franchise was *Final Fantasy*, an epic game that blended pagan mythology (druids and dragons) with science fiction (robots and space stations). First introduced in 1987, *Final Fantasy* has spawned 12 sequels and numerous side stories, and made Square Enix one of the most successful publishers in the industry. The game has also been adapted to film, television animated series, manga (Japanese comic books), radio plays, and full length novels.

Square Enix was also one of the first video game companies to take a focused approach to game development. In the late 1980s, the company established a policy of only developing games that would probably sell more than one million copies. In the mid 1990s as Sony and other entrants tried to challenge

Nintendo's dominance in consoles, Square (as the company was known prior to its acquisition of Enix Corporation in 2003) remained an exclusive Nintendo developer. It had to be sure that other console makers had enough market presence to support the company's sales targets. In the late 1990s and early 2000s, when Sony became the market leader, Square began developing exclusive titles for the PlayStation and PS2. It did not begin publishing titles for the Xbox until 2006.

When development costs skyrocketed with the launch of the Xbox 360 and PS3, Square Enix, like Take-Two, was well positioned to take advantage of market changes. The company's latest *Final Fantasy* installment was slated to be released in late 2009. After nearly five years of development, the *Final Fantasy* development team, headed by producer Yoshinori Kitase, felt an "unusual sort of pressure" to deliver "ten times the success and impact" of previous titles in the series (Crossly 2009).

Conclusion

The video game industry was one of many industries that were being transformed by the wide availability of technology. For example, musicians were creating professional quality compositions using inexpensive home studios and distributing their works on Internet sites like MySpace. Amateur photographers were uploading billions of photographs to Flickr and Wikipedia and distributing them free of charge. Craigslist provided free online classified advertising that all but eliminated classified ads in newspapers, which until recently had been a major source of revenue for companies like *The New York Times*.

For more than a century, companies relied on economies of scale to reduce development costs and bring new products to market. Today, many companies still believe in that twentieth century model. At IBM's Microelectronics Division, where the Cell processor was developed, chip designer David Shippy reiterated the mantra of bigger is better. "Great ideas, of which there is never a shortage, require significant monetary investment—top-notch salaries, employee benefits, office space, silicon test chips, lab space, and equipment," he explained (Shippy and Phipps 2009).

That may still be true for microprocessor design, but in the twenty-first century, that model is quickly being demolished by new community-based paradigms. Placing creative tools in the hands of the general populous created new challenges for large corporations that previously relied on economies of scale to reduce transaction costs. Chris Anderson, editor in chief of *Wired* magazine, refers to the "diseconomies of scale" associated with administrative costs and other expenses that smaller companies and individuals do not need to worry about. "Bigger companies have to place bigger bets," he writes, "but have less and less control over distribution and competition in an increasingly diverse marketplace. Those bets get riskier and the payoffs lower" (Anderson 2009). Everywhere from Wall Street to Detroit, "top-down companies of the 20th century" were being transformed into "industry ecosystems" dominated by free agents and startups.

In a market saturated with thousands of games, only a few titles will generate the sales needed to make big budget development ventures profitable. Studios that deviate from proven formulae or offer too many game titles risk losing considerable sums of money as they try to compete with low cost startups. Therefore, it was no wonder that developers felt "an unusual sort of pressure" to deliver the next blockbuster. The failure of a big budget title had the potential to bankrupt a company in the way that Free Radical Design was bankrupted by the failure of *Haze*. In such an environment, most publishers will continue to fund safe bets (games that use proven engines and follow well established story lines).

Publishers of big budget titles also need to have the resources to fund such projects. Therefore, only the largest and best-funded companies will survive. Smaller studios will increasingly need to partner with larger companies like Sony that can provide the funding needed for innovative projects. Consolidation can help pool resources provided that acquisitions are strategic. A good example was Square's acquisition of Enix Corporation. Both companies had a focus on role playing and fantasy games and the merged entity proved a good fit. Without an acquisition strategy, companies can find themselves in the same situation as EA with too many mediocre titles in too many categories. Companies need to focus, and not try to be "all things to all people," to ensure long-term success.

With hundreds of millions of dollars at stake, fewer publishers can afford to take risks on experimental game designs. That will be left to small studios that are either independently funded or that enter partnerships with larger firms. Companies like Media Molecule and Thatgamecompany have shown that opportunities abound for developers who want to redefine the way games are played the way Shigeru Miyamoto did in the 1980s.

11

Guitar Hero Nation

As we saw earlier, the Wii revolutionized the video game industry with its simple and easy-to-use controller. However, Nintendo is not the only company that is experimenting with new controllers and new game concepts. One of the fastest growing segments is party games like *Guitar Hero*, *Rock Band*, and *Dance Dance Revolution*. Nearly all of the games in this segment use simple and intuitive controllers ranging from plastic guitars and drums to dance pads and microphones. Although most of these games have been around much longer than the Wii, they have only recently surged in popularity. In this chapter we will review the history of music games and discuss their impact on gaming, music, and media.

The Triumph of Low Budget

In any media business, be it newspapers, film, or video games, content is king. Newspapers like *The Wall Street Journal* and *The New York Times* dominated the industry in the twentieth century, not for their elaborate layouts, but because they provided reliable journalism, a variety of stories, and useful content, such as stock quotes and film reviews. *The Wall Street Journal* has hardly changed in 100 years. The popular newspaper had few photographs, but its business content and analysis were second to none. Despite the 24-hour availability of television news and finance, and numerous online investment websites, *The Wall Street Journal* continues to enjoy a readership of more than two million people, including nearly one million long-term subscribers.

As we head into the second decade of the twenty-first century, many newspapers find themselves in financial trouble as more readers turn to the Internet for news. The decline in newspapers is not surprising. What is surprising is that newspapers have thrived for so long in a multimedia world that provides instant access to information from anywhere in the world. More than 50 years ago, the widespread adoption of television spelled doom for radio. After all, how could sound compete with the rich experience of video? Yet radio not only survived, it thrived. Today, listeners can choose from thousands of radio stations that make their feeds available on the Internet.

In film, interesting content often trumped expensive special effects. A case in point was *Juno*, a Canadian independent film about a teenager who becomes pregnant and decides to give her child up for adoption. With a budget of $7 million, it went on to gross more than $230 million in the box office. A few months later, *Dungeon Siege*, a fantasy film based on a popular computer game, was released at a cost of $70 million, but produced only $3 million in box office receipts after being labeled one of the worst movies ever made.

One of the most successful independent films was *Blair Witch Project*. In 1999, it became an overnight sensation, despite being shot over a period of eight days on a budget of only $22,000. The horror film purposely used home-video cameras and shaky footage to make it appear as footage recovered from film students who had gone missing in a Maryland forest. The low production value did not stop people from seeing the film. It grossed nearly $250 million worldwide. Similarly, the video sharing website YouTube hosts a variety of amateur content, ranging from laughing babies to spoofs of music videos. Despite the fact that most of the videos are extremely poor quality, YouTube has become one the most popular sites on the Internet.

The YouTube phenomenon is the basis for the 2008 film *Be Kind Rewind*, starring comedian Jack Black. When Black becomes magnetized after trying to sabotage a power plant, he accidentally erases all the VHS video tapes at a rental store managed by his best friend. The two buffoons then attempt to reshoot each of the films using a home video camera and homemade props, hoping that nobody will notice. Yet the remakes are so ridiculous that they become a sensation among viewers. Soon customers are coming from as far as neighboring states to rent the comical homemade films. The premise is, of course, that people are willing to look beyond low production value, and an obsolete medium like VHS, if they find the content to be entertaining.

The video game industry is no different. One of the top 10 best-selling games for the Xbox 360 was *Guitar Hero II*, a low-budget game in which players use a plastic guitar shaped controller to match the beat of an on-screen fret board. Although the graphics were primitive, people enjoyed the challenge and the music. It also followed the advice of another video game maxim, namely that it was easy to learn, but difficult to master. Compare *Guitar Hero* with *Lair*, a game developed for the PlayStation 3. After three years of development and a $20 million budget, gamers had high hopes for *Lair*, which boasted some of the most gorgeous visuals ever seen on any console. "But great visuals and sound mean absolutely nothing in *Lair*," wrote one reviewer. "There is nothing fun about it." *Lair* was the "ultimate example of how game play suffers when all the work goes into making everything look pretty" (VanOrd 2007).

Games and Music

The first music games were less about entertainment and more about education. *Miracle Piano Teaching System* by Software Toolworks was a perfect example. When the $500 program was released in 1990, it came with an NES cartridge, full piano-keyboard, floppy disks and a plethora of cables. Educators praised the system, which used games to help students learn the various notes and techniques necessary to master the piano. Nintendo's software review team gave it the highest rating of any third party title released for the system that year.

Commercially, however, *Miracle Piano* was a failure. Not even a $6 million advertising budget was enough to save the title. Parents thought it was expensive and kids thought it was boring. "Miracle is only worthwhile for someone genuinely interested in learning to play the piano," said one gamer in an online review.

> Miracle Piano *was a well-meaning but misguided attempt by my parents to get me to learn the piano. I mean, they bought the associated keyboard and stand, moved the NES into a bigger room so I could learn in comfort, and were just too nice about it for me to not be suspicious.* (GameSpot 2006)

Most kids enjoyed imitating their rock music heroes, whether lip-synching lyrics, playing air guitar, or tapping a rhythm with their hands or feet. Only a few were sufficiently dedicated to music to commit the time and effort needed to master a longer term learning program like *Miracle Piano*. The effort was simply too great for the small improvements that musicians achieved in the first few months of any music learning program. The premise behind later music programs like *Rock Band* and *Guitar Hero* is that an average gamer with absolutely no musical skill could pick up an instrument and play.

Eran Egozy and Alex Rigopulos founded Harmonix Music Systems in 1995 while conducting research on the role of music in video games at the Massachusetts Institute of Technology (MIT) Media Lab. Both were recent MIT graduates, Rigopulos in music and media and Egozy in electrical engineering and computer science. They sought to use games to make music creation more accessible to the masses. "Playing music is one of the most fundamentally joyful experiences that life has to offer," explained Rigopulos.

> Just about everyone tries at some point in their life to learn to play music: piano lessons as a kid, guitar lessons as a teenager, or whatever. The overwhelming majority of people give it up after six months or a year in frustration, just because it's too difficult to learn to play music the old-fashioned way. Of course, some people go on to become skilled musicians, but that's really a tiny minority of those who try. Consequently, this profound joy that comes from making music is only accessible to this tiny percentage of the people of the world. We created this company to try to invent new ways to give music-loving non-musicians a chance to play music. (Stone 2004)

As with most startups, Harmonix had a modest beginning. Its first product was a Windows PC game called *The Axe*. The game's interactive music videos featured animated characters and various instruments, including guitars, pianos, wind instruments, synthesizers and voice. The instruments were controlled by pressing buttons on the computer keyboard or joystick. Although reviewers were impressed by the detail in *The Axe*, which seemed to include "every single riff combination, chord, and trick," they were less impressed by the clumsy keyboard and joystick interface (Carson 2000).

Concurrently, several Japanese video game companies developed music titles that quickly became the latest rage among Japanese youth. The most important of these was *Dance Dance Revolution* (DDR) by Tokyo-based Konami Corporation. What distinguished *Dance Dance Revolution* was the use of an innovative controller known as a dance mat. The game required players to step on different squares on the mat corresponding to arrows that scrolled down the screen in synch with popular dance music tracks.

Dance Dance Revolution debuted in November 1998 as an arcade game built around a dance stage. A few months later, Konami released a home version for the PlayStation home video game console. The home version included a roll-out mat that plugged into the game console. Players danced on the mat in the same way as the arcade version. Parents and educators embraced the new game for its ability to combine physical fitness and game play.

Konami's other successful music games included *GuitarFreaks*, *DrumMania*, and *BeatMania*. Released in 1999, each of these arcade games featured a controller in the shape of an instrument. *GuitarFreaks* presented players with a plastic guitar with three buttons representing frets. Players pressed on the frets in synch with images displayed on the screen. *DrumMania* worked in much the same way, except that gamers interacted with an electronic drum set instead of a guitar. Finally, *BeatMania* simulated a DJ studio using a record spinning simulator to control game play.

Over the next several years, the popularity of music games surged in Japan. By 2003, Konami sold more than 4 million units of DDR to Japanese gamers. The game also began to build a following in Europe and North America where sales topped 1.5 million units and 1.0 million units respectively. To Rigopulos, the success of DDR and other Japanese music games affirmed his belief in the market potential of music games.

> *When we saw that happen, it really struck us that video gaming was the mass-market interactive medium, and it was the medium through which we wanted to achieve our mission of bringing the music-making experience to people who are non-musicians. (Stone 2004)*

In 2001, Harmonix released *Frequency*, a game that imitated *Dance Dance Revolution* in several ways. It included a number of dance songs which were visually represented by "jewels" which scrolled down the screen. However, instead of responding to these cues by stepping on a dance pad, players pressed buttons on a video game controller. Each "wall" on the game screen represented a different instrument. When a player completed a wall without mistakes, the wall started playing on its own, allowing the player to focus on another wall. *Frequency* won several video game awards and received positive reviews from every major video game critic. It also had the most appealing soundtrack of any game yet produced.

The game impressed Sony, which agreed to promote and distribute *Frequency* for its PlayStation 2 console. However, neither *Frequency* nor its sequel, *Amplitude*, reached a wide audience. "Sony, to their credit, said, 'alright, we don't really understand why this really great game didn't sell. Let's try again,'" explained Rigopulos in a 2004 interview.

We'd like to make more music games. But in order for that to happen, we need to sell, at a minimum, hundreds of thousands of units of each title, which is not a sales level we achieved with those games.

The challenge isn't really a developmental one, it's a marketing challenge. As I said, although music games have been enormously successful in Japan, and while we and our publishers believe that eventually music games will also explode in the U.S., it hasn't happened yet. It's sort of a chicken and egg problem. It's very hard to make games successful without a marketing budget. On the other hand, without a proven successful existing category, it's very hard to get that marketing budget. We're trying to break the music gaming category in the U.S., but Frequency *and* Amplitude *never had any substantial marketing support. (Stone 2004)*

Although Harmonix's early attempts at music games fared poorly, they won Harmonix a reputation as a capable development company and the only U.S. developer focused exclusively on the music subgenre.

Konami approached Harmonix in 2002 to develop a Karaoke game known as *Karaoke Revolution*. Konami had already developed a Japanese Karaoke game, known as *Dancing Karaoke DKara*, which combined dancing and singing. *Karaoke Revolution* would be developed exclusively for North America and Europe and focus strictly on singing. *Karaoke Revolution* was the first Harmonix game to incorporate a unique controller, in the form of a microphone. In 2003, *Karaoke Revolution* helped Harmonix post its first ever profit.

Guitar Hero

Given that Konami was the publisher of hit games like *GuitarFreaks* and *DrumMania*, it seemed natural for Harmonix to develop American versions of these instrument-based games. However, Rigopulos was reluctant to develop similar games for the U.S. market. He believed that Konami had only been able to launch home console versions of *GuitarFreaks* because the game already had a strong following in video game arcades. "When you're dealing with arcades and you're selling a $5,000 box, putting on a guitar controller is easy to make work in the business model," Rigopulos explained. In Japan, where music games were extremely popular, it made sense to develop home versions of these games. "They knew it was going to sell half a million units of the home version, so it was very low risk to manufacture half a million custom controllers."

In contrast, music games were an unproven concept in North America. Thus, Rigopulos hesitated to make the investment needed for a wide scale game launch.

> *It's very risky to spend that money because you're asking the consumer not just to buy a new game for fifty bucks, but to buy a custom controller that will work for just that one game when they probably don't even know what that game is yet. (Stone 2004)*

Yet there was no reason to think that a *GuitarFreaks* style game could not be successful outside Japan. After all, music was universal. At least that was the thinking behind the decision by Charles and Kai Huang to introduce the game in the United States. In the early 2000s, the Huang brothers founded a video game import and rental business known as RedOctane. In 2004, following the successful launch of *GuitarFreaks* in the Japanese home console market, they decided to import inexpensive guitar shaped controllers into the United States. However, they chose not to import the *GuitarFreaks* game itself, as it was too "focused on the Japanese consumer."

Instead, the Huang brothers approached Egozy and Rigopulos with a proposal to develop an American guitar game. "We thought that there was an opportunity to make music-based games [in North America], and to do that we needed to change the music," said Kai Huang.

> *For us, it was very logical that if we were going to do a music-based game for North America and Europe, it would have to be based on rock and roll. And if it was going to be based on rock, we knew that the first instrument had to be a guitar. And so, really, that's how we started with* Guitar Hero. *(Boyes 2007)*

Guitar Hero had an initial development budget of one million dollars, significantly less than the tens of millions typically spent on popular game titles. Not having anticipated the success of *Guitar Hero*, Harmonix agreed to a profit sharing and royalty agreement that left RedOctane as owner of the brand and most of the intellectual property. In the future, RedOctane would be free to hand the project to another developer, but it would be required to pay Harmonix a royalty on any releases based on its technology.

At the time, RedOctane did not have "any particularly grand ambitions other than needing a game," explained Rob Kay, lead developer for *Guitar Hero*.

> *Relatively speaking it was a low budget game [but] everyone here was really psyched to work on a rock guitar game. It really fit with people's interests here. We never thought about it being a massive success. We all just thought it would be fun to do. (Simons 2007)*

Kay took some existing guitar controllers and began work on a simple "Pong-style" game with dots floating down the screen. The player had to press one of several buttons on the guitar controller that corresponded to the dots on the screen.

At the same time, a design group worked on the art and visuals of the game. They borrowed heavily from the style of Konami's *Karaoke Revolution*, which featured animated performers rather than "the really abstract visuals" found in *Frequency* and *Amplitude*. By pulling design ideas from existing games, Harmonix was able to complete the program design in only nine months.

Licensing songs for use in the game proved to be one of the more challenging aspects of the game's design, explained Huang.

> *The licensing can take a very long time. We have to work with the music labels to get the clearances to be able to use the songs in the game, and then after we're done, we have to, in some cases, rerecord them and tune the songs a little bit to make them a little bit more fun to play for Guitar Hero. That process can take a very long time, and that's what really makes the selection of the songs such a time-consuming process. (Boyes 2007)*

Rhythm games appealed to a wide audience because "they can be very easy to pick up but very difficult to master," explained Huang.

> *When you look at how easy it is for rock fans or consumers to get into the Guitar Hero game, almost anybody can, whether you're five years old or 65 years old. Everybody can pick up the guitar, everybody knows what it is, and they can have a great time playing the game almost immediately. (Boyes 2007)*

However, as *Frequency* and *Amplitude* had shown, rhythm and a good soundtrack were not enough to attract customers. *Guitar Hero* had to offer something more. "When *Guitar Hero* was first talked about, it wasn't 'We're going to make an awesome beat matching game,'" Kay observed.

> It was "We're going to make players feel like rock stars." And I think the best ideas are ones that can be described in one line like that. The guitar controller "was all about immediacy," he added.
>
> Someone could come to the game, be handed a plastic guitar, and feel like a rock star within moments of playing. That ability to feel like Hendrix (or whoever) was in place from day one. It was great to know from the outset that we were on to something that was clearly fun.
>
> The overriding enjoyment for me is being able to put games straight into non-gamers hands and seeing them get it straight away. It's amazing what a barrier the standard joypad is. I think you only understand that when you take it away and put something more natural in its place... Custom controllers are the way forward in terms of engagement. (Simons 2007)

People understood the concept of a guitar the same way they understood a television remote control, a conductors' wand, or a baseball bat. It was the same concept that made the Wii and DS so popular.

Guitar Hero also improved on previous rhythm games by offering a career mode that allowed novice players to progress and increase their skills. New players started with easy songs and only three buttons. As they improved, the game presented more difficult songs that required use of up to five buttons. They started as a garage band and then progressed through the ranks toward virtual superstardom. This set *Guitar Hero* apart from other rhythm games like *Dance Dance Revolution*, as players could live out their fantasies of becoming rock stars.

Unexpected Hit

Guitar Hero's North America launch on November 8, 2005 was met with critical acclaim. "Music games have a tendency to be great fun for parties and such, but very few of them have ever struck that certain primal chord deep inside all of us," offered Chris Roper (2005) Editor-in-Chief of IGN. "*Guitar Hero* is one of those rare games that do just this."

> *While* Guitar Hero *draws very close comparison to Konami's* Guitar Freaks, *we have yet to see that series hit any console outside Japan. So while you can head over to an import-friendly arcade for your guitar gaming fix,* Guitar Hero *is your only option at home. But not only is* Guitar Hero *the only in-home option, it's the best you'll find there or in a coin-op house. Harmonix and RedOctane have nailed this one in almost every way, and while we can always wish for more, what's there is nearly perfect.*

Even though the game mechanics were similar to previous music games, reviewers were impressed by the realistic graphical backgrounds and a music soundtrack that featured iconic rocks songs from the likes of Jimi Hendrix and Ozzy Osbourne. They also liked the controller, which was patterned after a Gibson SG, one of the most recognizable electric guitars.

In its first year as a PlayStation 2 title, *Guitar Hero* racked up sales of more than $45 million. Rigopulos was more than pleased with the results, which were better than any game Harmonix had produced to this point. Even so, he was unprepared for the explosive popularity of the game's sequels.

> *We really didn't know it was going to become a hit game yet. We knew it was going to be more successful than any of our previous music games (it was still early enough that it was an exciting time), but the way it was all going to play out was not at all clear. (Van Zelfden 2007)*

The early success of *Guitar Hero* attracted more than admiration. In May 2006, Activision acquired RedOctane for $100 million on the belief that music games would represent "one of the fastest growing genres in the coming years." "The success we are seeing today is a strong indicator that *Guitar Hero* and the many potential extensions, new platform exploitations and international versions appear to be somewhat transition proof," noted Ron Doornik, an Activision director and key strategic advisor.

> *Consumers are responding to this product on current-generation platforms in a manner that defies traditional late-cycle behavior. We think the online capabilities of the next-generation platforms offer new and well differentiated opportunities to create additional revenues from*

downloadable music, which today represents one of the most popular
downloadable content categories. (Sinclair 2006)

A Winning Formula

Activision's acquisition of RedOctane left Harmonix uncertain about its future.
When RedOctane hired Harmonix to develop *Guitar Hero,* it left the door open
to hire another developer. And while Activision was quick to sign long term
contracts with key RedOctane employees, Harmonix was left out in the cold.

RedOctane and Harmonix also disagreed on the future of the *Guitar*
Hero series. Harmonix wanted "a bigger and more ambitious endeavor,"
while RedOctane sought to maintain the winning formula of the *Guitar Hero*
franchise.

When RedOctane decided to replace Harmonix with a more experienced
developer, Rigopulos was not surprised. He recognized that RedOctane's
investment in the project gave it the right to move the project in any direction
it wanted to.

> *They were coming to us as a company that was basically the same size*
> *as us, and they were writing the checks to finance the game, and betting*
> *the farm on the game. So I think they're rightfully the owner of that IP.*
> *(Boyer 2007)*

Although RedOctane's decision to hire another developer proved "very
emotionally intense" for Harmonix employees, the *Guitar Hero* franchise
continued to reach new heights. In November 2006, RedOctane released *Guitar*
Hero II, the last version to be developed by Harmonix.

Guitar Hero II was "the best music game ever released," exclaimed Chris
Roper (2006).

> Guitar Hero II *expands upon the smash-hit original game in almost*
> *every way with a greatly expanded (and arguably better) track list,*
> *improved multiplayer support, a practice mode and more. The result*
> *is a game that seems to have almost everything you could have wished*
> *for in the sequel.*

With multiplayer support, *Guitar Hero II* quickly became the ultimate party game. College dormitories adopted it for parties and social gatherings. Night clubs began to offer *"Guitar Hero* Nights" where patrons could play their favorite songs or compete against other patrons for prizes. Afterwards, club-goers bought their own game so they could practice for the next competition. In some cases, people who never played video games before purchased consoles just so they could practice *Guitar Hero.* "We never intended for it to happen," admitted Greg LoPiccolo, Harmonix VP of product development, "but once we saw it take place, it was kind of perfect" (Zezima 2007).

By the time RedOctane released an Xbox 360 version of the game, sales were already setting new records. In the all important holiday season, *Guitar Hero II* was the second best-selling game. Sales revenue continued to be strong throughout 2007, eventually reaching $200 million.

Rock Band

In November 2006, not long after Activision's acquisition of RedOctane, MTV Games offered to purchase Harmonix for $175 million in cash. MTV was a subsidiary of Viacom Inc., an important media company with significant interests in television and film. However, in 2007 Viacom found itself in a difficult position, as the new media forms competed for consumers' attention. More recent changes were "so dramatic that revenue has flattened out."

To a beleaguered entertainment industry, video games represented an opportunity. In 2007, U.S. industry revenues from video games increased 28.4 percent. Over the same period, the music industry saw revenues decline by 10 percent, while the film industry grew by a modest 1.4 percent. Entertainment Software Association President, Michael Gallagher highlighted the industry's achievements.

> The video game industry set the pace over all others in 2007, with record-breaking sales, off-the-charts consumer demand, and innovation reaching from galactic exploration to guitar simulation. On average, an astonishing nine games were sold every second of every day of the year. (Bangeman 2008)

Harmonix was the most significant of Viacom's video game acquisitions. Nevertheless, Michael Pachter, a leading video games analyst, criticized the deal. "Would you pay $150 million dollars for someone who ripped off Guitar Freaks?" he asked. Given that RedOctane retained both the brand and intellectual property for *Guitar Hero*, he wondered what Harmonix could offer MTV.

At a time when Harmonix's future was up in the air, MTV's offer was a godsend for Eran Egozy and Alex Rigopulos. After losing the most important project of their careers, they now had the funds to pursue bigger and better things. MTV not only infused Harmonix with cash, it gave the developers freedom to undertake "bigger and more ambitious endeavors" than they could have pursued under RedOctane. One such endeavor was *Rock Band*.

According to Rigopulos, *Rock Band* "takes the core premise of *Guitar Hero* and expands it tenfold" (Plunkett 2007). It melded the best elements of *Guitar Hero* and *Karaoke Revolution* while adding a *DrumMania* style drum controller. Players could cooperate in a career mode that mimicked the adventures of a fictional *Rock Band* as it progressed from a garage band to pop stardom, or they could participate in a "band quick play" mode that allowed anyone to join the game at any time.

When Harmonix unveiled *Rock Band* at the Electronic Entertainment Expo (E3) 2007, it quickly became the talk of the show. Attendees were impressed by the playlist that included Black Sabbath, David Bowie, Rush, and Foo Fighters. Clearly MTV Games had used "its music-industry muscle" to win over A-list performers. But what really won over the media was the game's ability to simulate an entire band, including drums, vocals, bass, and guitar. *Rock Band* won the coveted "Best in Show" award and was declared the "greatest party game ever" by several media outlets.

By the time Harmonix released *Rock Band* on November 20, 2007, the game was already causing a sensation. *Rolling Stone* called it the "most anticipated video game of the year," despite the fact that at $169, it was one of the most expensive video games to ever hit store shelves, more expensive even than some game consoles. That didn't stop *Rock Band* from selling out in the midst of the holiday season. Within a week, *Rock Band* kits were selling for over $300 on eBay.

Rock Band went on to sell approximately 5 million units in its first year. Yet its success in the marketplace was undermined by a lack of profitability. Game controllers proved more expensive to manufacture than anticipated, while quality control problems resulted in a much higher than normal number of warranty repairs. As a result, *Rock Band* became the biggest contributor to a 3 percent decline in Viacom's overall operating margin. Phillippe Dauman, President and CEO of Viacom tried to alleviate the concerns of investors. "On a more positive note," he began, "ancillary fees grew 12 percent for the quarter."

> *Worldwide ancillary revenues rose an impressive 62 percent with Rock Band continuing to be the biggest driver of our growth. Next year, we expect Rock Band to begin to generate increasingly meaningful bottom-line results as well. (Viacom, Inc. 2008)*

Although getting the game into the hands of players proved to be an expensive undertaking, once the game was in place, it offered a number of ways to earn additional revenue. One was to sell add-ons, such as new songs, levels, or theme packages. By 2008, *Rock Band* players were buying an average of one million downloadable items every nine days through online services such as Xbox Live and PlayStation Network.

It also gave Viacom an opportunity to try new forms of music distribution and to cross-market the game with other Viacom products.

A New Form of Music Distribution

Although the Internet opened up new avenues for the distribution of entertainment content, it also created new challenges. Consumers had long been able to copy music they owned from CDs to personal computers. Even so, consumers usually had to purchase a CD or borrow one from a close friend or relative in order to make a digital copy. In 1999, Northeastern University student Shawn Fanning developed a file-sharing service known as Napster that allowed Internet users to swap songs for free online. Although Napster was eventually shut down, new file-sharing services quickly took its place. By 2007, more music was being distributed through free file-sharing services than through any other medium. The record industry tried to fight back by suing, or threatening to sue, individuals who shared music over the Internet, but to no avail. Album sales declined every year from 2000 to 2008, as record stores across the country closed their doors forever.

As the record industry spiraled into oblivion, online music sales through retail sites such as Apple iTunes, Amazon MP3, and Rhapsody surged. Sales of digital music, however, remained small compared to pre-Internet record sales.

Video games, such as *Rock Band* and *Guitar Hero* offered artists an entirely new way to distribute music. The success of these games offered some hope to artists willing to pioneer the new medium. Aerosmith was the first band to license an entire game based on its music. *Guitar Hero: Aerosmith* delivered 25 songs in an interactive format that featured the likenesses of band members. The game sold more than half a million copies at $50 each during in its first week, compared with only 160,000 copies of the group's last CD over the same time period.

Other bands took notice. Shortly afterward, acts like Metallica and Guns and Roses signed their own distribution agreements with Activision and Harmonix. Despite the new hope offered by video games, not all music was suitable to beat matching games like *Rock Band* and *Guitar Hero*. "There are actually just a handful of bands that have this really deep catalog of music that people would have a lot of fun playing," admitted Huang.

Guitar Hero proved a boon to some lesser known bands. Dragonforce, which was practically unknown before *Guitar Hero*, saw its single "Through the Fire and Flames" vault to the top 100 after being featured in the game.

Despite these successes, Bob Lefsetz, a music industry consultant, was doubtful of the long-term potential of *Rock Band*.

> *Four years from now, will kids be standing in front of their flat screens flicking the levers on plastic guitars or will they be playing something different? One thing you know about the music industry: It can't get enough of a good thing. If it finds something successful, it runs it into the ground. (Dow Jones 2008)*

Lefsetz had a point. Nintendo almost destroyed the Mario brand in the 1990s by trying to extend the franchise too far. Not only did the quality of the games decline, people grew tired of the famous plumber. *Guitar Hero* and *Rock Band* appeared to be following the same path, as prices for games like *Rock Band 2* and *Guitar Hero Aerosmith* plummeted. By the 2008 holiday season, band kits that once sold for $99 had to be discounted to $30 or less.

Nevertheless, Harmonix, RedOctane, and Konami continued to release new rhythm games and spin-offs of existing titles. Konami's *Rock Revolution* tried to capitalize on the *Guitar Hero* craze, but the effort was too little and too late. Within months, the title was collecting dust in the remainder bins of retailers. Nintendo tried its hand at the genre with *Wii Music*, a game that used the Wii Remote and Wii Fit Balance Board to simulate musical instruments. However, sales were so poor that Amazon began giving the game away free with every Wii console purchase.

To reignite interest in the genre, Harmonix enlisted the support of the two remaining Beatles to create *The Beatles: Rock Band*. However, at $249, Harmonix may find that the game is so overpriced that not even the lads from Liverpool will be able to stimulate interest in the title.

Whether *The Beatles* is a success or a failure will not change the long-term impact rhythm games have had on the video game industry. Like the DS stylus and Wii Remote, they have proven that simplicity and ease of use are more important to most consumers than graphics. More importantly, they demonstrate the need to make the game interface appear intuitive and natural, so that anyone can pick up a game and play.

Conclusion

The history of the video game industry is littered with promising products that failed for one reason or another. Developers, engineers, and marketing executives need to be cognizant of the fact that the most advanced and carefully designed products will be rejected by consumers if they do not meet their needs. Consumers need to understand the utility the product can provide in their daily lives. The usefulness of a product might be clear to its creator, but is it clear to consumers? Promotional activities (e.g., advertising, public relations, sales promotion, direct marketing) that create awareness and inform customers are necessary for all new products. However, if a product is really new or a radical innovation, promotional efforts should focus on educating the public about the product and its benefits. This can be done by accessing the services of social networking sites, by getting products in the hands of opinion leaders, and by demonstrating the product in different locations, including non- traditional venues.

If we look at video game consoles today, they contain many of the features of now defunct products that were introduced years or even decades ago. For example, in 1993 the 3DO Multiplayer was more than a gaming device; it was a complete home entertainment unit that would eventually act as a terminal for Internet access, a cable box for high definition television playback, and a music player capable of high fidelity sound. They were features that were ahead of their time and although the Multiplayer failed, we find its innovative features in products ranging from game consoles, to DVRs and Apple TV. Likewise, the Dreamcast was the first console to offer true real-time online gaming. It too failed, but the technology behind the Dreamcast lives on today in Xbox Live and the PlayStation Network.

Having been inspired by the Nintendo Wii, console makers are beginning to focus their efforts on making games easier to use. For example, Microsoft is working on Project Natal, a technology that will eliminate controllers completely.

Once projects like Natal overcome technical and economic hurdles, they will need to be accepted by the public. Today's most promising technologies by no means guarantee success. At any point along the way, something could go wrong. However, even if they end up in the same graveyard as the 3DO Multiplayer, Atari Jaguar, and Sega Dreamcast, history has shown that useful technologies will always find their way into the mainstream. The question is not if, but when and by whom.

By focusing on the key successes and failures of the video game industry, we hope that technology managers will be better prepared to assess the viability of their products and successfully bring them to market. As such we provide the following summary of key lessons as a quick reference for product managers, engineers and developers.

- Your product must have unique benefits that provide value to customers.

New product success depends on offering customers benefits that are important to them and that they can't get from another competitor. To achieve this, firms need to have a deep understanding of their customers. The ideal development process includes the customer at multiple points in the process to ensure that the product is meeting their requirements.

- Performance matters, but content is king.

Powerful consoles inevitably fail if they don't have compelling games to offer consumers. The Sega Saturn was one of the best consoles of the mid 1990s, but it failed because it lacked games. The 3DO Multiplayer had games, but most of them were of poor quality. In contrast, the Nintendo DS and Wii are low on performance, but high on content.

- Beware of the performance oversupply.

When products begin to exceed consumer performance needs, performance becomes a less important factor in purchasing decisions. If your product competes on performance, it is important to be first with faster and more powerful-performance specifications. However, you need to be aware that at some point, the mass market consumer will not be able to distinguish performance differences in your products or those of your competitors. When this happens, if you have not added other features that are attractive to customers, you will lose out to competitors that have "good enough" performance but offer other attributes that customers value. Performance oversupply can happen in software, hardware, and services and is one of the most common performance traps in the video game industry.

- Patience is a virtue.

When Nintendo cancelled the Play Station project in 1991, Sony could have launched its own console within a few months. Instead, Sony chose to wait several more years so that it could build up developer relationships and ensure that it had good games to offer when its own redesigned PlayStation was launched. Sega chose to launch the Saturn early and it failed miserably. Microsoft paid a heavy toll with the Xbox 360, both by insisting on being first to market at all costs, and for its lack of experience in hardware engineering. Consoles are not like software. They can't be fixed remotely after the fact by issuing software patches. When you are talking about cutting edge technology that exceeds the performance of some of the most advanced computers on the planet, you can't afford to take shortcuts.

- Price is not a defining feature.

Many people feel that 3DO Multiplayer's failure and the PS3's initially poor sales were due to high prices. Instead, other factors determined the outcome of these consoles. In its first two years on the market, the Wii commanded prices on the grey market that were as high as the PS3. In other words, Nintendo offered consumers the features they wanted, and consumers were willing to pay a premium to get them. 3DO and Sony did not.

- Take advantage of diversity.

Some of the most important innovations in the video game industry have come from artists and musicians who bring fresh ideas to the table. Diversity is often looked at as an employment equity issue when, in fact, it can become a competitive advantage. Diversity of culture, gender, education, profession, and personal interests can help bring fresh ideas to product design and innovation. Therefore, if you are interested in really new and radical innovation, look for unconventional backgrounds when hiring new staff members.

- Plan for the best, but be prepared for the worst.

Sega failed as a hardware company, not because its products were not successful, but because it lacked the financial resources to compete against better funded competitors like Sony and Microsoft. With better financial backing, the Sega Dreamcast might have been as successful as Xbox.

- Adhere to industry standards and dominant designs.

Nintendo lost market share to Sony, Sega, and Microsoft when it used proprietary media, such as cartridges and mini-disks. Instead, they should have adhered to industry standard CDs and DVDs. Sony relinquished its share of the portable music market to Apple and Microsoft because of the company's unwillingness to accept mp3 as a dominant design. In both cases, Nintendo and Sony insisted that users adopt their format even after other formats had achieved widespread consumer acceptance.

- Most copy protection schemes fail.

Even the most draconian copy protection schemes will be defeated by enterprising hackers. Almost every game system has been hacked as companies play cat and mouse with program updates that try to defeat the latest hack. Even hardware copy protection can be defeated. Enterprising gamers found ways to easily hack the Xbox to turn it into a Linux PC. Atari created cartridges that zapped the NES circuits that prevented unauthorized games from being used on the console. The examples are endless. With the PS3, Sony took the opposite approach when it encouraged the use of alternative operating systems and allowed users to upgrade their hard drives with off-the-shelf components.

- The only way to combat piracy is to compete with it.

Companies that try to combat piracy directly usually do themselves more harm than good. Anti-piracy measures such as DRM and cartridges end up frustrating legitimate consumers, even as determined pirates find ways to defeat the best anti-piracy technologies. Yet many companies have failed to learn the lessons of Nintendo and continue to use self-defeating technologies as a way to combat piracy.

The recent PC game *Spore* is one example of how anti-piracy measures continue to backfire. *Spore* used a copy protection scheme known as SecurROM that not only prevented copying but imposed limits on the way the game was used. When a DRM-free version of the game was posted on BitTorrent, it became the most popular pirated game in history. The reason—the pirated version did not impose restrictions and therefore was considered a better product than the legal version. The only effective way to fight piracy is to offer unique benefits that are costly to copy, such as consumer support, attractive covers and game manuals.

- Avoid complexity, embrace complexity.

Complexity makes it difficult for consumers to access products and utilize their full functionality. The infamous 15-button controller for the Atari Jaguar is a perfect example. Compare it to the six-button Wii Remote controller. That said, the more powerful a technology becomes, the more inherently complex it is, whether it is the number of transistors on a microchip or the number of chips on a motherboard. The key is to make the complexity invisible to the customer. If programmers are your customers, it means making easy-to-use development tools. If gamers are your customers, it means simplifying controllers and creating easy to navigate on-screen menus.

- Offer fewer options.

Product options can help you customize your product to meet specific consumer needs. For example, Dell Computers turned mass customization into an art form as it rose to be one of the most successful PC manufacturers in the world. However, too many options can cause confusion and turn off potential customers. The PlayStation 3 and Xbox 360 came in a variety of configurations, which caused less savvy buyers (such as parents) to avoid buying a console. The Nintendo Wii, like the Model T Ford, demonstrated that a product can be more successful when it comes in one color, one configuration, and one price.

- Use social networks to create product awareness.

The most successful product launches have been preceded by extensive word-of-mouth campaigns. Sony gave away 5,000 PlayStation consoles to opinion leaders, Microsoft created a free online game called *OurColony* to announce the Xbox 360, and Nintendo became the first video game company to participate in the AARP annual conference. The important lesson is to get your product into the hands of people who can influence the purchasing behavior of others. Whether that means participating in conferences and online forums, giving away free products, or demonstrating your products at various venues depends on who you want to reach. However, planning such activities takes time and should occur long before the product launch

- Practice open innovation.

Sony has found that partnering with independent studios allows it to remain at the forefront of game development. Sega attracted development for its Dreamcast console by working with Microsoft to create easy-to-use development tools. In today's world, it is important to practice open innovation so that you can discover new technologies and products and bring fresh ideas to your existing products. Coined by Henry Chesbrough (2003), open innovation implies using internal and external knowledge and sources to accelerate innovation. No longer can any firm expect to create, design, and develop new products completely by themselves. If Microsoft had outsourced the hardware design for the Xbox 360, the company might have had to deal with fewer system failures.

- Do not overextend successful franchises.

Nintendo's Mario became one of the most recognized characters in America in the 1980s. Among children he was more recognizable than Mickey Mouse. However, Nintendo overused the Mario franchise in the 1990s, releasing multiple Mario titles each year, and almost killed the brand in the process. Instead, companies need to constantly bring new ideas to the market to keep consumers interested. Mario was successful when sequels were released less frequently and each sequel offered unique levels and gameplay.

- Avoid complacency.

Success can be your own worst enemy. The more successful you become, the harder competitors will work to find ways to compete with your products. At the same time, success makes it more likely that you will continue providing the same products and services that made you successful, even if the market and industry are changing. Nintendo became complacent in the 1990s, thereby allowing Sony, Sega, and Microsoft to bring superior products to market and steal market share. Nintendo is once again becoming complacent, relying too heavily on avatar-based (Mii) sports games to drive sales. Meanwhile, Sony and Microsoft are developing new interfaces that may surpass the Wii Remote in easy-of-use and functionality, while Apple is making inroads in casual games through the development of iPhone applications. Continuous innovation is imperative for success, regardless of what industry you are in.

- Nothing lasts forever.

Companies cannot rely on successful products to maintain their lead forever. Magnavox, Atari, Nintendo, Sega, and Sony have each in turn dominated the video game market and each saw their lead slip away after they failed to deliver products the market wanted. In each case, it was content, not technology, that drove sales. Today, Microsoft has the most advanced gaming network on the planet—Xbox Live, but the commoditization of networking is allowing competitors to rapidly close the gap. To maintain industry leadership, companies must always be looking for new ways to bring value to customers.

The video game industry is unique in that it is fast-changing, competitive, and has seen many different firms achieve success and failure in rapid succession. Ultimately, the most successful innovations are the ones that provide significant value to customers based on a keen understanding of customer needs.

Epilogue

Throughout the book we have shown numerous examples of companies that have succumbed to the performance trap. In the video game industry 3DO, Sega, Microsoft, and Sony are all prime examples. Yet we should not dismiss the value of performance under the right circumstances. Performance can be a selling point if it provides value to the customer in terms of new functions and features. Consider Blu-ray. The value proposition was the PlayStation 3's ability to play high definition movies. To film aficionados, Blu-ray was an important selling point, but to many people, it simply did not make enough difference. Some did not have high definition televisions that could take advantage of Blu-ray. Others did not see enough difference between the 480p resolution of standard DVDs and 1080p of Blu-ray.

Eventually, high definition will be the new standard, broadband will be ubiquitous, and Sony and Microsoft will reduce costs sufficiently to offer lower-priced consoles. When that time comes, Nintendo will need to update the graphics and features of the Wii to remain competitive within the video game market. Already the base price of the Xbox 360 is less than Wii, making cost a less compelling consideration for buyers. And the PS3 might not be far behind. Already, Sony CFO Nobuyuki Oneda claims that "the cost reductions since we introduced the PS3 are very substantial and on schedule...about 70 percent, roughly speaking." That means that each PS3 now costs roughly $300 to make, after adjusting for the recent rise in the Japanese Yen.

As more people upgrade their home entertainment systems, they will want to take advantage of features not currently available on the Wii, such as high-definition graphics, online movie streaming, and media storage. Sony believes that many Wii users will migrate to the PS3. "We think [the Wii's success] is good for the business," claimed Peter Dille, senior vice president of marketing at Sony Computer Entertainment America.

There's a perspective here that, if we all believe that the Wii and Nintendo are doing something that hasn't been done—i.e., bringing more people into gaming—that's a good thing. Now, if those people get hooked on gaming and they want to continue with their gaming habit, then many of them will figure out "Okay, what else can I do?" and "wouldn't a high-definition gaming experience be of interest to me?" (Nutt 2009)

The question is whether Microsoft and Sony can make their consoles intuitive and easy to use. Both companies continue to make progress in the development of casual games targeted to the same non-traditional gamers who were originally attracted to the Wii. Microsoft's first attempt to challenge Nintendo came with the introduction of Xbox 360 Arcade in 2007. Like the Wii, it was aimed at casual gamers and came bundled with five games (*Boom Boom Rocket, Feeding Frenzy, Luxor 2, Pac-Man Championship Edition,* and *Uno*). For the Christmas 2008 season, Microsoft offered a special edition Arcade console that also came bundled with *Sega Superstars Tennis* for a price of $199. Microsoft's strategy seems to have paid off as its decline in market share relative to Nintendo slowed in the last quarter of 2008 and first quarter of 2009.

Although Microsoft showed no sign of toppling Nintendo from its first place position any time soon, its ability to reach new consumers with low-priced consoles bundled with casual games highlights the need for Nintendo to continue to innovate. Sony has also made inroads into the casual gaming market by partnering with independent game studios to produce experimental games like *Flower* and *Pixeljunk,* and in October 2008 Sony filed a patent for a motion controller that operated through a combination of video tracking and ultrasonic sounds. Microsoft has gone a step further with a development project known as Natal that involves the creation of a tracking device that can completely eliminate the need for a controller.

Microsoft's Project Natal

We have extolled the virtues of simplicity, whether it is simplicity in design, simplicity in game rules, simplicity in programming environments, or simplicity in controller layouts. Nevertheless, it is important to distinguish between visible and invisible complexity. From the user's point of view, it does not matter how complex the hardware is inside the box, as long as the gaming experience lives up to customers' expectations.

When designing the next *Grand Theft Auto* or *Call of Duty*, it may not matter if the control scheme is complex since the target market is core gamers who are probably familiar with the controller layout. On the other hand, targeting older gamers and new gamers involves creating products that are easy to pick up and play. In some cases, it may involve creating advanced interfaces and complex artificial intelligence algorithms.

Over the years, the game controller has become a significant barrier between non-gamers and game consoles. For companies like Microsoft that wanted the console to be a complete entertainment hub for the entire family, the controller has been the main obstacle. As consoles became more powerful and games became more complex, console makers added new buttons to give gamers command over increasingly complex game functions. Game controllers that originally began with two buttons soon had four, then eight, and even fifteen buttons. As we saw earlier, Nintendo took full advantage of this performance trap to leap ahead of the competition with its Wii remote.

But performance doesn't always have to be a trap. Powerful processing capabilities can also be used to provide greater accessibility and more intuitive interfaces. For example, in the 1980s, Apple took advantage of increasingly powerful computer graphics to create a window-based desktop computer that eliminated the need to memorize dozens of keyboard commands. Instead, computer users used a graphical interface to execute commands with the click of a mouse. Today, almost everyone uses some form of window-based solution, regardless of operating system.

However, keyboards still have their place. Not only are they used for entering text, they provide quick access to macro commands that control sound volume, printing, and other features. Keyboard commands also provide greater flexibility to advanced users and programmers who can design their own macros and shortcuts so that they can issue complex command sequences quickly. Even computer gamers often prefer keyboards to game controllers for their added flexibility and quick access to game commands.

Fast forward to E3 2009 where Microsoft unveiled Project Natal, a 3-D camera prototype that promises to have as profound an impact on video gaming as windows had on home computing. "For far too many people, the controller is a barrier separating video-game players from everyone else," explained Don Mattrick, head of Microsoft's Interactive Entertainment Business at the Microsoft press conference. With Natal, Mattrick and his colleagues hoped to remove that barrier by eliminating the controller. When combined with facial recognition and voice recognition, Natal became a complete artificial intelligence solution that could only be possible on a system as powerful as the Xbox 360. Although Project Natal is not expected to be commercially available until late 2010, once it becomes available, Microsoft expects it to become the core of the Xbox 360 experience.

Project Natal utilized a 3-D camera that is able to sense depth under varying light conditions, essentially mimicking human vision. "The 3-D sensor itself is a pretty incredible piece of equipment providing detailed 3D information about the environment similar to very expensive laser range finding systems but at a tiny fraction of the cost," explained Johnny Chung Lee (2009), a researcher at Microsoft's Applied Sciences group. "Depth cameras provide you with a point cloud of the surface of objects that is fairly insensitive to various lighting conditions allowing you to do things that are simply impossible with a normal camera."

Chung Lee recalled how "jaws dropped with amazement" when he showed Project Natal to some of his colleagues in academia.

> The human tracking algorithms that the teams have developed are well ahead of the state-of-the art in computer vision in this domain. The sophistication and performance of the algorithms rival or exceed anything that I've seen in academic research, never mind a consumer product. At times, working on this project has felt like a miniature "Manhattan project" with developers and researchers from around the world coming together to make this happen.

On various video game forums, the reaction to Natal was mixed. Some thought Natal represented the wave of the future, while others were skeptical that it would have much real world application. Skeptics wondered how camera sensors could replace the functions of a controller in first person shooter games. In fact, motion sensing will not replace the traditional controller, just as the mouse did not replace the keyboard after Apple introduced the Macintosh. Although it is true that the controller has been a major barrier for non-gamers, it is nevertheless the product of years of evolution. For dedicated gamers, handheld controllers provide a level of interaction that would otherwise be impossible. Neither Natal nor any other alternative control scheme will change that.

However, nothing will prevent developers from combining 3-D cameras, voice recognition, and traditional controllers to provide a more immersive experience that will appeal to gamers and non-gamers alike. Some games will continue to use standard controllers exclusively, others will use camera sensors exclusively, and some will use a combination of the two.

Natal will offer gamers new ways to navigate menus and perform non-gaming functions. It can be combined with traditional controllers to add new options. For example, in a battle sequence, instead of pressing the "O" button to duck and cover, the player can use physical gestures while still using the buttons for other functions, like pulling the trigger of a gun. In promotional videos, Microsoft showed a Natal player driving a car by moving her hands. Many gamers will still want to have something physical to touch, whether it is a real steering wheel or a steering wheel shaped controller with buttons to control actions such as gear changes.

Nintendo's Iwata responded to Microsoft's announcement by revealing that his company had tried motion cameras years earlier, but rejected the concept. The technology used in the Wii remote provided better results, he said. Although Iwata's statements implied that camera sensors were somehow inferior, in truth it was the Wii's limited processing ability that forced Nintendo to settle on the Wii remote. Natal captured 48 points on the human body in 3-D and processed them in real time with a level of detail that pushed the limits of the most advanced computers on the market. The Wii simply did not have enough processing power to accurately process 3-D visual data.

Nintendo deserves praise for its achievements. Given the Wii's antiquated processor, lack of hard drive, and limited memory, the Wii remote was a cost effective and functional alternative that helped rescue Nintendo's home console business and forced the industry to rethink its business model. It was also the driving force behind Microsoft's Project Natal and similar efforts by Sony and Ubisoft. Nintendo didn't follow the industry leaders, acknowledged Microsoft's Phil Spenser.

> We took a little bit of inspiration from that when we thought about where we are going to go. We love the work Nintendo has done in the past, and with Natal we thought that we needed to take a similar revolutionary step. (Game Trailers 2009)

However, without a major upgrade, it is hard to see how the Wii can compete against technologies like Natal. Peter Pachal (2009), a technology editor at NBC Universal, agreed that Natal would be as "game-changing as the Wiimote." Yet he wondered if Microsoft had the competency needed to bring the technology to market. "Given the company's checkered past, there's a chance it might screw up Natal, too," he said.

Already, there are signs that the Wii may have peaked. In March 2009, the PS3 surpassed the Wii in Japan as the best selling console after a year of declining Wii sales. One reason may be Nintendo's reliance on the motion controller as a selling point. As time goes on, games begin to look increasingly similar. Take *Wii Sports Resort*, released in the summer of 2009. *Sports Resort* was similar in appearance and function to the many sports games developed for the Wii, including the *Wii Sports* pack that is included with the console. The main difference was the use of a precision accessory known as Wii Motion Plus, which could be purchased as part of a controller package for $80, or as a separate add-on for $20. However, only programs designed for Motion Plus could take advantage of the extra precision.

Developers seemed uncertain of the value proposition of a more precise controller. Unlike *Wii Fit*, which brings an entirely new dimension to the Wii experience, Motion Plus had limited value to Nintendo's core market of casual gamers. The Wii's unique selling proposition was its ease of use, interactivity, and emphasis on social gaming, none of which was appreciably improved by the use of Motion Plus. At the same time, Nintendo could quickly lose its standing as an innovator if it continues to focus on avatar-centered sports games.

The Future of PlayStation

Before the launch of the PS3, Sony seemed to be doing everything right. It offered backwards compatibility, quality development tools, and a large library of games. In addition, the price of the PS2 was comparable to other systems on the market. Then Sony abandoned its model for success to follow the same performance trap that resulted in the demise of 3DO and the Sega Dreamcast. However, the setbacks experienced by the PS3 are not insurmountable. Sony has lowered the price, offered more exclusive titles, and restored rumble.

Developers continue to struggle with the challenges of programming games for a system as complex and unique as the PS3 with its Synergistic processing elements (SPEs). However, as more developers become familiar with the distinctive features available on the Sony console, they will create more innovative games like *Flower* and *Little Big Planet* that take advantage of the PS3's capabilities. But progress remains slow.

The future of the PS3 depends entirely on the ability of developers to take advantage of its powerful processing ability. "On paper, the PlayStation 3's Cell engine is more capable than the Xbox 360's triple-core Xenon CPU," noted Carl Nelson (2007), founder of hardcoreware.net.

> However, the Xbox 360 is much easier to develop for. In other words, a lot of the Cell's power is going to waste. Although that is expected to change eventually, as always seems to happen with Sony's consoles (compare early PS2 games to current games, and the same goes for PS1), one year later we're still waiting for someone to fully exploit the system. Another indication that the PS3 is harder to develop for is the fact that almost all multiplatform games arrive weeks — if not months — after their 360 versions.

By 2009, the situation was beginning to change. "It looks like PS3's Cell architecture is finally beginning to flex its muscle," Nelson (2009) observed. "It is possible that the 360 has already met its full potential, and the PS3 is still getting there, at least where AAA exclusives are concerned."[1] Nelson was particularly impressed by certain PS3 exclusive titles like *Metal Gear Solid 4* and *Killzone 2*, both of which offered some of the best graphics and gameplay seen on any platform to date.

"We think the SPEs remain an underutilized resource," noted Scott Pease, Development Director for Neversoft Entertainment. "The Cell architecture … can surpass everything available in the current gen," added Dominique Duvivier, a programmer for Ubisoft Montreal. She admitted that at first, nobody in her company was "sure of what we could do," but "programmers are getting used to this kind of programming model. Ubisoft expects a lot of progression in the quality of games, helped on the content side by the storage capacity of the Blu-ray disk, and the non-optional hard drive."

At Ubisoft's Shanghai office, developers were making strides in their ability to program for the PS3. "We have to admit, the very different architecture of the PS3 was challenging at first," declared creative director Stanislas Mattra.

---

1   The term "AAA exclusives" refers to high quality big budget titles like *Halo 3* and *Killzone 2*.

> *This is the same architecture that forces you to rethink your work,*
> *opening your mind to new development areas and gameplay possibilities*
> *using the SPUs rather than stick to well known solutions. That's the*
> *reason why most developers now target the PS3 as their main platform.*
> (PlayStation 2009b)

This is consistent with the findings of Rebecca Henderson and Kim Clark (1990), who argue in their classic article on architectural innovation that "radical innovation establishes a new dominant design and, hence, a new set of core design concepts embodied in components that are linked together in a new architecture." The PS3 architecture not only stimulates new and innovative ways of thinking about program design, but it could also be creating a new industry standard.

One of the key advantages of the PS3 architecture was its ability to support distributed programming, which is "the current and future standard" according to Mattra. Distributed programming allowed developers to take advantage of the multiple processing elements within the Cell processor. Basically, the program is split up into units that can be handled simultaneously rather than sequentially. However, "getting there is not easy," noted Alain Tascan, General Manager of Electronic Arts in Montreal, Canada. "One has to resolve multiple complex data structures and data pathing problems" (*PlayStation* 2009b).

Redmond Washington-based Zipper Interactive created an "SPU boot camp" to train its developers to work with the PS3's synergistic processors. Even so, the company "could only leverage 10 percent of the SPU's potential," explained company founder Brian Soderberg. However, that 10 percent provided "massive gains."

> *This is the system under which we have found it possible to create a*
> *game with 256 networked characters, all skinned, in vast poly-rich*
> *environments, without sacrificing visual fidelity, without making*
> *concessions. We have scratched the surface of this machine's potential*
> *and it has allowed us to create what was once considered impossible.*
> (PlayStation 2009b)

The question is whether or not Sony will continue to build upon the technology it developed for the PS3. If it does, "we should enter the golden age of the PS3 soon," predicted EA Vice President Philip Holt. Afterwards, if the PlayStation 4 is designed as an improvement of existing PS3 architecture,

Sony could be well positioned to once again lead the market. By then the PS3 programming environment will be very familiar to developers, allowing studios to create a larger number of quality launch titles. If the system offers backwards compatibility, PS3 owners will be more inclined to upgrade. And an expanded PlayStation Network could give Xbox Live a run for its money. Of course, all of these are big "ifs."

By now, Sony should have learned that performance is not the most important factor in consumer purchasing behavior. Better graphics and sound can greatly enhance a game, but so can other features, such as intriguing story lines, challenging game play, and the ability to participate in group play, either at social gatherings or online. Sony is building alliances with some of the most innovative development studios. Now it must leverage those relationships to enhance gameplay using currently available technology.

Many developers feel that the PS3 continues to be underutilized, but as they build greater competence, they will be able to further evolve next generation gameplay without the need for another major hardware upgrade. Once programmers become accustomed to the new way of thinking required by the Cell processor, the PS3 will become "easier to develop for than the competition," claims Hermen Hulst, Managing Director of Guerrilla Games, "provided one approaches it with the right mindset" (*PlayStation* 2009b). The last thing that developers want is to have to start over again. That could set them back far enough in the learning curve that Microsoft will have an even greater opportunity to move ahead of Sony in the console wars.

All this suggests that the next PlayStation needs to be an extension of existing technology, just as the Wii was an extension of the GameCube. Even as Nintendo was able to redefine gaming without a significant upgrade to the hardware, so too can Sony find new ways to differentiate its PlayStation brand, provide value to consumers, and win over the hearts and minds of developers. "It's a developer's dream to think about your next game and how you can improve," explained Glen Schofield of Electronic Arts, "but thinking about the next console is even better. I just hope it's still a few years away—we're still learning new ways to squeeze more out of the PS3 even today" (*PlayStation* 2009b).

Sony might even want to delay introducing the next generation PlayStation for several years to give game developers more time to leverage the full capabilities of the current system. The risk, of course, is that Nintendo and

Microsoft will develop and launch their next generation console platforms before Sony.

Regardless of what happens, the technologies currently being developed are not going to disappear. Sooner or later, they will find their way into gaming consoles or other related products. How long it will take will depend on whether console makers and software developers can learn to avoid the types of performance traps discussed in this book and create products that are both fun and easy to use.

Bibliography

Abrams, D. 2008. CAG Community Xbox 360 Failure Survey Results. *Cheap Ass Gamer* [Online March] Available at: http://www.cheapassgamer.com/forums/showthread.php?t=175137 [accessed: 15 April 2008].

Acohido, B. 2006. Nintendo hopes Wii Spells Winner. *USA Today*. 15 August, 3B.

Akass, C. 2007. PS3 To Win Console War. *Personal Computer World*. 25 January.

Akihito, A. 1998. Gambling behaviors among college students: A preliminary investigation. *The Bulletin of Mukogawa Women's University*. (48), 21–28.

Allen, D. 2004. *Customer Satisfaction Research Management: A Comprehensive Guide to Integrating Customer Loyalty and Satisfaction Metrics in the Management of Complex Organizations*. Milwaukee: ASQ Quality Press.

Amazon.com. 2009. *Shaun White Snowboarding* Customer Reviews [Online] Available at: http://www.amazon.com/review/R88FCB81TJ9XP/ [accessed: 23 March 2009].

American Psychological Association. 2000. Press Release: Violent Video Games Can Increase Aggression [Online 23 April] Available at: http://www.apa.org/releases/videogames.html [accessed: 17 April 2007].

Amjadali, S. 2006. A Gamer's Paradise. *Herald Sun*. 12 March, 88.

Anderson, C. 2009. The New Economy. *Wired*. 17 June, 99.

Apple, Inc. 2008. Press Release: iPhone SDK Downloads Top 250,000 [Online 9 June] Available at: http://www.apple.com/pr/library/2008/06/09iphone_sdk.html [accessed: 26 July 2009].

Ashley, V. 2009. Microsoft Profit Falls for First Time in 23 Years. *The New York Times*. 24 April, B1.

Ayers, R. 2006. Review: *Real World Golf*. *The Entertainment Depot* [Online] Available at: http://www.entdepot.com/ps2/article_1448.php [accessed: 4 August 2009].

Baker, C. 2009. OnLive's 'Cloud Gaming' Could be a Game-Changer. *Wired* [Online 24 March] Available at: http://www.wired.com/gamelife/2009/03/cloud-gaming/ [accessed: 16 July 2009].

Bangeman, E. 2006. Sony Taking Big Hit on Each PS3 Sold; Xbox 360 in the Black. *Ars Technica* [Online 16 November] Available at: http://www.arstechnica. com/news.ars/post/20061116–8239.html [accessed: 21 March 2007].

Bangeman, E. 2008. Growth of Gaming in 2007 Far Outpaces Movies, Music. *Ars Technica* [Online 24 January] Available at: http://www.arstechnica.com/ news.ars/post/20080124-growth-of-gaming-in-2007-far-outpaces-movies-music.html [accessed: 16 September 2008].

BBC News. 2005. Muted hello for Xbox 360 in Japan [Online 10 December] Available at: http://news.bbc.co.uk/1/hi/technology/4517362.stm [accessed: 7 May 2008].

BBC News. 2007. PlayStation 3 Launched in Europe [Online 23 March] Available at: http://news.bbc.co.uk/1/hi/technology/6474045.stm [accessed: 4 May 2009].

Beenstock, S. 1998. Marketing Focus: Market raider: How Sony Won the Console Game. *Marketing*. 10 September.

Belluck, P. 2006. As Minds Age, What's Next? Brain Calisthenics. *The New York Times*. 27 December, 1.

Berardini, C. 2007a. Wistron to Discontinue Production of Xbox 360. *Team Xbox* [Online 26 March] Available at: http://news.teamxbox.com/xbox/13096/ Wistron-to-Discontinue-Production-of-Xbox-360/ [accessed: 23 October 2007].

Berardini, C. 2007b. Xbox Disc Replacement Program Kicks Off. *Team Xbox* [Online 3 April] Available at: http://news.teamxbox.com/xbox/13175/Xbox-Disc-Replacement-Program-Kicks-Off/ [accessed: 28 April 2008].

Berardini, C. 2007c. Robbie Bach: Xbox Will Be Profitable Next Year. *Team Xbox* [Online 4 May] Available at: http://news.teamxbox.com/xbox/13401/Robbie-Bach-Xbox-Will-Be-Profitable-Next-Year/ [accessed 7 May 2008].

Berger, C. et al. 1993. Kano's Methods for Understanding Customer-defined Quality. *The Center for Quality Management Journal*. 2 (4), 1–37.

Berghammer, B. 2006. The Revolution Gets a Name: Wii. *Game Informer* [Online 27 April] Available at: http://www.gameinformer.com/News/Story/200604/ N06.0427.1154.38678.htm [accessed June 18, 2007].

Bishop, T. 2009. Q&A: Microsoft's Robbie Bach on economy, Zune glitch and iPhone. *Tech Flash* [Online 8 January] Available at: http://www.techflash. com/QA_Microsofts_Robbie_Bach_on_games_phones_and_Zune_glitch37268609.html [accessed: 26 January 2009].

Boone, M. 2001. *Managing Interactively*. New York: McGraw-Hill.

Bowditch, G. 2008. *Grand Theft Auto* Producer is Godfather of Gaming. *The Times* [Online 27 April] Available at: http://www.timesonline.co.uk/tol/news/ uk/scotland/article3821838.ece [accessed: 28 August 2008].

Boyer, B. 2007. Harmonix Talks *Guitar Hero*, New Music Franchise. *GamaSutra* [Online 22 January] Available at: http://www.gamasutra.com/php-bin/news_index.php?story=12477 [accessed: 21 August 2008].

Boyer, B. 2008. Pachter: Smash Bros, Wii To Drive $850m In March U.S. Sales. *GamaSutra* [Online 14 April] Available at : http://www.gamasutra.com/php-bin/news_index.php?story=18233 [accessed: 16 April 2008].

Boyes, E. 2007a. Q&A: RedOctane's Kai Huang. *GameSpot* [Online 16 April] Available at: http://www.gamespot.com/news/6169125.html [accessed: 23 July 2008].

Boyes, E. 2007b. Xbox 360s investigated by *Watchdog*. *GameSpot* [Online 14 February] Available at: http://www.gamespot.com/news/6165896.html?page=3 [accessed: 16 April 2008].

Boyes, E. 2009. Crytek Purchases Free Radical, Says Company Scriptwriter. *1Up News* [Online 3 February] Available at: http://www.1up.com/do/newsStory?cId=3172598 [accessed: 17 April 2009].

Brightman, J. 2006. PC Gaming on the Rise. *Business Week* [Online 28 February] Available at: http://www.businessweek.com/innovate/content/feb2006/id20060228_545385.htm [accessed: 29 June 2007].

Brightman, J. 2007. Carmack on id Mobile, Crap Games, and Why iPod Sucks. *Game Daily* [Online 15 November] Available at: http://www.gamedaily.com/games/doom-rpg/mobile/game-features/carmack-on-id-mobile-crap-games-and-why-ipod-sucks/4674/71158/ [accessed: 26 July 2009].

Brightman, J. 2008. Interview: Take-Two's Ben Feder Talks GTA, Wii, MMOs and More. *Game Daily* [Online 28 July] Available at: http://www.gamedaily.com/articles/features/interview-taketwos-ben-feder-talks-gta-wii-mmos-and-more/?biz=1 [accessed: 20 May 2009].

Brightman. J. 2009. NPD: PC Game Sales Fall 14% in 2008, *Game Daily* [Online 15 January] Available at: http://www. gamedaily.com/articles/news/npd-pc-game-sales-fall-14-in-2008/ [accessed: 13 April 2009].

Buchanan, M. 2009. Apple is Serious about Gaming: Steals Xbox Senior Director of Strategy. Gizmodo [Online 30 April] Available at: http://gizmodo.com/5234256/apple-is-serious-about-gaming-steals-xbox-senior-director-of-strategy [accessed: 31 July 2009].

Burrill, W. 1993. Game Boy a Video Dinosaur Despite Many Shortcomings, Hand-held Unit is Selling Well. *The Toronto Star*. 13 March, J-4.

Callaham, J. 2008. Over $3 million in sales (so far) for Garry's Mod. *Game Daily* [Online 3 December] Available at: http://news.bigdownload.com/2008/12/03/over-3-million-in-revenue-so-far-from-garrys-mod/ [accessed: 23 May 2009].

Campbell, S. 2007. Report Shows HDTV Sets Likely to See Major Growth, TMCnet [Online 28 June] Available at: http://www.tmcnet.com/voip/ip-communications/articles/8029-report-shows-hdtv-sets-likely-see-major-growth.htm [accessed: 24 July 2007].

Carson, M. 2000. *The Axe. Kick Start News* [Online] Available at: http://www.kickstartnews.com/reviews/productivity/the_axe.html [accessed: 17 July 2008].

Carter, D. and Rovell, D. 2003. *On the Ball.* Upper Saddle River: Financial Times Prentice Hall

Caulfield, B. 2008a. Games Girls Play. *Forbes* [Online 14 March] Available at: http://www.forbes.com/2008/03/13/casual-gaming-women-tech-personal-cx_bc_0314casual.html [accessed: 21 May 2009].

Caulfield, B. 2008b.The Xbox Trap. *Forbes* [Online 24 April] Available at: http://www.forbes.com/2008/04/24/microsoft-xbox-earnings-tech-ebiz-cx_bc_0424xbox.html [accessed: 3 August 2009].

Centers for Disease Control. 1999. Press Release: Obesity Epidemic Increases Dramatically in the United States. [Online 26 October] Available at: http://www.cdc.gov/OD/OC/MEDIA/pressrel/r991026.htm8 [accessed: 17 April 2007].

Chen, B. 2009. iPhone, You Phone, We All Wanna iPhone. *Wired* [Online 27 June] Available at: http://www.wired.com/thisdayintech/2009/06/dayintech_0629/ [accessed: 26 July 2009].

Chesbrough, H. 2003. *Open Innovation: The New Imperative for Creating and Profiting from Technology.* Boston: Harvard Business Press.

Chesbrough, H., Vanhaverbeke, W. and West, J. 2006. *Open Innovation: Researching a New Paradigm.* New York: Oxford University Press.

Chmielewski, D. 2006. Marketing Moms. *The Los Angeles Times.* 25 December, C-1.

Chronis, G. 2001a. Winners are Many in War of Consoles. *Video Business.* 26 November.

Chronis, G. 2001b. Restocking Keeps Xbox Rockin'. *Video Business.* 17 December.

Chung Lee, J. 2009. *Procrastineering – The Personal Blog of Johnny Chung Lee* [Online 1 June] Available at: http://procrastineering.blogspot.com/2009/06/project-natal.html [accessed: 7 June 2009].

Cifaldi, F. 2006. Analysts: FPS 'Most Attractive' Genre for Publishers. *Gamasutra* [Online 21 February] Available at: http://www.gamasutra.com/php-bin/news_index.php?story=8241 [accessed: 17 April 2009].

Clark, S. 2008. PlayStation Store Movie Downloads Review Part 2. *Variety* [Online 17 July] Available at: http://www.videobusiness.com/blog/1730000173/post/1420030142.html [accessed: 12 July 2009].

Classic Gaming Museum. 1999. 3DO FAQ [Online 10 February] Available at: http://www.classicgaming.com/3dotoday [accessed: 6 July 2009].

Clements, R. 2009. Flower Review. *IGN* [Online 9 February] Available at: http://ps3.ign.com/articles/952/952529p1.html [accessed: 24 April 2009].

Chaplin, H. and Ruby, A. 2005. *Smartbomb: The Quest for Art, Entertainment, and Big Bucks in the Videogame Revolution.* Chapel Hill: Algonquin.

Chen, Y. and Tsai, J. 2007. Wistron Quits on Xbox 360. *Digitimes* [Online 14 November] Available at: http://www.digitimes.com/systems/a20071113PD219.html [accessed 27 August 2008].

Christensen, C. 1997. *The Innovator's Dilemma.* Boston: Harvard Business School Press.

Christiansen, C., Suarez, F. and Utterback, J. 1998. Strategies for Survival in Fast-Changing Industries. *Management Science.* 44, 207–220.

Cohen, K. 2007. Alienware, Out of This World Success. *Hispanic Trends.* February/March, 26–30.

Combs, J. 2008. NEC, The Hudson Bee and TurboGrafx-16: From Japan to the USA, a Turbocharged Competition. *Game Trader.* [Online March] Available at: http://www.videogametrader.com/2009/03/16/nec-the-hudson -bee-and-turbografx-16-from-japan-to-the-usa-a-turbocharged-competition/# [accessed: 2 July 2009].

Consumer Electronics Daily. 2006. Don't Write Off Nintendo's 'Revolution,' Analysts Say [Online 10 March] Available at: http://www.cedailynews.com/2006/03/index.html [accessed: 20 February 2007].

Consumer Reports. 2001. DVD Players. December.

Consumer Reports. 2008. Buzzword: Staycation. [Online 24 April] Available at: http://www.blogs.consumerreports.org/home/2008/04/staycation.html [accessed: 18 January 2009].

Cordeira, J. 2005. *Wipeout Pure* Review. *Gaming Age.* [Online 22 March] Available at: http://www.gaming-age.com/cgi-bin/reviews/review.pl?sys= psp&game=wipeout_pure [accessed: 25 July 2009].

Cornelisse, B. 2008. Media Molecule Interview. *VG Chartz* [Online 3 November] Available at: http://news.vgchartz.com/news.php?id=2454 [accessed: 19 May 2009].

Crawford. C. 1992.The History of Computer Games: The Atari Years. *The Journal of Computer Game Design* [Online] Available at: http://www.erasmatazz.com/library/JCGD_Volume_5/The_Atari_Years.html [accessed: 1 June 2007].

Croal, N. 2000. The Art of the Game. *Newsweek.* 6 March, 60.

Croal, N. 2007. Confession is Good for the Soul: Why Microsoft Must Be More Forthcoming About the Xbox 360's Flaws--Or Initiate a Recall. *Newsweek* [Online 10 July] Available at: http://blog.newsweek.com/blogs/levelup/archive/2007/07/10/why-microsoft-must-be-more-forthcoming-about-xbox-360-flaws-or-initiate-a-recall.aspx [accessed: 16 May 2008].

Crossly, R. 2009. *Final Fantasy* Team Balancing Costs with Creativity. *Develop Magazine.* [Online 5 May]. Available at: http://www.developmag.com/news/31792/Final-Fantasy-team-balancing-costs-with-creativity [accessed: 20 May 2009].

Davies, P. 2003. Nintendo Interviews: Miyamoto Speaks! *Computer and Video Games* [Online 13 May] Available at: http://www.computerandvideogames.com/article.php?id=91537 [accessed: 6 July 2007].

Davis, R. 2001. *Frequency* Review. *GameSpot* [Online 19 November] Available at: http://www.gamespot.com/ps2/puzzle/frequency/review.html [accessed 1 August 2009].

Deming, W. 1982. Improvement of Quality and Productivity through Action by Management. *National Productivity Review.* Winter, 12–22.

Dillon, B. 2008. Jenova Chen, Designer of Flow. *Notes on Game Dev* [Online 27 October] Available at: http://www.notesongamedev.net/people/design-interviews/jenova-chen/ [accessed: 24 April 2009].

D'Innocenzio, A. 2001. Sega Set to Leave Dreamcast Behind: Game Console Dies due to Poor Sales. *The National Post.* 31 January, C20.

Divnich, J. 2009. New Versus Old. *Game Informer.* July, 12.

Doree, A. 2006. Hirai: Motion Sensing Beats Rumble. *Kikizo* [Online 3 October] Available at: http://games.kikizo.com/news/200610/009.asp [accessed: 13 June 2007].

Dow Jones Newswire. 2008. Sales of Viacom's '*Rock Band*' Sing, But Profits Fall Flat, Dow Jones Newswire [Online 31 July] Available at: http://money.cnn.com/news/newsfeeds/articles/djf500/200808051254DOWJONESDJONLINE000412_FORTUNE5.htm [accessed 1 August 2009].

Dvorak J. 2005. Sony's New PlayStation 3 Game Machine Will Use an Advanced 2-teraflop CPU Being Developed Jointly by IBM, Sony, and Toshiba. *PC Magazine,* 22 March, 53.

Economist, The. 1993. Nintendo; Game Over? 20 November.

Economist, The. 2008. Play On. 18 December.

Economist, The. 2009. Playing a New Game. 18 April, 72.

Ekberg, B. 2007. *WWE SmackDown! vs. RAW 2008* First-Look. *GameSpot* [Online 30 March] Available at: http://www.gamespot.com/wii/action/smackdownvsraw2008/news.html?sid=6168373&mode=previews [accessed: 2 July 2007].

Electronic Gaming Business. 2003. Earnings Roundup: Software Up, Hardware Down, Prospects Mixed for Sony, Nintendo, and Atari [Online 13 August] Available at: http://findarticles.com/p/articles/mi_m0PJQ/is_9_1/ai_110307539/ [accessed: 4 August 2009].

Electronic Gaming Monthly. 2005. Sony and Microsoft Take the Next-Gen Battle to the Japanese Front. 1 October, 18.

emarketer, 2009. Traffic Spikes for Ad-Supported Games [Online 19 February] Available at: http://www.emarketer.com/Article.aspx?R=1006906 [accessed: 22 May 2009].

Emery, C. 2009. Detour Bar Maker Files Bankruptcy on Peanut Recall. *Reuters UK* [Online 17 February] Available at: http://uk.reuters.com/article/fundsNews2/idUKN1736922020090217 [accessed: 23 February 2009].

Ewers, J. 2006. Cisco's Connections. *US News and World Report*. 26 June.

Fahey, M. 2008. Sony Patents Ultrasonic Waggle Controller Technology. *Kotaku* [Online 30 October] Available at: http://www.kotaku.com/5071145/sony-patents-ultrasonic-waggle-controller-technology [accessed: 23 March 2009].

Farhan, H. 2006. E3 2006: PlayStation 3 and Nintendo Wii. *Anantech* [Online 16 May] Available at: http://www.anandtech.com/tradeshows/showdoc.aspx?i=2757 [accessed: 6 June 2007].

Farley, C. 2001. In Fantasy's Loop, Time 100: The Next Wave. *Time* [Online 28 May] Available at: http://www.time.com/time/magazine/article/0,9171,999983,00.html [accessed: 16 June 2009].

Feldman, C. E3 06: Analysts React Swiftly to Console News. *GameSpot* [Online 11 May] Available at: http://www.gamespot.com/news/6150398.html [accessed 6 June 2007].

Fenlon, B. 2002. Game's Violence Bloody Alluring. *The Toronto Sun*. 31 October, 44.

Flavelle, D. Microsoft's Xbox 360 the Holiday's Most Elusive Gift. *The Toronto Star*. 8 December, D1.

Fleming, D. 1996. *Powerplay: Toys as Popular Culture*. Manchester: Manchester University Press.

Fletcher, J. 2009. *Wii Sports Resort* Features Golf and Table Tennis? *Joystiq* [Online 18 May] Available at: http://nintendo.joystiq.com/2009/05/18/wii-sports-resort-features-golf-and-table-tennis?icid=sphere_blogsmith_inpage_joystiqnintendo [accessed: 5 June 2009].

Foster, R. 1986. *Innovation: The Attacker's Advantage*. New York: Summit Books.

Fortune. 2009. 100 Best Companies to Work For. 2 February, 72.

Fritz, B. 2006. Sony Gets its Game On. *Daily Variety*. 10 May, 1.

Fritz, B. 2008. Litigious Note on 'Guitar'. *Daily Variety*. 12 March, 2.

Frommer, D. 2009. iPhone Apps A Hot Acquisition Market. *Silicon Valley Insider* [Online 29 April] Available at: http://www.businessinsider.com/iphone-apps-a-hot-acquisition-market-2009-4 [accessed: 29 April 2009].

Game Informer. 2009. Atari President Phil Harrison Looks Into the Future. April, 18.

GameSpot. 2006. The Miracle Piano Teaching System Reviews [Online 16 March] Available at: http://www.gamespot.com/nes/action/miraclepiano/player_review.html [accessed: 24 June 2009].

GameSpot. 2007. Shigeru Miyamoto Interview [Online 12 July] Available at: http://www.gamespot.com/video/942009/6174769/shigeru-miyamoto-interview [accessed: 16 July 2007].

GameSpot UK. 2001. Microsoft Denies Xbox Dreamcast Rumours [Online 26 January] Available at: http://news.zdnet.co.uk/emergingtech /0,1000000183,2083985,00.htm [accessed: 27 February 2009].

Game Trailers. 2009. Microsoft Video Game, E3 09: Phil Spencer Interview Part I [Online 5 June] Available at: http://www.gametrailers.com/video/e3–09-microsoft/50988 [accessed: 8 June 2009].

Gaming Today. 2007. *Rock Band* on eBay [Online 1 December] Available at: http://news.filefront.com/rock-band-on-ebay-you-how-much-for-it/ [accessed: 15 September 2008].

Gantayat, A. 2006. E3 2006: Kutaragi Claims PS3 Too Cheap? *IGN* [Online 9 May] Available at: http://ps3.ign.com/articles/706/706133p1.html [accessed: 20 June 2007].

Gardiner, R. 1994. *Games for Business and Economics*. New York: Wiley.

Gaudiosi, J. 2007. How the Wii is Creaming the Competition. *Business 2.0*. 25 April.

Gay Gamer. 2009. Capcom Bringing PS1 Games To PSN. Eventually [Online 18 March] Available at: http://www.gaygamer.net/2009/03/capcom_bringing_ps1_games_to_p.html [accessed: 18 May 2009].

Gershenfeld, A., Loparco, M., and Barajas, C. 2003. *Game Plan: The Insider's Guide to Breaking In and Succeeding in the Computer and Video Game Business*. New York: St. Martin's Press.

Gibbon, D. 2007. '*Halo 3*' Cost £15 million to Develop. Digital Spy [Online 28 December] Available at: http://www.digitalspy.co.uk/gaming/a82352/halo-3-cost-gbp15-million-to-develop.html [accessed: 28 August 2008].

Gladwell, M. 2002. *The Tipping Point*. Newport Beach, CA: Back Bay Books.

Globe and Mail, The. 1996. Video Games Too Violent, Report Says. 6 December, C13.

Globe and Mail, The. 2005. Proprietary Worries Delayed New Sony Products, Top Executive Admits. 21 January, B12.

Good, O. 2009. Indie Devs Turn to In-Game Ads After Piracy Strike. *Kotaku* [Online 21 May] Available at: http://www.kotaku.com/5264139/indie-devs-turn-to-in+game-ads-after-piracy-strike [accessed: 23 May 2009].

Goodavage, J. 1972. *Spacewar!* A Computer Game Today, Reality Tomorrow. *Saga*. November, 35.

Grant, C. 2006. Sony Declares "Full-on Assault" on Xbox Live. *Joystick* [Online 31 January] Available at: http://www.joystiq.com/2006/01/31/sony-declares-full-on-assault-on-xbox-live/ [accessed: 25 April 2008].

Grant, C. 2007. September NPD: Xbox 360 Takes the Lead, *Halo 3* to Thank. *Joystick* [Online 18 October] Available at: http://www.joystiq.com/2007/10/18/september-npd-xbox-360-takes-the-lead-halo-3-to-thank/ [accessed: 28 April 2008].

Graser, M. 1999. Sega Dreamcast Tops 1 mil Mark. *Variety*. 24 November, 4.

Gross, N. and Brandt, R. 1994. Sony has some very Scary Monsters in the Works. *Business Week*. 23 May, 116.

Gruener, W. 2009. Nintendo Wii Surrenders Market Share in Weak Game Console Market. *TG Daily* [Online 17 July] Available at: http://www.tgdaily.com/content/view/43289/113/ [accessed 21 July 2009].

Guardian, The. 2000. Sony Set for Total Entertainment. 24 February, 2.

Haber, S. et al. 2003. If Piracy is the Problem, Is DRM the Answer? in *Digital Rights Management: Technological, Economic, Legal and Political Aspects*, edited by E. Becker et al. Berlin:Springer-Verlag, 224–233.

Hachman, M. 2006. Universal Backs out of Blu-ray. *PC Magazine* [Online 19 September] Available at: http://www.pcmag.com/article2/0,2817,2017527,00.asp [accessed: 3 August 2009].

Hamel, G. 2000. *Leading the Revolution*. Boston: Harvard Business School Publishing.

Hara, Y., McGrath, D. and Yoshida, J. 2006. '06 Had Sony Singing the Blues. *Video Imaging DesignLine* [Online 28 December] Available at: http://www.videsignline.com/196800222 [accessed: 3 August 2009].

Harding, R. and Nutall, C. 2009. Nintendo "Rejected" Rivals' Choice of Technology. *Financial Times* [Online 4 June] Available at: http://www.ft.com/cms/s/0/dfcdde86–513e–11de–84c3–00144feabdc0.html [accessed: 7 June 2009].

Harding-Rolls, P. and Keen, B. 2005. Digital Distribution of Games: Growth Opportunities and Forecasts to 2010. *Screen Digest*. August, 17–19.

Harris, C. 2008. Nintendo DSi Hands-on. *IGN* [Online 5 November] Available at: http://ds.ign.com/articles/927/927128p1.html [accessed: 25 July 2009].

Hartley, A. 2008. Jasper-based Xbox 360s beat RRoD Problems. *Tech Radar* [Online 1 December] Available at: http://techradar.com/news/gaming/jasper-based-xbox-360s-beat-rrod-problems-489725 [accessed: 7 May 2009].

Haynes, J. 2007. PS3 Updated to 1.50. *IGN News* [Online 24 January] Available at: http://ps3.ign.com/articles/758/758306p1.html [accessed: 12 April 2007].

Hax, A. and Wilde, D. 2001. *The Delta Project: Discovering New Sources of Profitability*. New York: Palgrave.

Henderson, R. and Clark, K. 1990. Architectural Innovation: The Reconfiguration of Existing Product Technologies and the Failure of Established Firms. *Administrative Science Quarterly*, 35, 9–30.

Herman, L. 2008. Handheld Video Game Systems, in *The Video Game Explosion: A History from PONG to PlayStation and Beyond*, edited by M. Wolf. Westport: Greenwood Press, 143–48.

Hiatt, B. 2008. Rock Games Battle for the Bands. *Rolling Stone*. 7 August, 7–8.

High Fidelity Review. 2004. DVD-Audio Sales Five Times Higher than SACD Sales [Online 22 April] Available at: http://highfidelityreview.com/news/news.asp?newsnumber=18483611 [accessed: 5 April 2007].

Hillis, S. 2007. Microsoft says 'Halo' 1st-week Sales were $300 mln. *Reuters* [Online 4 October] Available at: http://uk.reuters.com/article/technologyNews/idUKN0438777720071005 [accessed: August 2008].

Hinkle, D. 2009. Patent Shows Wiimote was Originally a GameCube Peripheral. *Joystiq* [Online 9 January] Available at: http://nintendo.joystiq.com/2009/01/09/patent-shows-wiimote-was-originally-a-gamecube-peripheral/ [accessed: 21 July 2009].

Holden, W. 2007. Juniper Research Predicts Mobile Games Market to Reach $10bn by 2009, Driven by Emerging Markets and Casual Gamers. *Juniper Research* [Online 7 November] Available at: http://juniperresearch.com/shop/viewpressrelease.php?pr=63 [accessed: 26 July 2009].

Hsu, D. and Bettenhausen, S. 2007. Battle Station. *Electronic Gaming Monthly*. March, 60–72.

Huang, C. 2008. The Real *Guitar Hero*. *The Straits Times*. 17 June.

Hussman, W. 2007. How to Sink a Newspaper. *The Wall Street Journal*. 5 May, A15.

IGN. 2009. Top 100 Game Creators of All Time [Online 23 February] Available at: http://games.ign.com/top-100-game-creators/1.html [accessed: 16 June 2009].

Immersion Corporation. 2006. *Immersion Corporation Introduces Next-Generation Vibration Technology for Video Console Gaming Systems* [Online 19 June] Available at: http://ir.immersion.com/releasedetail.cfm?ReleaseID=201102 [accessed 4 May 2009].

Independent, The. 2009. Music Industry Decides that all the World's a Stage [Online 3 January] Available at: http://www.independent.co.uk/arts-entertainment/music/features/music-industry-decides-that-all-the-worlds-a-stage-1222854.html [accessed: 18 January 2009].

Irish Times, The. 2008. 'Grand Theft Auto' Makers Reject $2bn Takeover Offer. 26 February, 23.

Ishizawa, M. 1994. 'Fantasy' Creator Sticks to Proven Path Square Co. Rebukes Nintendo Rivals, Reaffirms Strategy of Targeting Super Famicom Megahits. *The Nikkei Weekly*. 26 December, 8.

Islam, F. 2002. Making Money in Video Games not Child's Play. *The Observer*. 5 May, 8.

Izawa, E. 2000. The Romantic, Passionate Japanese in Anime, in *Japan Pop! Inside the World of Japanese Popular Culture*, edited by Craig, T. New York: M.E. Sharpe, 141–142.

Jenkins, D. 2005. PopCap Games Releases Open Source Framework. *Gamasutra* [Online 9 March]. Available at: http://gamasutra.com/php-bin/news_index. php?story=5084 [accessed: 22 May 2009].

Jenkins, D. 2007. Nintendo Full Year Results Show Rapid Gain, *Gamasutra* [Online 26 April] Available at: http://gamasutra.com/php-bin/news_index. php?story=13682 [accessed 9 July 2007].

Johansson, J. and Nonaka, I. 1996. *Relentless: The Japanese Way of Marketing*. New York: HarperBusiness.

Johnson, S. 2006. *Everything Bad is Good for You*. New York: Riverhead Trade.

Jones, A. 2007. Interview: C&VG's Miyamoto Interview. *N-Europe* [Online 22 March]. Available at: http://www.n-europe.com/news.php?nid=4563 [accessed: 20 March 2007].

Jones, G. 2007. Sony PS3 Hit by £10m in Cancellations. *Brand Republic Daily News* [Online 27 March] Available at: http://www.brandrepublic.com/ BrandRepublicNews/News/646182/Sony-PS3-hit-10m-cancellations/ [accessed: 28 June 2007].

Juran, J. and Gryna, F. 2001. *Quality Planning and Analysis: From Product Development through Use*. New York: McGraw-Hill.

Kairer, R. 2005. Tapwave Discontinues Zodiac Business. *Palm Info Center* [Online 27 July] Available at: http://www.palminfocenter.com/news/7990/tapwave-discontinues-zodiac-business/ [accessed: 24 July 2009].

Kane, Y. 2007. Beyond *Pokémon*: Nintendo DS Goes To School in Japan. *The Wall Street Journal*. 11 July 11, A1.

Kasavin, G. 2006. Review of *Resistance: Fall of Man*. *GameSpot* [Online 15 November] Available at: http://www.gamespot.com/ps3/action/ insomniacshooter/review.html?om_act=convert&om_clk=gssummary&tag= summary;review [accessed: 20 February 2007].

Kelly, M. 2008. Not Just Lag: How Nintendo Fumbled Online Play. *Kombo* [Online 4 April] Available at: http://wii.kombo.com/article.php?artid=11651 [accessed: 20 July 2009].

Kennedy, S. 2005. Dreamcast 2.0. *1up* [Online 4 November] Available at: http:// www.1up.com/do/feature?cId=3145154 [accessed: 27 February 2009].

Klepek, P. 2006. Are Wii Ready? Nintendo's Revolution Renamed. *1up* [Online 27 April] Available at: http://www.1up.com/do/newsStory?cId=3150013 [accessed: 18 June 2007].

Klepek, P. 2007a. NPD Releases December Numbers. *1up* [Online 11 January] Available at: http://www.1up.com/do/newsStory?cId=3156365 [accessed: 21 August 2008].

Klepek, P. 2007b. Sony: Rumble is a Last Generation Feature. *1up* [Online 26 February] Available at: http://www.1up.com/do/newsStory?cId=3157501 [accessed: 23 April 2009].

Klepek, P. 2007c. NPD: 30% of Xbox 360 Owners Aware of HD Graphics. *1up* [Online 8 August] Available at: http://www.1up.com/do/newsStory?cId=3161833 [accessed: 26 January 2009].

Klepek, P. 2008. CES 2008: The Future of PSP. *1up* [Online 8 January] Available at: http://www.1up.com/do/newsStory?cId=3165293 [accessed: 25 July 2009].

Kohler, C. 2006. Sony's Online Free-for-All. *Wired* [Online 20 October] Available at: http://www.wired.com/gaming/gamingreviews/news/2006/10/71982 [accessed: 22 May 2009].

Kohler, C. 2008. Q&A: 90 Minutes with Miyamoto, Nintendo's Master of Amusement. *Wired* [Online 27 June] Available at: http://www.wired.com/gamelife/2008/06/interview-90-mi/ [accessed: 4 June 2009].

Korzeniowski, P. 2008. The TV Ad Exodus, Part 1: Beyond the 30-Second Spot. *E-Commerce Times* [13 September] Available at: http://www.ecommercetimes.com/story/must-read/64460.html [accessed: 16 September 2008].

Kuchera, B. 2007a. Microsoft to Extend Warranty against Red Rings of Death to 3 Years. *Ars Technica* [Online 5 July] Available at: http://arstechnica.com/gaming/news/2007/07/microsoft-to-extend-warranty-against-red-rings-of-death-for-3-years.ars [accessed 16 April 2008].

Kuchera, B. 2007b. Report: Gamers Largely Clueless about Next-gen Console Media Capabilities. *Ars Technica* [Online 9 August] Available at: http://arstechnica.com/gaming/news/2007/08/report-gamers-largely-clueless-about-next-gen-console-media-capabilities.ars [accessed: 21 April 2009].

Kuchera, B. 2008a. Xbox 360 Failure Rates Worse than Most Consumer Electronics. *Ars Technica* [Online 14 February] Available at: http://arstechnica.com/gaming/news/2008/02/xbox-360-failure-rates-worse-than-most-consumer-electornics.ars [accessed: 16 April 2008].

Kuchera, B. 2008b. Why Microsoft Should be Worried about New Npd Sales Figures. *Ars Technica* [Online 14 March] Available at: http://arstechnica.com/gaming/news/2008/03/why-microsoft-should-be-worried-about-new-npd-sales-figures.ars [accessed: 16 May 2008].

Kuchera, B. 2008c. A Crumbling Tower: Sony Lays Siege to the 360's Weak Spots. *Ars Technica* [Online 17 August] Available at: http://arstechnica.com/news.ars/post/20080817-microsoft.html [accessed: 27 August 2008].

Kuchera, B. 2009. $80 Controller: Nintendo Announces Date, Price of MotionPlus. *Ars Technica* [Online 14 April] Available at: http://arstechnica.com/gaming/news/2009/04/while-the-nintendo-wii-may.ars [accessed: 19 April 2009].

Lagrace, M. 2006. Open Source Science: A New Model for Innovation. *HBS Working Knowledge* [Online 20 November] Available at: http://hbswk.hbs.edu/item/5544.html [accessed: 9 June 2009].

Lai, M. 2009. Xbox 360 to host 1 vs 100 Xbox Live Points Prize. *Punch Jump* [Online 7 July] Available at: http://news.punchjump.com/article.php?id=8207 [accessed: 16 July 2009].

Lee, E. 2007. 100 Million iPods Sold Since 2001. *San Francisco Chronicle*. 10 April 2007, C1.

Leek, M. 2005. Game On. *The San Jose Mercury News*. 2 January, 40.

Leichtman Research Group. 2007. Press Release: Over Half of U.S. Households Subscribe to Broadband Internet [Online 7 June] Available at: http://www.leichtmanresearch.com/press/060707release.html [accessed: 24 July 2007].

Lefton, T. 1994. Play It Loud; Nintendo Goes After MTV Generation. *Adweek*. 27 June.

Lemos, R. 1998. US Report: Windows CE Lands its Sega Dream Machine. *ZdNet* [Online 22 May] Available at: http://www.news.zdnet.co.uk/software/0,1000000121,2068408,00.htm [accessed: 27 February 2009].

Leonard-Barton, D. 1998. *Wellsprings of Knowledge: Building and Sustaining the Sources of Innovation*. Boston: Harvard Business School Press.

Levine, D. 1993. Nintendo Urges Groups Representing Mentally Handicapped to Zap Sega Ads. *Adweek*. 15 November.

Levy, C. 2009. Dead Discs: Blu-ray's Failure to Launch Signals end of Spinning Media. *TG Daily* [Online 23 June] Available at: http://www.tgdaily.com/content/view/42950/99/ [accessed: 22 July 2009].

Levy, S. 1993. Hey, it's More than a Game. *The New York Times*. 18 July, 7–8.

Levy, S. 2009. Young's Frankenstein. *Wired*. July, 54.

Li, R., Kennedy, S. and Bertrand, J. 2006. What the Cell is Going On? *The PlayStation Official Magazine* [Online 28 November] Available at: http://www.1up.com/do/feature?cId=3155393 [accessed: 28 June 2007].

Lichfield, J. 1991. Game Up as Nintendo Admits Price-fixing. *The Independent*. 11 April, 28.

Lieberman, J. 1993. Label Games—or Else. *USA Today*. 6 December, 10A.

Lowood, H. 2006. A Brief Biography of Computer Games, in *Playing Video Games*, edited by P. Vorderer and J. Bryant. Mahwah, New Jersey: Lawrence Erlbaum Associates, 25–32.

Mainelli T. 2000. The Sony Emotion Engine: Will PlayStation 2 Replace your PC? [Online 1 February] Available at: http://www.archives.cnn.com/2000/TECH/computing/02/01/emotion.engine.idg [accessed: 28 June 2007].

Mantle, R. 2005. SACD is Dead [Online 1 April] Available at: http://ultraaudio.com/opinion/20050401.htm [accessed: 5 April 2007].

Markoff, J. 1993. Market Place; Investors can only Guess Which Video Game Device will Conquer. *The New York Times*. 9 September, D-6.

Markoff, J. and Richtel, M. 2006. Battleground for Consoles Moves Online. *The New York Times* [Online 18 October] Available at: http://www.nytimes.com/2006/10/18/technology/18game.html?_r=1&pagewanted=2 [accessed: 2 August 2009].

Marriott, M. 2004. From Sony, a Hand-held Entertainment Center. *The New York Times*. 13 May, 7.

Marriott, S. TurboExpress Biography. All Game [Online] Available at: http://www.allgame.com/platform.php?id=17673 [accessed: 24 July 2009].

Martin, M. 2007. Repair specialists refuse to take 360s. *Games Industry* [Online 28 June] Available at: http://www.gamesindustry.biz/articles/repair-specialists-refuse-to-take-360s [accessed: 15 April 2008].

Matthews, M. 2009. NPD: Behind the Numbers, February 2009. *Gamasutra* [Online 21 March] Available at: http://www.gamasutra.com/view/feature/3969/npd_behind_the_numbers_february_.php [accessed: 23 March 2009].

Matzler, K. and Hinterhuber, H. 1998. How to Make Product Development Projects More Successful by Integrating Kano's Model of Customer Satisfaction into Quality Function Deployment. *Technovation*. 18, 25–38.

McDonald, M. 2005. Koji Kondo Interview. *Electronic Gaming Monthly* [Online 3 May] Available at: http://www.1up.com/do/feature?pager.offset=0&cId=3140040 [accessed 18 June 2009].

McDougall, P. 2007. Microsoft Xbox 360 Sales Plunge 60% as Problems Mount. *Information Week* [Online 20 July] Available at: http://www.informationweek.com/news/personal_tech/showArticle.jhtml?articleID=201200157 [accessed: 3 August 2009].

McDougall, P. 2008. Microsoft Drops Player Fees on Games for Windows Live. *Information Week* [Online 23 July] Available at: http://www.informationweek.com/news/windows/operatingsystems/showArticle.jhtml?articleID=209600008 [accessed: 16 July 2009].

McElroy, J. 2009. Joystiq Survey: Xbox 360 E74 Errors on the Rise Since NXE. *Joystiq* [Online 19 March] Available at: http://www.joystiq.com/2009/03/19/joystiq-survey-xbox-360-e74-errors-on-the-rise-since-nxe [accessed: 29 April 2009].

McGill, D. 1989. Now, Video Game Players Can Take Show on the Road. *The New York Times*. 5 June, D-6.

McKenna, A. 2005. Analysts Predict Xbox 360 will Beat PlayStation 3. *The Inquirer* [Online 30 September] Available at: http://www.theinquirer.net/en/inquirer/news/2005/09/30/analysts-predict-xbox-360-will-beat-playstation-3 [accessed: 7 May 2008].

McLaughlin, R. The History of *Final Fantasy VII*. *IGN* [Online] Available at: http://retro.ign.com/articles/870/870770p6.html [accessed: 8 July 2009].

McShea, T. 2008. *Shaun White Snowboarding* Review. *GameSpot* [Online 16 November] Available at: http://www.gamespot.com/xbox360/sports/shaunwhitesnowboarding/review.html [accessed: 23 March 2009].

Media Molecule. 2006. *Press Release: Media Molecule Sign Exclusive Deal With Sony Computer Entertainment Europe* [Online September] Available at: http://www.mediamolecule.com/Sep06Media_Molecule.pdf [accessed: 19 May 2009].

Melanson, D. 2006. A Brief History of Handheld Video Games. *Engadget* [Online 3 March] Available at: http://www.engadget.com/2006/03/03/a-brief-history-of-handheld-video-games [accessed: 11 April 2007].

Melekian, B. 2007. But Coach, I Practiced in the Living Room. *The New York Times*. 15 March, 8.

Merritt, R. 2005. Sony Claims PlayStation 3 Performance Edge. *Electronic Engineering Times*. 23 May, 33.

Metcalf, J. 2008. Inside Source Reveals the Truth About Xbox 360 "Red Ring of Death" Failures. *8bitJoystick* [Online 19 January] Available at: http://www.8bitjoystick.com/2008/01/inside-source-reveal-the-truth-about-xbox-360-red-ring-of-death-failures.html [accessed: 23 February 2009].

Michel, A. and Shaked, I. 1996. Lessons from Failed Corporate Marriages. *Strategy + Business*, Fourth Quarter.

Microsoft Corp. 1998. Press Release: Microsoft, Sega Collaborate on Dreamcast [Online 21 May] Available at: http://www.microsoft.com/presspass/press/1998/May98/Segagmpr.mspx [accessed: 15 July 2009].

Microsoft Corp. 1999. Press Release: Microsoft Announces Windows CE Toolkit for Dreamcast [Online 16 March] Available at: http://www.microsoft.com/presspass/press/1999/mar99/toolkitpr.mspx [accessed 9 July 2009].

Microsoft Corp. 2005a. Press Release: Microsoft Teams With MTV to Provide Exclusive Sneak Peek at the Debut of the Next-Generation Xbox, Microsoft.com, April 11, 2005 Available at: http://www.microsoft.com/presspass/press/2005/apr05/04-11MTVXboxPR.mspx [accessed 24 October 2007].

Microsoft Corp. 2005b. Press Release: Xbox 360 Officially Announced, Team Xbox [Online 12 May] Available at: http://news.teamxbox.com/xbox/8233/Xbox-360-Officially-Announced/ [accessed: 6 May 2008].

Microsoft Corp. 2007a. Press Release: Microsoft Unites Xbox and PC Gamers with Debut of Games for Windows — LIVE [Online 14 March] Available at: http://www.microsoft.com/presspass/press/2007/mar07/03-14G4WandXboxLIVEPR.mspx [accessed: 16 July 2009].

Microsoft Corp. 2007b. Press Release: Xbox 360 Warranty Coverage Expanded [Online 5 July] Available at: http://www.xbox.com/en-GB/support/systemsetup/xbox360/resources/warrantyupdate.htm [accessed: 16 April 2008].

Microsoft Corp. 2007c. Press Release: Peter Moore Resigns From Microsoft to Return to Northern California [Online 17 July] Available at: http://www.microsoft.com/Presspass/press/2007/jul07/07-17MooreMattrickPR.mspx [accessed: 16 April 2008].

Microsoft Corp. 2008. Press Release: Xbox 360 and Netflix Team Up [Online 14 July] Available at: http://www.xbox.com/en-US/community/events/e32008/articles/0714-netflixteamup.htm [accessed: 26 January 2009].

Microsoft Corp. 2009. Press Release: Description of the E74 error message warranty extension [Online 14 April] Available at: http://support.microsoft.com/kb/969905 [accessed: 29 April 2009].

Midway Games. 2007. Q1 2007 Midway Games Earnings Conference Call. *Fair Disclosure Wire*. 3 May.

Mielke, J. 2008. A Day in the Life of Nobuo Uematsu. *1Up* [Online 15 February] Available at: http://www.1up.com/do/feature?cId=3166165 [accessed: 16 June 2009].

Mindlin, A. 2006. It Seems Girls Go for Computer Games, Too. *The New York Times*, 17 April 17, C-3.

Miyamoto, S. 2003. Miyamoto Interview. Computer and Video Games [Online 16 May] Available at: http://www.miyamotoshrine.com [accessed: 20 March 2007].

Mohr, J., Sengupta, S. and Slater, S. 2004. Marketing of High-Technology Products and Innovations, 2nd Edition. Upper Saddle River, NJ: Prentice Hall.

Moore, G. 2002. *Crossing the Chasm*. New York: HarperCollins.

Moore, P. 2006. E3 Financial Analyst Briefing, Interactive Entertainment Business, Entertainment and Devices Division. Microsoft Corp. [Online 9 May] Available at: http://www.microsoft.com/msft/download/Transcripts/FY06/PeterMoore050906.doc [accessed: 24 October 2007].

Moore, P. 2007. Open Letter from Peter Moore. Microsoft Corp. [Online 5 July] Available at: http://www.xbox.com/en-GB/support/petermooreletter.htm [accessed: 16 April 2008].

Morford, M. 2005. There's Sex in my Violence. Anyone Game? *The San Francisco Chronicle*. 22 July, E1.

Morgan, R. 2008. Handheld Games Museum [Online] Available at http://www.handheldmuseum.com/Mattel/FB.htm [accessed: 22 July 2009].

Morris, C. 2006. An Experiment Failed: Majesco Learns a Hard Lesson about the Video Game Industry. *CNN Money* [Online 24 January]. Available at: http://money.cnn.com/2006/01/23/commentary/game_over/column_gaming/ [accessed: 19 May 2009].

Nader, P. et al. 2008. Moderate-to-Vigorous Physical Activity from Ages 9 to 15 Years. *Journal of the American Medical Association (JAMA)*, 300(3), 295–305.

Nelson, C. 2007. Playstation 3 vs. XBOX 360 – One Year Later. *Hardcore Ware* [Online 20 November] Available at: http://www.hardcoreware.net/ playstation-3-vs-xbox-360-one-year-later/ [accessed: 30 June 2009].

Nelson, C. 2009. Playstation 3 vs. XBOX 360 – Two Years Later. *Hardcore Ware* [Online 12 January] Available at: http://www.hardcoreware.net/ playstation-3-vs-xbox-360-two-years-later/ [accessed: 30 June 2009].

New York Times, The. 1999. Video Battlers Stick by Their Games. 20 June, 26.

Next Generation. 2007. Nintendo Rejects Wii Shortage Plot [Online 28 March] Available at: http://www.next-gen.biz/index2.php?option=com_content&task=view&id=5050 [accessed 1 August 2007].

Nikkei Weekly, The. 1994. Nintendo Easing Iron Grip on Programmers. 2 May, 8.

Nikkei Weekly, The. 1999. Game Developer Sees Role-playing as Winning Strategy. 22 February, 11.

Nintendo of America. 2007. What is Wii? Wii Remote [Online] Available at: http://wii.nintendo.com/controller.jsp [accessed: 6 June 2007].

Nintendo of America. 2007. *Q&A from Nintendo Analyst Meeting* [Online 27 April] Available at: http://press.nintendo.com/object?id=7657 [accessed: 9 July 2007].

Nintendo Company Ltd. *Consolidated Sales Transition by Region* [Online] Available at: http://www.nintendo.co.jp/ir/library/historical_data/pdf/consolidated_sales_e0806.pdf [accessed: 23 July 2009].

Nintendo Company Ltd. 2005. *Analysis of Operations and Financial Review, Annual Report 2005*. Kyoto: Nintendo.

Nintendo Company Ltd. 2007. *Q&A from Nintendo Analyst Meeting* [Online 27 April] Available at: http://press.nintendo.com/object?id=7657 [accessed: 9 July 2007].

Nintendo Company Ltd. 2008. *Financial Results Briefing for the Nine Month Period Ended December, 2008, Supplementary Information* [Online] Available at: http://nintendo.co.jp/ir/pdf/2009/090130e.pdf [accessed: 23 March 2009].

Nintendo Power. 2007. A Developing Revolution. June, 74–77.

Niizumi, H. 2003. *Dance Dance Revolution* hits 6.5 million in Sales. *GameSpot* [Online 23 December] Available at: http://www.gamespot.com/xbox/puzzle/ddrxbox/news.html?sid=6084894 [accessed: 17 July 2008].

Niizumi, H. 2006. 24 Wii VC devs ID'd. *GameSpot* [Online 14 September] Available at: http://www.gamespot.com/news/6157639.html [accessed: 10 July 2007].

Nowak, P. 2006. Living Room New Internet Battlefield, *The National Post*, December 28, 2006, p. FP1.

NPD Group, The. 2005. TRSTS Reports. In *Emerging Trends In Computer Entertainment*, Sony Computer Entertainment America Investor Presentation, January 2006

Nutall, C. 2008. *Spore* hit by DRM Protest. *Financial Times* [Online 8 September] Available at: http://blogs.ft.com/techblog/2008/09/spore-hit-by-drm-protest/ [accessed: 26 July 2009].

Nutall, C. 2009. Microsoft's Portal into a Virtual World 'S Moving Sense of Motion. *Financial Times* [Online 3 June] Available at: http://www.ft.com/cms/s/0/cb386de2-4fd6-11de-a692-00144feabdc0.html [accessed: 7 June 2009].

Nutt, C. 2009. Catching Up With PlayStation: Peter Dille On Sony In 2009. *Gamasutra* [Online 21 April] Available at: http://www.gamasutra.com/view/feature/4000/catching_up_with_playstation_.php [accessed: 24 April 2009].

Nystedt, D. 2006. Digital Music Sales Triple in 2005. *PC World*. 20 January, 28.

O'Brian, J. 2007. Wii will Rock You. *Fortune*. 11 June, 82–92.

OECD. 2001. *The Development of Broadband Access in the OECD Countries*. Working Party on Telecommunication and Information Services Policies, Organization for Economic Co-operation and Development. Paris: OECD Publications.

Oldenburg, D. 1989. Consummate Consumer. *The Washington Post*. 17 October, C-5.

Orr, D. and DeCarlo, S. 2007. Asia's Fab 50 Companies. *Forbes* [Online 6 September] Available at: http://www.forbes.com/global/2007/0917/074.html [accessed: 3 August 3, 2009].

Ortutay, B. 2007. Want a Wii? Get in line. *USA Today* [Online 29 June] Available at: http://www.usatoday.com/tech/gaming/2007-06-29-wii-demand_N.htm [accessed: 2 July 2007].

Ortutay, B. 2008. Take-Two's *Grand Theft Auto IV* tops $500M in week 1 sales. *USA Today* [Online 7 May] Available at: http://www.usatoday.com/money/topstories/2008-05-07-1908764460_x.htm [accessed: 28 August 2008].

Pacheco, D. 1994. Rating the Games, Labels to Help Parents Choose. *The Denver Post*. 29 October, E12.

Palmer, S. 1999. Record Sales on the Horizon for Dreamcast. *PC Dealer*. 13 October, 4.

Parker, P. 2007. '*Rock Band*' is Greatest Party Game Ever. *The Albuquerque Tribune*. 19 December.

Pashal, P. 2009. SHIFT: Why Project Natal is Future of Gaming (and how Microsoft Could Screw it up). *Dvice* [Online 4 June] Available at: http://www.dvice.com/archives/2009/06/shift-why-proje.php [accessed: 7 June 2009].

Patel, N. 2007. Sony's SonicStage CP Contains Playlist Security Hole. *Engadget* [Online 31 October] Available at: http://www.engadget.com/2007/10/31/sonys-sonicstage-cp-contains-playlist-security-hole/ [accessed: 27 March 2009].

Peckham, M. 2008. *Rock Band* Downloads Boom, Hit "Double Platinum." *PC World* [Online 18 January] Available at: http://blogs.pcworld.com/gameon/archives/006327.html [accessed: 1 August 2009].

Phan, M. 2004. Acclaim Files for Bankruptcy. *Newsday* [Online 2 September] Available at http://www.newsday.com/technology/ny-bzaklm020904,0,6663839.story [accessed: 28 June 2009].

Pinckard, J. 2005. Xbox 360 Crashes, Defects Reported. *1up* [Online 23 November] Available at: http://www.1up.com/do/newsStory?cId=3145847 [accessed: 28 April 2008].

Plastic Bamboo. 2006. Nintendo DS Museum Guide [Online 31 October] Available at: http://www.plasticbamboo.com/2006/10/31/nintendo-ds-museum-guide/ [accessed 13 July 2007].

PlayStation Official Magazine, The. 2009a. Blu-ray of Sunshine. April, 11.

PlayStation Official Magazine, The. 2009b. PlayStation State of the Union: The Developers (Part One). July, 59.

PlayStation Official Magazine, The. 2009c. PlayStation State of the Union: The Developers (Part Two). August, 54.

Plunkett, L. 2007a. Harmonix, MTV, EA to Bring us *Rock Band*. *Kotaku* [Online 2 April] Available at: http://www.kotaku.com/gaming/rock-band/harmonix-mtv-ea-to-bring-us-rock-band-248792.php [accessed: 16 September 2008].

Plunkett, L. 2007b. Apple Opens iPhone, iPod Touch, Games Sure to Follow. *Kotaku* [Online 17 October] Available at: http://www.kotaku.com/gaming/apple/apple-opens-iphone-ipod-touch-games-sure-to-follow-312172.php [accessed: 26 July 2009].

Poole, S. 2000. *Trigger Happy: Videogames and the Entertainment Revolution*. New York: Arcade Publishing.

Popkin, H. 1995. Virtual Boy. *St. Petersburg Times*. 18 December, 1D.

Prahalad, C.K and Ramaswamy, V. 2003. *MIT Sloan Management Review* [Online 15 July] Available at: http://www.sloanreview.mit.edu/the-magazine/articles/2003/summer/4442/the-new-frontier-of-experience-innovation/ [accessed: 1 June 2009].

Radd, D. 2006. Opinion: Wii Won't Rock You. *Game Daily* [17 November] Available at: http://www.biz.gamedaily.com/industry/feature/?id=14501 [accessed: 8 May 2007].

Rawlings, A. 2006. TAB Event – "Super Escher" Exhibition. *Tokyo Art Beat* [Online December] Available at: http://www.tokyoartbeat.com/tablog/entries.en/2006/12/super_escher_at_bunkamura_muse.html [accessed 10 July 2007]

Regnér, P. 1999. *Strategy Creation and Change in Complexity – Adaptive and Creative Learning Dynamics in the Firm*, published doctoral dissertation, Stockholm: Institute of International Business, Stockholm School of Economics.

Reichheld, F. 1990. Zero Defections: Quality Comes to Services. *Harvard Business Review*. September – October, 105 – 111.

Richtell, M. 2007. Nintendo Throws Down Again. *The New York Times* [Online 23 July] Available at: http://bits.blogs.nytimes.com/2007/07/23/nintendo-throws-down-again-not-the-way-you-think [accessed: 24 July 2007].

Richtell, M. 2008. Electronic Arts Forecasts Weaker Profit in 2009. *The New York Times*. 10 December, 9.

Ries, A. and Ries, L. 2002. *The Fall of Advertising*. New York: HarperCollins.

Robinson, A. 2009. PSP: 50 million Sold. *Computer and Video Games* [Online 13 February] http://www.computerandvideogames.com/article.php?id=208211%3fcid [accessed 25 July 2009].

Rogers, E. 1983. *Diffusion of Innovations*. 3rd edition. New York: The Free Press.

Rogers, E. 2003. *Diffusion of Innovations*. 5th edition. New York: The Free Press.

Rogers, J. 2008. Smashing Failure. *Slate*. [Online 27 March] Available at: http://www.slate.com/id/2187562 [accessed 3 July 2009]

Rojas, P. 2006. The Engadget Interview: Reggie Fils-Aime, Executive Vice President of Sales and Marketing for Nintendo, *Engadget* [Online 20 February] Available at: http://www.engadget.com/2006/02/20/the-engadget-interview-reggie-fils-aime-executive-vice-preside/ [accessed: 25 July 2009].

Roper, C. 2005. *Guitar Hero*, Turn it up to 11 and rock the #@$& out. *IGN* [Online 2 November] Available at: http://ps2.ign.com/articles/663/663674p1.html [accessed: 18 August 2008].

Roper, C. 2006. *Guitar Hero II* Review. *IGN* [Online 3 November] Available at: http://ps2.ign.com/articles/743/743905p1.html [accessed 21 August 2008].

Rosmarin, R. 2006. Why *Gears of War* Costs $60. *Forbes* [Online 19 December] Available at: http://www. forbes.com/2006/12/19/ps3-xbox360-costs-tech-cx_rr_game06_1219expensivegames.html [accessed: June 28, 2007].

Rushe, D. 2009. DVD Sales Slump Challenges Hollywood. *The Times* [Online 4 July] Available at: http://business.timesonline.co.uk/tol/business/industry_sectors/leisure/article6639171.ece [accessed: 13 July 2009].

Ryans, A. et al. 2000. *Winning Market Leadership : Strategic Market Planning for Technology-Driven Businesses*. Etobicoke: Wiley.

Sabbagh, D. 2008. How the Format War was Won – Sony Outspent, Outsold Toshiba. *The Times*. 21 February, 53.

Samiljan, T. 2007a. *Rock Band*: A First Look at the Biggest Thing Since *Guitar Hero*. *Rolling Stone* [Online 17 July] Available at: http://www.rollingstone.com/rockdaily/index.php/2007/07/12/rock-band-a-first-look-at-the-biggest-thing-since-guitar-hero/ [accessed: 15 September 2008].

Samiljan, T. 2007b. *"Rock Band"*: A Hands-On Test of the Most Anticipated Video Game of the Year. *Rolling Stone* [Online 16 August] Available at: http://www.rollingstone.com/rockdaily/index.php/2007/08/16/rock-band-a-hands-on-test-of-the-most-anticipated-video-game-of-the-year/ [accessed: 15 September 2008].

Satariano, A. 2009. Sony Faces Heat From Game Publishers to Cut PS3 Price. *Bloomberg News* [Online 16 March] Available at: http://www.bloomberg.com/apps/news?pid=20601101&sid=aiHCQM2xNCmU [accessed: 17 April 2009].

Schonfeld, E. 2008. *Spore* and the Great DRM Backlash. *The Washington Post* [Online 14 September] Available at: http://www.washingtonpost.com/wp-dyn/content/article/2008/09/14/AR2008091400885.html [accessed: 17 July 2009].

Schwartz, B. 2004. *The Paradox of Choice: Why More is Less*. New York: Harper Collins.

Shaffer, H. et al. 2003. *Futures at Stake: Youth, Gambling, and Society*. Reno: University of Nevada Press.

Shah, S. 2009. iPhone Gaming. *GameSpot* [Online 20 April] Available at: http://www.gamespot.com/features/6208133/index.html [accessed: 26 July 2009].

Shapiro, E. 1991a. Sony, Nintendo's Partner, Will Be a Rival, Too. *The New York Times*. 1 June, 36.

Shapiro, E. 1991b. Nintendo and Minnesota Set a Living-Room Lottery Test. *The New York Times*. 27 September, A-1.

Sharma, A. and Silver, S. 2009. BlackBerry Storm is off to Bit of a Bumpy Start. *The Wall Street Journal*. 26 January, B1.

Sheff, D. 1993. *Game Over*. New York: Random House.

Sheth, J. 2007. *The Self-Destructive Habits of Good Companies and How to Break Them*. Upper Saddle River, NJ: Wharton School Publishing.

Shimbun, A. 2000. Interview: Nintendo. *Core Magazine* [Online 20 October] Available at: http://www.web.archive.org/web/20001109163700/http://www.coremagazine.com/news/3157.php3 [accessed: 18 June 2009].

Shippy, D. and Phipps, M. 2009. *The Race for the New Game Machine*. New York: Kensington.

Shoemaker, B. 2001. *Lunar 2: Eternal Blue* Complete Review. *GameSpot* [Online 3 January] Available at: http://www.gamespot.com/ps/rpg/lunar2eternalblue/review.html [accessed: 18 May 2009].

Sid, V. 2006. Nintendo DS Shortage Strikes Japan, Leads to $300 Prices. *GamePro* [Online 10 January] Available at: http://www.gamepro.com/news.cfm?article_id=51053 [accessed 13 July 2007].

Siegler, M. 2008. Netflix comes to the Xbox 360. Did Microsoft just Destroy the Apple TV? *Venture Beat* [Online 14 July] Available at: http://www.venturebeat.com/2008/07/14/netflix-comes-to-the-xbox-360-did-microsoft-just-destroy-the-apple-tv/ [accessed: 1 March 2009].

Siklos, R. 2006. MTV will Acquire Maker of Music-oriented Games, *The New York Times* [Online 26 September] Available at: http://www.nytimes.com/2006/09/22/business/media/22mtv.html [accessed 1 August 2009].

Simons, I. 2007. *Inside Game Design*, London: Laurence King Publishers.

Sinclair, B. 2006a. Moore on 360 Launch: "Nothing's Perfect." *GameSpot* [Online 9 January] Available at: http://www. gamespot.com/news/6142087.html [accessed: 28 April 2008].

Sinclair, B. 2006b. Wii Dev Costs Fraction of PS3's, 360's. *GameSpot* [Online 5 May] Available at: http://www.gamespot.com/wii/driving/cars/news.html?sid=6149154 [accessed: 20 February 2007].

Sinclair, B. 2006c. E3 06: Activision buys RedOctane. *GameSpot* [Online 9 May] Available at: http://www.gamespot.com/news/6149653.html [accessed: 21 August 2008].

Sliwinski, A. 2007. Scratch That: The Xbox 360 Might Damage Discs After All. *Joystick* [Online 16 April] Available at: http://www.joystiq.com/2007/04/16/scratch-that-the-xbox-360-might-damage-discs-after-all/ [accessed: 28 April 2008].

Sliwinski, A. 2008. Wii Outsold PS3 3-to-1 in Japan During '07; Xbox Pens Memoir on Neglect. *Joystick* [Online 7 January] Available at: http://www.joystiq.com/2008/01/07/wii-outsold-ps3-3-to-1-in-japan-during-07-xbox-pens-memoir-on/ [accessed: 7 May 2008].

Smith, E. 1989. Now the Hottest Video Games are Handheld – and in Color. *Business Week*. 11 December, 127

Snider, M. 2002. Car-theft Video Game Should See Big Sales — and Big Outcry. *USA Today*. 30 October, 4D.

Snow, B. 2007a. Feature: Six Reasons the Xbox 360 is in Trouble. *Game Pro* [Online 20 July] Available at: http://www.gamepro.com/microsoft/xbox360/ games/features/124008.shtml [accessed: May 2008].

Snow, B. 2007b. The 10 Worst-Selling Handhelds of All Time. *Game Pro* [Online 30 July] Available at: http://www.gamepro.com/article/features/125748/the-10-worst-selling-handhelds-of-all-time/ [accessed: 24 July 2009].

Solomon, M. 2003. *Conquering Consumerspace*. New York: AMACOM.

Sony Computer Entertainment Inc. 2006a. *Cell Broadband Engine Fact Sheet*. 23 October.

Sony Computer Entertainment Inc. 2006b. *PlayStation 3 System Fact Sheet*. 18 December.

Sony Computer Entertainment Inc. 2007. *Cumulative Production Shipments of Hardware / PlayStation 2* [Online March] Available at: http://www.scei.co.jp/ corporate/data/bizdataps2_e.html [accessed: 18 April 2007].

Soviero, M. 1993. Magic Box. *Popular Science*. December, 100–104.

Stang, B. 2007. *The Book of Games Volume 2*. Ottawa:GameXplore N.A.

Steen, P. 2009. An Interview with ThatGameCompany: *Flower*. *Gamezine* [Online 17 March] Available at: http://www.gamezine.co.uk/features/formats /playstation3/an-interview-with-thatgamecompany-flower-$1281103.htm [accessed: 24 April 2009].

Sterling, J. 2008. Ten Golden Rules of Videogame Fanboyism. *Destructoid*. [Online 27 April] Available at: http://www.destructoid.com/ten-golden-rules-of-videogame-fanboyism-83502.phtml [accessed: 4 May 2009].

Stone, D. 2004. Interview with Alex Rigopulos. *Game Critics* [Online 31 March] http://www.gamecritics.com/feature/interview/rigopulos/page01.php [accessed: 17 July 2008].

Stuart, E. 2009. Warm and Fuzzy Makes a Comeback. *The New York Times* [Online 6 April] Available at: http://www.nytimes.com/2009/04/07/business/ media/07adco.html [accessed: 23 May 2009].

Stuart, K. 2008. Peter Moore Interview *The Guardian* [Online 11 September] Available at: http://www.guardian.co.uk/technology/gamesblog/2008/sep/11 /playstation.microsoft [accessed: 18 September 2008].

Surrette, T. 2006. Wii tops Game Critics' Best of E3 2006. *GameSpot* [Online 31 May] Available at: http://www.gamespot.com/news/6152135.html [accessed: 6 June 2007].

Sutton, R. 2002. *Weird Ideas That Work*. New York: Free Press.

Suominen, J. 2007. *The Past as Future: Nostalgia and Retrogaming in Digital Culture, Proceedings of the 7th International Digital Arts and Cultures Conference.* Perth, Australia. 15–18 September 2007, Available at: http://users.utu.fi/jaasuo/suominen-dac2007-paper.pdf [accessed: 29 July 2009].

Superplay Magazine. 2003. Miyamoto Interview. [Online 23 April] Available at: http://www.miyamotoshrine.com/theman/interviews/230403.shtml [accessed: 18 June 2009].

Surette, T. 2007. Xbox Live: 6 million Strong and Counting. *GameSpot* [Online 6 March] Available at: http://www.gamespot.com/news/6166851.html [accessed 12 March 2007].

Sydney Morning Herald, The. 2007. Most Kids 'Unaffected' by Violent Games [Online 1 April] Available at: http://www.smh.com.au/news/National/Most-kids-unaffected-by-violent-games/2007/04/01/1175366055463.html[accessed: 29 June 2007].

Takahashi, D. 2007a. Xbox 360 Failures: A Loyal Fan Returns Seven Machines. *The Mercury News* [Online 22 February] Available at: http://blogs.mercurynews.com/aei/2007/02/22/xbox_360_failures_a_loyal_fan_returns_seven_machines/ [accessed: 15 April 2008].

Takahashi, D. 2007b. An Interview with Nintendo's Super Game Designer Shigeru Miyamoto. *San Jose Mercury News* [Online 29 July] Available at: http://blogs.mercurynews.com/aei/2007/07/an_interview_with_nintendos_super_game_designer_shigeru_miyamoto.html [accessed: 1 August 2007].

Takahashi, D. 2008a. PopCap Games Executive Interview: Don't be Stupid, Have Fun. *Venture Beat* [Online 21 April]. Available at: http://www.venturebeat.com/2008/04/21/popcap-games-executive-interview-dont-forget-about-the-fun/ [accessed: 22 May 2009].

Takahashi, D. 2008b. Xbox 360 Defects: An Inside History of Microsoft's Video Game Console Woes. *Venture Beat* [Online 5 September] http://www.venturebeat.com/2008/09/05/xbox-360-defects-an-inside-history-of-microsofts-video-game-console-woes/3/ [accessed: 27 February 2009].

Taub, E. 2006. Nintendo at AARP Event to Court the Grayer Gamer. *The New York Times.* 30 October, 8.

Taylor, A. 2006. The Birth of the Prius. *Fortune* [Online 24 February] http"//money.cnn.com/magazines/fortune/fortune_archive/2006/03/06/8370702/index.htm [accessed: 2 December 2008].

Taylor, J. 2005. It's a Gaming Console! It's an Entertainment Hub! *Fast Company.* December, 41.

Thom, G. 2006. Xmas Joy for Xbox. *Herald Sun.* 11 October, C03.

Thomas, L. 2009. The Wii Update You've Waited For. *IGN* [Online 25 March] Available at: http://wii.ign.com/articles/966/966290p1.html [accessed: 22May 2009].

Thorsen, T. 2004. Microsoft Raises Estimated First-day *Halo 2* Sales to $125 million-plus. *GameSpot* [Online 10 November] Available at: http://www. gamespot.com/news/2004/11/10/news_6112915.html [accessed: 28 April 2008].

Thorsen, T. 2005. Ad Campaign Offering Glimpse of Next-gen Xbox? *GameSpot* [Online 6 April] Available at: http://www.gamespot.com/news/2005/04/06/ news_6121811.html [accessed: 24 October 2007].

Thorsen, T. 2006. Nintendo Posts $456.6 million Profit. *GameSpot* [Online 26 October] Available at: http://www.gamespot.com /news/6160557.html [accessed: 9 July 2007].

Thorsen, T. 2007. NPD: $1.25B in US Game Sales Kick off '07. *GameSpot* [Online 21 February] Available at: http://www.gamespot.com/wii/action/ thelegendofzelda/news.html?sid=6166199 [accessed: 16 March 2007].

Thorsen, T. 2008a. *Spore*, Sega Monkey-ing around on iPhone. *GameSpot* [Online 6 March] Available at: http://www.gamespot.com/pc/strategy/spore/news. html?sid=6187307 [accessed: 26 July 2009].

Thorsen, T. 2008b. *Wii Music* Sells under 81,000 in Oct. *GameSpot* [Online 15 November] Available at: http://au.gamespot.com/news/6201159.html [accessed: 17 July 2009].

Thorsen, T, 2009. Xbox 360 Failure Rate 23.7%, PS3 10%, Wii 2.7% – Study, *Gamespot* [Online 2 September] Available at http://www.gamespot.com/ news/6216691.html [accessed March 1, 2010].

Thorsen, T. 2009a. US Retail PC Game Sales Down $210 million in '08. *GameSpot* [Online 28 January] Available at: http://www.gamespot.com/pc/strategy/ spore/news.html?sid=6203825 [accessed: 22 May 2009].

Thorsen, T. 2009b. PS3 Manufacturing Costs Down Around 70%. *GameSpot* [Online 31 July] Available at: http://www.gamespot.com/news/6214569. html?part=rss&tag=gs_news&subj=6214569 [accessed: 3 August 2009].

Time. 1993. The Best Products of 1993. 19–25 December.

Time. Mind-Meltingly Bad Video Game Movies [Online] Available at: http:// www.time.com/time/specials/packages/completelist/0,29569,1851626,00. html [accessed 4 July 2009].

Time Warner. 2008. Press Release: Warner Bros. Entertainment to Release Its High-Definition DVD Titles Exclusively in the Blu-Ray Disc Format Beginning Later this Year [Online 4 January] http://www.timewarner.com/ corp/newsroom/pr/0,20812,1700383,00.html [accessed: 13 July 2009].

To Buy or Not to Buy: The Game Developer's Dilemma, Part 2: Total Cost of Ownership. 2008. Emergent Game Technologies White Paper. Calabasas, California: Emergent Technologies. June 2008.

Tochen, D. 2007. Square Enix Working on PS3, Vista MMORPG. *GameSpot* [Online 19 April] Available at: http://www.gamespot.com/news/6147946. html [accessed: 5 March 2007].

Todd, T. 2006. Knives are out for a November to Remember. *The Gazette.* 30 September, 14.

Toor, M. 1991. The Bottom Line: Lynx hunts Nintendo's Game Boy. *Marketing.* 14 March.

Topkin, M. 1992. Reported Link to Gambling is Absurd. *St. Petersburg Times.* 1 February, C-6

Torgan, C. 2002. Childhood Obesity on the Rise. *Word on Health* [Online June] Available at http://nih.gov/news/WordonHealth/jun2002/childhoodobesity. htm [accessed: 17 April 2007].

Totilo, S. 2006a. West Virginia Adds *"Dance Dance Revolution"* To Gym Class. *MTV News* [Online 25 January] Available at http://www.mtv.com/news/ articles/1521605/20060125/index.jhtml?headlines=true [accessed 17 July 2008].

Totilo, S. 2006b. The Revolution has a Name: Nintendo Wii. *MTV News* [Online 27 April] Available at http://www.mtv.com/news/articles/1529658/20060427/ index.jhtml [accessed: 18 June 2007].

Totilo, S. 2008. Sony Explains how PSN can Trump Xbox Live. *MTV News* [Online 24 July] Available at http://multiplayerblog.mtv.com/2008/07/24/ sony-explains-how-psn-can-trump-xbox-live/ [accessed: 27 August 2008].

Tu, K. 2008. XBOX 360 Gets New Chipset. *Tom's Guide* [Online 8 May] Available at: http://www.tomsguide.com/us/microsoft-xbox-game,news-1284.html [accessed 18 May 2009].

USA Today. 1998. Top-selling Video Games for March. 17 April, 17E.

Utterback, J. 1994. *Mastering the Dynamics of Innovation.* Boston: Harvard Business Press.

VanBurkleo, M. 2009. Indie Week: Day One – What Does It Mean To Be Indie? *Game Informer* [Online 20 April] Available at: http://www.gameinformer. com/NR/exeres/6d46990a-b2c1-45d2-a74c-ecb0669536a1.htm [accessed: 25 April 2009].

VanOrd, K. 2007. *Lair* is a Beautiful Disaster. *GameSpot* [Online 31 August] Available at: http://www.gamespot.com/ps3/action/lair/review.html [accessed: 19 February 2009].

Van Zelfden, N. 2007. Musical Chairs. *Games Industry* [Online 14 February] Available at: http://www.gamesindustry.biz/articles/musical-chairs [accessed: 21 August 2008].

Verbatim, Ltd. 2008. Press Release: Pioneer Increases Disc Size to 500GB [Online 5 August] Available at: http://www.blu-ray.com/news/?id=1616 [accessed: 26 January 2009].

Vestal, A. 2002a. The History of Console RPGs. *GameSpot* [Online March] Available at: http://www.gamespot.com/features/vgs/universal/rpg_hs/nes1.html [accessed: 19 June 2009].

Vestal, A. 2002b. The History of *Zelda*. *GameSpot* [Online August] Available at: http://www.gamespot.com/gamespot/features/video/hist_zelda/index.html [accessed: 11 June 2009].

Vestal, A. 2003. The History of *Final Fantasy*. *Gamespot*. Available at: http://www.gamespot.com/features/vgs/universal/finalfantasy_hs/sec1_7_2.html [accessed: 15 June 2009].

Viacom, Inc. 2008. Q2 2008 Viacom Earnings Conference Call. *Fair Disclosure Wire*. 29 July.

Vossekuil, B. et al. 2002. The Final Report and Findings of the Safe School Initiative: Implications for the Prevention of School Attacks in the United States. *United States Secret Service and United States Department of Education* [Online May] Available at: http://www.secretservice.gov/ntac/ssi_final_report.pdf [accessed: 19 April 2007].

Watts, S. 2008. Report Claims Xbox 360 Failure Rates at 16%. *1up* [Online 13 February] Available at: http://www.1up.com/do/newsStory?cId=3166259 [accessed: 16 April 2008].

West, M. 2008. *The Japanification of Children's Popular Culture*. Lanham: Rowman & Littlefield.

Wheelwright, S. 1992. *Revolutionizing Product Development: Quantum Leaps in Speed, Efficiency, and Quality*. New York: Free Press.

White, M. 1994. *The Material Child: Coming of Age in Japan and America*. Berkeley: University of California Press.

Wielage, M. 1988. The Rise and Fall of Beta. *Videofax*. Spring, 28–29.

Williams, M. 2007. Sony Ships 1 Million PS3s in Japan, Seen Missing Target. *Information Week*, 16 January.

Wind, J. and Mahajan, V. 2001. *Digital Marketing: Global Strategies from the World's Leading Experts*. New York John Wiley & Sons.

Wingfield, N. 2007. Microsoft's Videogame Efforts Take a Costly Hit. *The Wall Street Journal*. 6 July.

Wolf, M. 2007. Intentional Scarcity: For Nintendo, How Long is the Lack of Wii's a Good Thing? *ABI Research* [Online 27 April] Available at: http://www.abiresearch.com/Blog/Digital_Home_Blog/338 [accessed: 1 August 2007].

Wolf, M. 2008. *The Video Game Explosion: A History from PONG to PlayStation and Beyond*. Westport: Greenwood Press.

Wolverton, T. 2009. E3: Nintendo Getting a Bit Complacent? *The San Jose Mercury News* [Online 2 June 2009] Available at: http://blogs.mercurynews.com/aei/2009/06/02/e3-nintendo-getting-a-bit-complacent/ [accessed: 5 June 2009].

Woo, J. 2005. Winning the Good Fight. *GameAxis Unwired*. September, 12.

Wortham, J. 2009. Unofficial Software Incurs Apple's Wrath. *The New York Times*. 13 May, B1.

Wyman, W. 2006. Miyamoto on Wii. *GameSpot* [Online 22 August] Available at: http://www.gamespot.com/news/6156175.html [accessed 16 June 2009].

XNA Creators Club. 2009. *Download History Now Available* [Online 28 March] Available at: http://creators.xna.com/en-US/news/downloadhistorynews [accessed: 22 May 2009].

Yam, M. 2007. Netflix Statistics Show HD DVD More Popular than Blu-ray Disc. *Daily Tech* [Online 10 October] Available at: http://www.dailytech.com/article.aspx?newsid=9202 [accessed: 26 January 2009].

Yam, M. 2007a. SCEA CEO Says PS3 Will Be Difficult to Cost Reduce. *Daily Tech* [Online 23 January] Available at: http://www.dailytech.com/article.aspx?newsid=5810 [accessed: 7 March 2007].

Yam, M. 2007b. Retailers Estimate Xbox 360 Failure Rate High as 33 Percent. *Daily Tech* [Online 2 July] Available at: http://www.dailytech.com/Retailers+Estimate+Xbox+360+Failure+Rate+High+as+33+Percent/article7892.htm [accessed: 24 April 2008].

Yeniyurt, S. and Townsend, J. 2003. Does Culture Explain Acceptance of New Products in a Country? An Empirical Investigation. *International Marketing Review* 20(4), 377–395.

Yoshida, J. 2008. The Truth about Last Year's Xbox 360 Recall. *EE Times* [Online 9 June] Available at: http://www.eetimes.com/showArticle.jhtml?articleID=208403010 [accessed: 12 June 2008].

Zeidler, S. 2009. Netflix says 1 million Xbox Members use Movie Service, *Reuters* [Online 5 February] Available at: http://uk.reuters.com/article/filmNews/idUKTRE5145SF20090205 [accessed: 1 March 2009].

Zezima, K. 2007. Virtual Frets, Actual Sweat. *The New York Times*. 17 July, 1.

Ziegler, C. 2007. The Apple iPhone. *Engadget* [Online 9 June] Available at: http://www.engadget.com/2007/01/09/the-apple-iphone/ [accessed: 26 July 2009].

Zito, K. 1999. Dreamcast Is Season's Hot Hardware. *The San Francisco Chronicle*. 2 December, C3.

Index

3DO Company 42, 50–52, 58, 67–68, 92, 98, 143, 211–213, 219, 224
accelerometer 96, 119
Acclaim Entertainment 21, 59
Activision 22, 144, 204–206, 209
Age of Empires xiii
Alienware 76–77
Alzheimer's disease xiii, 3
Amazon.com 97–98, 140, 155, 164, 178, 190, 209–210
American Association of Retired Persons 3, 150
Apple 28, 47, 51, 76, 79, 92–93, 95–99, 108, 123, 136, 147, 214, 216, 221–222
  iPhone 28, 87, 95–99, 134, 136, 140, 217
    App Store 98,
  iPod 92–93, 108, 133–134
  iTunes 133–134, 140, 209
  Macintosh 51, 133, 222
  Pippin 95, 97
Apple TV 139–140, 211
artificial intelligence 2, 113, 172, 174, 221–222
AT&T 51, 96
Atari 10, 15–16, 20–21, 32, 34, 37–38, 41, 50, 52–53, 58, 67–68, 80–87, 127, 152, 171, 178, 212, 214, 217
  2600 (console) 66
  Jaguar 50, 52, 143, 212, 215

Lynx 80, 82–83, 87
ATRAC 95, 133–134, 141

Baer, Ralph 1
Bach, Robert J. 106, 137–138
backward compatibility 38, 88, 124–126, 149, 160–162
beta testing 72
Betamax 4–5, 94, 132, 134, 141
Bejeweled 171, 178–179, 182
Blockbuster Inc. 35, 86, 140
Blu-ray Disk Association 135
Brain Age xiii, xiv, 79, 88–90
broadband Internet 31, 58, 62, 67, 73, 103, 105, 157, 168, 219,
Bungie Software 62, 71
Burnout Paradise 27, 120
Bushnell, Nolan 15, 32

Call of Duty 120, 221
casual gaming 66, 98, 134, 157, 167–168, 171, 175–183, 186, 190, 216, 220, 224
CD-ROM 41, 43, 49, 53–56, 171, 180
Cell Processor, *see* IBM Cell Processor
Christensen, Clayton 12, 75
cloud gaming 7, 77
cognitive drivers 127
Coleco 14–15, 40, 110
community-based development 96–97, 171, 180, 182, 193

compatibility 149

complacency 78, 166–169, 216

complexity 20, 23–24, 149, 172–173, 215, 220–222

copy protection 55, 61, 97, 134, 214

core rigidities 176

Craigslist 114, 193,

culture, role of 32, 39, 41, 213; see also compatibility

Dance Dance Revolution xiii, 163, 195, 198–199, 203

demographics 20, 39, 56, 74, 82, 89, 94, 144, 164, 171, 176, 187

development tools 53, 59, 67, 98, 171–174, 181, 194, 215–216, 224

digital rights management, see copy protection

diffusion of innovation 57, 128, 148–150

Dille, Peter 74, 117, 128, 185–186, 219

disruptive innovation 12

dominant design 54–56, 94, 141, 214, 226

Donkey Kong 9, 11–15, 17–18, 25, 27–28, 82, 89, 124, 172, 187

DOOM 66–67

Dragon Quest 19

Dreamcast, see Sega Dreamcast

DS, see Nintendo DS

Dual Shock 3 controller 119

early adopters 1, 57, 96, 105, 109, 128, 175

eBay 104, 114, 116, 118, 184, 207

Egozy, Eran 198, 201, 207,

Electronic Arts 3, 7, 50, 62, 190–191, 226–227

Electronic Entertainment Expo (E3) 104, 145–148, 166, 188, 207, 221

Electronic Gaming Monthly xi, 20

Emotion engine 60, 117, 125

engine, see game engine

Enix Corporation 19, 193, 194; see also Square Enix

Entertainment Software Ratings Board (ESRB) xii, 121

Final Fantasy 19, 21–23, 25, 37, 74, 86, 126, 172, 178, 192

Final Fantasy VII 22, 55, 57, 184

Final Fantasy XIII 23, 193

Famicom, see Nintendo Entertainment System

Fils-Aime, Reginald 89, 148

Flower 185–187, 189, 220, 225

Frequency and Amplitude 199–203

gambling 29–33

Game Boy, see Nintendo Game Boy

game engine 66–67, 174, 186, 192, 194

Game Gear, see Sega Game Gear

GameCube, see Nintendo GameCube

Gametrak 159

Genesis, see Sega Genesis

Gladwell, Malcolm 103, 111,

Grand Theft Auto (game franchise) xiii, 23, 43, 126, 163, 191–192, 221

great videogame crash of 1983 7, 14–16, 18, 25, 66

Guitar Hero xiv, 154, 195–197, 200–207, 209–210

GuitarFreaks 199–201

Halo 56, 62, 163, 179, 225

Harrison, George 20, 149, 158

Harrison, Phil 115, 118

Hawkins, William M. 50–51, 190

Haze 174, 194

HD-DVD 131–132, 135–137, 139
High Definition Television
        (HDTV) 51, 77, 103, 118,
        157, 168, 211, 219
Hirai, Kazuo 115, 118, 120–121
Hudson Soft 36–37

IBM 47, 77, 101, 106–107
    Cell processor 51, 113, 117,
            122–123, 189, 193, 225–227
    cost 117
    PowerPC processor 51, 123, 145
    Xenon processor 51, 225
Imanishi, Hiroshi 11, 43, 156
Immersion Corporation 119
Intel Corporation 54, 70, 72
iPhone, *see* Apple iPhone
iPhone Dev Team, *see* Jailbreak
iPod, *see* Apple iPod
iTunes, *see* Apple iTunes
Iwata, Satoru 44, 90–91, 143–144,
        158, 168–169, 181, 223

Jailbreak 97, 99
Japan Victor Company Ltd.
        (JVC) 4, 132

Kano model 120
Karaoke Revolution 200, 202, 207
Konami 198–200, 202, 204, 210
Kondo, Koji 25–26
Kutaragi, Ken 26, 48–49, 53,
        115, 124, 133, 147

late adopters 4, 128–129, 135
LCD, *see* liquid crystal display
Legend of Zelda, The 9, 14, 17–19,
        22, 37, 57, 86, 121
liquid crystal display 54–55

LittleBigPlanet 187–189, 225
The Lord of the Rings 17, 103

Mario Bros. 9, 11, 14–16, 18, 28,
        37–41, 84, 124, 187, 191, 216
Mario Kart 9, 18, 155
Massachusetts Institute of
        Technology 65, 198
Master System, *see* Sega
        Master System
maven 103, 105, 111
Media Molecule 187–189, 194
Memory Stick 92–94
Metal Gear Solid 57, 178, 184, 186, 225
Microsoft
    acquisition strategy 62, 68–71, 102
    Office 67, 103
    Windows 5, 65, 68–69,
            75–76, 102, 175
    Xbox 7, 29, 34, 43, 61–62, 65, 69–70,
            72, 95, 119, 128, 143, 214
    Xbox 360 6–7, 73, 101–112,
            114–116, 119–128, 137–139,
            160, 162, 213, 215–216, 225
    controller 119–120; *see*
            also Project Natal
    CPU, *see* IBM Xenon processor
    development, *see* XNA
    hardware failures 6, 109–111
    HD-DVD player 104,
            131–132, 135, 137, 139
    online services, *see* Xbox Live
    OurColony viral campaign
            102–103, 215
    pricing 104–105, 157, 219
Zune 92, 108
mini disk, *see* Nintendo GameCube
        mini-disk format
Minnesota State Lottery 31, 33
Miracle Piano Teaching System 197

M.I.T., *see* Massachusetts
    Institute of Technology
Miyamoto, Shigeru 7, 9–18, 23–28,
    38, 40, 44, 88, 144, 151, 158,
    164, 172, 176, 192, 194
Moore, Peter 59–60, 62, 69,
    73, 102, 107, 112
mp3 format 79, 87, 91–93, 133–
    134, 141, 177, 209, 214
MTV 103–104, 206–207

N64, *see* Nintendo Ultra 64
Nakamura, Masaya 35
Namco Ltd. 10, 35, 54, 57, 178
Natal, *see* Project Natal
NEC 26, 36, 38, 41, 50, 58, 83, 85–87
    TurboExpress 83
    TurboGrafx-16 36, 38
NES, *see* Nintendo
    Entertainment System
netbook 1, 76–77
Netflix 75, 131, 137–141, 157
Nintendo
    DS xii, 1, 4, 7, 10, 24, 29, 45,
        87–93, 98, 119, 124, 184, 212
    DSi 91, 94–95
    Game Boy 79–89, 91, 99
    Game Boy Advance
        86–88, 91–92, 124,
    GameCube 29, 43–45, 51,
        61–62, 114, 119, 124, 128,
        143, 145, 147, 163, 227
        mini-disk format 43, 61, 214
    Revolution (Wii prototype)
        89, 143–146
    Ultra 64 42, 43, 54–56, 61, 153
    Virtual Boy 85–86

Wii xii, xiv, 4, 23–24, 29, 101,
    105, 110, 114, 121, 123–124,
    128–129, 145–169, 210–213,
    215–216, 219–221, 223–224
    controller, *see* Wii Remote
    development 173
    downloadable content 182–183
    online services 153–155
    pricing 118, 152–153
    supply shortages 157–159
Nintendo Entertainment System
    15–16, 20–21, 26, 29–32, 34–39,
    41–42, 48, 56–57, 81, 86, 97,
    136, 152–153, 197, 214
Nintendo Network 30–34
Nintendo Power 20, 36
Nintendogs 9, 88–89
Nokia N-Gage 87, 96
Nomad, *see* Sega Nomad
Nvidia 70, 72

observability 150
Ogha, Norio 48–49
open innovation 184–187, 216
outsourcing 72, 216

Pac-man 15–16, 18, 87, 175,
    177, 182, 220
Panasonic 50–52, 135; *see also*
    Blu-ray Disk Association;
    3DO Company
paradox of choice 160–163
performance oversupply
    75–76, 212–213
peripherals 15, 159, 163, 168
Philips Electronics N.V. 40, 49–50, 135
piracy 41, 43, 54–56, 61, 181, 214–215
PlayStation, *see* Sony PlayStation

Pokémon 20, 90, 191
PopCap Games 156, 178–180, 182
pricing strategy 82–85, 93–94, 96,
        114–118, 127–129, 140, 143,
        147, 153, 157, 162, 213
product life cycle 24, 40, 128–
        129, 168, 175, 204
Project Natal 7, 78, 211–212, 220–224
PSP, *see* Sony PlayStation Portable
PSP Go 94–95, 140
Psychonauts 188

quality control 21,72, 108, 208

Radar Scope 10, 18
red ring of death, see Xbox 360
        hardware failures 6, 109–111
RedOctane 201–202, 204–207, 210
relative advantage 149
retrogaming 177–178
Ricoh Company Ltd. 14, 37
Rigopulos, Alexander 198–201, 205, 207
Rock Band 176, 190, 195, 197, 206–210
royalties 35, 50–52, 105, 135,
        181–182, 201
rumble, *see* vibration feedback

SACD, *see* Super Audio
        Compact Disk
Sakaguchi, Hironobu 19, 23, 26
scarcity marketing 34, 91, 158
SD, *see* Secure Digital
SDK, see software development kit
Secure Digital 91, 93–94
SecurROM, *see* copy protection
Sega
    Dreamcast 7, 58–62, 67–70,
        73, 102, 120, 128, 143,
        211–212, 214, 216, 224
    Game Gear 84–85, 99,

    Genesis 36, 38–39, 41, 50, 85, 178
    Master System 38
    Nomad 85
    Saturn 53, 58–59, 61, 183, 212–213
Shaun White Snowboarding:
    Road Trip 164–166
Sixaxis controller 118–119, 126
SNES, *see* Super Nintendo
    Entertainment System
software development kit 98; *see*
    also development tools
Sonic the Hedgehog 39, 41, 84, 187
Sony
    PlayStation 2 29, 43, 60–62, 72,
        92, 105–106, 113–114, 118–119,
        124–129, 143, 156, 160–161
    CPU, *see* Emotion engine
    PlayStation 3 xi, 1, 6–7, 75,
        101, 105–106, 108, 110,
        113–129, 143–147, 155–165,
        213–215, 219, 224–227
    Blu-ray drive 131, 134–137
    controller, *see* Sixaxis; *see*
        also Dual Shock 3
    CPU, *see* IBM Cell processor
    development 172–173, 193
    downloadable content
        22, 183–185
    pricing 114–118, 147, 157
    third party titles 188, 190
    PlayStation One 42–43, 47–50,
        53–57, 67, 84, 95, 156, 164,
        184, 188, 193, 213, 215
    PlayStation Portable 1, 7, 87,
        91–95, 99, 124, 140, 157
    Trinitron 49, 132
    Walkman 49, 83, 132–133, 141
Spore 97, 190, 214
Square Company 25, 57, 193–194;
        see also Square Enix

Square Enix 7, 172, 190, 192–193
Spacewar 65–66
standards 4, 29, 50, 54, 94–95,
     98, 123, 141, 214
Steam 180–181
strategy making at the
     periphery 12–13
Super Audio Compact Disk
     95, 134, 141, 162–163
Super Mario Bros. 14, 16–18, 25, 82, 86
Super Mario 64 9, 58
Super Nintendo Entertainment
     System 26, 41, 49–50, 56, 86, 95
Synergistic processing elements,
     see IBM Cell Processor

Take-Two Interactive 7, 191–193
Tapwave Zodiac 87
Tengen Inc. 34, 37, 39
Tetris 79–82, 84, 92, 171, 177, 179
Thatgamecompany 185, 194
THQ Inc. 156, 173
TiVo 92, 139–140
Toshiba 132, 135–137
Tretton, Jack 93, 113, 116,
     121–122, 127, 183
trialability 149
Trinitron, *see* Sony Trinitron
Trojan horse strategy 117, 135–137
TurboGrafx-16, see NEC
     TurboGrafx-16

Uematsu, Nobuo 25–27
Universal Media Disk
     (UMD) 91, 93–94

VHS 4–5, 132, 141, 196
Viacom 206, 208
vibration feedback 9, 118–120,
     123, 147, 153, 224
viral marketing 102–105, 148–150
Virtual Boy, *see* Nintendo Virtual Boy

Walkman, *see* Sony Walkman
Warner Bros. 136–137
Wii, *see* Nintendo Wii
Wii Fit xiv, 10, 149, 163–164,
     166, 192, 210, 224
"Wii for all" (television
     commercial) 151–153
Wii Remote 4, 24, 28, 119, 126,
     146–147, 150, 153, 156, 159–160,
     165–166, 210, 215–216, 221, 223
Wii Sports 121, 149, 152, 154,
     163, 166, 173, 224
World of Warcraft 74, 180

Xbox, *see* Microsoft Xbox
Xbox Live 6–7, 34, 60, 62, 65,
     73–75, 77, 103–105, 110, 126,
     138–140, 153–154, 173, 180,
     182–183, 208, 211, 217, 227
XNA 172, 182

Yamauchi, Hiroshi 10–11,
     13–15, 25, 30, 41
YouTube 98, 187–188, 196

Zelda: Twilight Princess 18, 121, 173

Zune, *see* Microsoft Zune

About the Authors

David Wesley is a Research Manager at Northeastern University's College of Business Administration in Boston. His case studies on companies like Adidas, Hewlett-Packard, and Nintendo have appeared in numerous management textbooks and have been consistently ranked among the best-selling cases at Harvard Business School Publishing and Ivey Publishing.

Professor Gloria Barczak is the head of the marketing department at Northeastern University and former director of the Executive MBA program. She is a founding member of the Institute for Global Innovation Management and was recently recognized as one of the top innovation management scholars in the world by the Journal of Product Innovation Management.

If you have found this book useful you may be interested in other titles from Gower

Convergenomics:
Strategic Innovation in the Convergence Era
Sang M. Lee and David L. Olson
Hardback: 978-0-566-08936-7
e-book: 978-0-566-08937-4

Relationship Economics:
The Social Capital Paradigm and it's Application to
Business, Politics and Other Transactions
Lindon J. Robison and Bryan K. Ritchie
Hardbback: 978-0-566-09169-8
e-book: 978-0-566-09170-4

Risk Strategies:
Dialling Up Optimum Firm Risk
Les Coleman
Hardback: 978-0-566-08938-1
e-book: 978-0-566-08939-8

GOWER